The Value and Momentum Trader

Founded in 1807, John Wiley & Sons is the oldest independent publishing company in the United States. With offices in North America, Europe, Australia, and Asia, Wiley is globally committed to developing and marketing print and electronic products and services for our customers' professional and personal knowledge and understanding.

The Wiley Trading series features books by traders who have survived the market's ever changing temperament and have prospered—some by reinventing systems, others by getting back to basics. Whether a novice trader, professional or somewhere in-between, these books will provide the advice and strategies needed to prosper today and well into the future.

For a list of available titles, visit our Web site at www.WileyFinance.com.

The Value and Momentum Trader

Dynamic Stock Selection Models to Beat the Market

GRANT HENNING

WILEY

John Wiley & Sons, Inc.

Published by John Wiley & Sons, Inc., Hoboken, New Jersey.
Published simultaneously in Canada.

For general information on our other products and services or for technical support, please contact our Customer Care Department within the United States at (800) 762-2974, outside the United States at (317) 572-3993 or fax (317) 572-4002.

Wiley also publishes its books in a variety of electronic formats. Some content that appears in print may not be available in electronic books. For more information about Wiley products, visit our web site at www.wiley.com.

Library of Congress Cataloging-in-Publication Data:

Henning, Grant, 1941–
    The value and momentum trader : dynamic stock selection models
to beat the market / Grant Henning.
        p. cm. – (Wiley trading; 442)
    Includes bibliographical references and index.
    ISBN 978-0-470-48173-8
    1. Stocks–Prices.   2. Investment analysis.   3. Portfolio management.
4. Speculation.   I. Title.
    HG4636.H46 2009
    332.63'22–dc22

                                                        2009021674

Printed in the United States of America

10 9 8 7 6 5 4 3 2 1

This book is dedicated to
Lydia, Jonathan, Madison, Lincoln, Elgin, and Naomi,
the next generation of faithful stewards.

Contents

List of Tables and Figures

Foreword

E ach year during the past five years, Dr. Grant Henning has been invited to speak to a group of finance-majored students at the Smeal
College of Business of The Pennsylvania State University about his
personal investment experience and his trading system. His speeches have
always been well received. When he asked me to write this foreword, I was
honored, knowing the immense investment performance and experience
he has in the market. As a colleague of Grant at The Pennsylvania State
University, I have personal knowledge of his qualifications and ability as
an active trader and I am glad that he has put the results of his 20 years of
research into this book. I wish I had read this book years ago, and I enjoy
reading it today, finding pearls of wisdom to improve my own trading.

Grant's approach to the market, and in this book, is both unique and
integrated. He is not simply a fundamentalist, a technical analyst, a value
investor, or a momentum investor, but rather he is a pragmatist. Over the
past 20 years, he has developed a fundamental-technical hybrid system,
which has built on the two stock selection systems he developed earlier:
(1) a growth-momentum technical system and (2) a value-earnings fundamental system. He has demonstrated that the fundamental variables can
provide value information, while the technical variables offer timing information. He has also demonstrated that it is possible to realize an average
gain of 10 percent per month through the design of appropriate trading
systems and through the skillful implementation of these systems.

Among the various investment approaches, including momentum,
value, growth, fundamental and technical analysis, Grant has chosen the
best elements of each approach and has fine tuned his trading system
according to changes in market conditions. Through his independent research, Grant has designed a trading system that works well in both bull
and bear markets.

I met with Grant last fall (2008) and asked him why he wrote this book
and gave away his trading secrets. He laughed and replied "My approach
to trading does not produce zero-sum gains. If other people end up chasing
the same stocks that I am chasing, that will only drive their prices higher.

Thus, it could be argued that the more persons there are who adopt these trading systems, the better it will be for me and for them."

This book is valuable to everyone who is interested in personal investment, irrespective of his or her background and expertise in the stock market. It relates the obvious as well as the more subtle nuances of stock selection process that distinguish between successful and unsuccessful traders. To become successful investors and traders, all you need is to take this knowledge and to work with it.

Dr. Charles Cao
Smeal Chair Professor of Finance
The Pennsylvania State University
University Park, Pennsylvania
May 2009

Preface

This book is offered as a resource to those who seek success in stock market trading. I especially wish to pass it on to my children and grandchildren and nephews and nieces as a tool for good stewardship of the resources that have been entrusted to them. I am keenly aware of the fact that there are many books written on the subject of stock market trading, and many of them are in my own library. However, you will find this book unique in that it actually describes several mathematical models for stock selection. It therefore has potential for greatly enhancing performance over most other anecdotal references. In the best of worlds, readers will adapt these models to their own needs and trading styles and will add their own personal refinements.

There are many ways to succeed in stock trading, and this is a summary of only a few of those approaches. However, the methods outlined here have been tried and tested over many months and years of market warfare in both bull markets and bear markets. They are the end products of more than 20 years of trading of stocks, options, mutual funds, and commodities, and the past decade has been one in which I have traded for a living. They are offered in the profound belief that market activity is not random, but like other natural phenomena in the wider creation, it follows certain predictable patterns and rules. As Albert Einstein once mused, "God does not play dice with the universe," and I believe this is as true in market phenomena as it is in weather patterns or in the motions of planetary bodies. If we look carefully, we can see that market undulations can be as beautiful as the waves of the sea washing on the shoreline. There is both science and art here, like surfing on a perfect wave, and the sheer thrill of interacting with rhythmic market phenomena is difficult to match in any other profession. Perhaps this is why Einstein is also reported to have said that, if he had it to do over again, he would have become a professional stock trader.

As I share the information in this book, I am mindful of the day my father proudly announced to me that he had imparted skills to me that would enable me to make a living in any economic situation that might present itself. He had taught my brothers and me his trade of landscape gardening—how to plant and maintain lawns and gardens. Although I have never subsequently practiced landscape gardening for a living, but only as a hobby, I can fully understand his satisfaction at knowing that his children could be self-supporting. It is with a similar satisfaction that I am sharing what I have learned about stock market trading. I am fully convinced that, if done correctly, this is an income-producing pursuit that can enable ordinary people who do not own a seat on any stock exchange to become self-supporting and can be of benefit to individuals and communities. It is also a way to take advantage of one of the key benefits we are offered as citizens of a free, democratic, and capitalistic society—that is, the right to own shares in our public corporations and to exchange those shares actively in a beneficial manner.

Acknowledgments

Special thanks are due to my editor, Bill Falloon, for his supportiveness and wise guidance regarding matters of title choice, cover design, CD concept, and a myriad of other editorial details. My thanks also to the editorial staff of John Wiley & Sons, especially Meg Freeborn for the really important and difficult professional work of putting the manuscript into final book format.

In addition I want to thank Professor Charles Cao of The Pennsylvania State University Smeal College of Business Department of Finance for his helpful encouragement and collegial friendship extending over many years.

Thanks to my wife Ruth for her lasting encouragement, gifted exhortation, and the constant reminder that all things are possible with the enablement that comes through trust.

Most of all, my thanks are due to my son Jeffrey for his trading insights, frequent phone calls, race car and other analogies, enthusiastic feedback, and the creative divergence variable that has proven to be another window on market inefficiency.

The Value and Momentum Trader

CHAPTER 1

A Philosophy of Trading

What is trading after all? How can it best be understood? What are its possibilities, limitations, and goals? Is it subject to moral and ethical constraints? Can there be an underlying philosophy of trading? These are some of the questions that are considered in this initial chapter.

ANALOGIES

Stock market trading can be both highly rewarding and extremely dangerous to your financial health. It is a kind of perpetual warfare with many enriching spoils and hidden hazards. It is like climbing in steep, rocky terrain with the simultaneous reward of new vistas and the peril of falling. It often reminds me of the passage in Psalm 18 where David recounts that God "makes my feet like hind's feet, and sets me on my high places." If you have ever watched a mountain goat run up a steep mountain precipice, you get the picture. It takes special feet there to avoid catastrophic falls. Whether those "trading feet" need be a created endowment or an acquired trait is an open question. What is clear is that not every person should get involved in stock trading, and no one should rush into it without thorough preparation. There is a saying that "To fail to prepare is to prepare to fail," and nowhere is this more certain than in the domain of equities trading.

Trading is analogous to farming, where the farmer must carefully choose the crop to be planted and the appropriate location of the fields for planting that particular crop. It is then necessary to prepare the soil

1

thoroughly, plant the seeds at the best time, monitor growth, care for the plants, and then to harvest the product at the right time and deliver it to the right market at the right price. It is hard, sacrificial work, and there are always factors outside of one's control. It is a tribute to Providence and to human stamina that the farmer is ever even able to make a living. There are, however, many types of crops favorable for different soils, climates, and seasons that make success something within the realm of possibility. In the end, however, much of the farmer's success may be attributed to his network of family and friends that provide him or her with information and behavior modeling that extend necessary skills from generation to generation.

Trading is also analogous to fishing. There are many kinds of fishing, just as there are many approaches to trading. There is deep-sea bottom fishing, mountain-stream fly fishing, lakeside bobber fishing, winter ice fishing, and commercial net fishing, to name just a few kinds. In each approach, other factors such as seasonality, types of lures, time on task, and so on also come into play. It is possible to catch fish by any of those methods, just as it is possible to be successful using a variety of approaches to trading stocks. What methods one ultimately adopts depends on available resources, proximity to particular kinds of fish, and many personality and temperamental preferences. It is probably a good thing that styles of fishing differ, as do styles of trading. Otherwise the fish and profits would soon disappear in certain overfished areas.

Yet another analogy for stock trading is that of designing race cars. Every possible consideration is given to competitive advantage, whether through engine modifications, use of superior tires, or aerodynamic improvements. As important as tire tread may be, if one focuses exclusively on tires and neglects other considerations, the race will be lost. In the same way with stock trading, if one considers only technical charting or earnings per share or book value to the exclusion of other concerns, success will prove elusive. One must take into consideration a variety of factors simultaneously. And even if you manage to develop the perfect race car that is far superior to the competition, skill at driving and the skill of the repair crew in the pit may well decide the outcome. So it is that, even if you develop the ultimate stock selection system, skill at executing individual trades or at portfolio management may finally determine success or failure. To carry the race car analogy one step further, there are always factors outside of one's control, such as an oil slick on the track or a collision with another race car, that can take you out of the race altogether. It is crucial to manage these risks in order to survive to compete in yet another race.

One more analogy for trading is provided by the hunter. Near my home in the mountains stands a tree with a folding chair tied high up on its trunk. The chair has now rusted and fallen into disuse. But at one time it was affixed to the tree by a hunter in avid search of prey. I can imagine him seated there for hours at a time waiting for some unsuspecting turkey or deer. The chair stands as a stark reminder of the trader's need for proper positioning, skill with appropriate weaponry, and enduring patience. Even before those assets, the hunter needs a mindset that tells him there will be a reward for his trouble. It is this confidence that helps him scope out his position and endure discomfort for many hours and days at a time. For the trader there is a similar need for confidence that hard work will pay off. Even though it is highly unlikely that sitting in that chair will now produce the same level of satisfaction after years of encroachment by development, the principles are still valid. And in the same way, the trader cannot expect to hold his positions forever with the same assurance of reward.

The game of chess provides another analogy for stock trading. In chess, as in trading, it is critical to have a firm grasp on an appropriate opening strategy that includes a memorized set of contingency plans. Every move, whether it is passive or aggressive, involves some level of risk, so the player must continually assess potential threats. The chess player, like the stock trader, is constantly seeking advantage through exchanges, whether the advantage is asset-related or merely positional. In both chess playing and stock trading, one must not let intense emotion cloud clear thinking. In both pursuits, when positions are extremely complicated, one must be guided by a set of dependable principles.

One final analogy for trading that comes to mind is one that can be borrowed from the field of linguistics. Trading has its own vocabulary and syntax. It is important to know the meanings of the words and the rules for their usage. But in actual communication there is a kind of Chomskyan distinction between competence and performance. The rules of successful trading competence can be described with a certain degree of specificity just like the syntax of a language, but the execution of those rules in actual performance will vary in ways that are much more difficult to describe and may have situational nuances that defy description and prescription. Just as a person will frequently generate creative new sentences never used before and never to be used again, and yet those sentences may be in full conformity to the rules of syntax, semantics, morphology, and phonology—so it is with trading. Having a well-defined trading system does not pre-empt the possibility of creative moves that may never be repeated in the same way, and yet those moves may be perfectly appropriate to any particular trading situation that presents itself and may comply completely with purposeful guidelines.

PRAGMATISM

The ultimate test of a trading system is how it works for the person using it. Seen from this perspective, trading is one of the most pragmatic activities imaginable. Here I am reminded of Thomas Edison and his invention of the incandescent light bulb. He tried many substances as conductors before he found that tungsten filament would produce light under the proper conditions. Edison never learned the precise molecular qualities of tungsten that caused it to produce light where other elements had failed; understanding and proposing a theory of molecular luminescence were not his goals. He merely wanted to find a better way to produce light. Once he found his answer, he abandoned the search for other conducting elements. His task then was merely to refine the implementation of the discovery he had made. Similarly, the stock trader wants to adopt a trading system that has a high monetary yield. The goal is not to understand and promulgate a better theory of microeconomics. He may never fully comprehend why his trading system actually works for him, while other trading systems do not work so well. Pragmatism can lead to appropriate solutions without the distractions of rigorous theoretical accommodation.

Inherent in most expressions of pragmatism is a common-sense belief that natural phenomena tend to follow established rules and predictable patterns. This view is not compatible with extreme versions of random walk theory that would maintain that market behavior is chaotic and not susceptible to description, prediction, or harnessing in any scientific sense. If I believed that market phenomena were totally random and did not conform to predictable patterns, I would have abandoned trading long ago and put my money in a mattress and walked away. The reality is that mathematicians have no single satisfying definition of randomness. If randomness is defined as "equiprobability of outcomes," then you cannot know if phenomena are random unless you can specify all possible outcomes and can test all possible occurrences to verify that they are equally distributed. If randomness is defined as "unpredictability of outcomes," then you cannot know if randomness occurs unless all possible attempts at prediction by all possible methods have been exhausted. If randomness is defined as "lacking identifiable pattern," then you cannot know if it exists unless all possible occurrences can be examined for the presence of any possible pattern. Chaos could not possibly even be recognized unless there existed some orderly field against which to evaluate it. This is not to say that stock market phenomena are simple, uncomplicated, and easily understood. Someone has said that trying to understand stock market phenomena by most common scientific means is like trying to understand moving water by catching it in a bucket. This may be why pragmatism is so appealing. It allows us to stop our searching whenever we find that our methods are working for the intended purpose.

At the same time, some varieties of pragmatism can have their own dangers. Have you ever watched a baseball game and seen the batters walking up to home plate? Some batters have an elaborate routine that they follow religiously. Perhaps they will rub their hands in the dust and then pick up three bats. After two swings with three bats, they discard one bat and swing twice with two bats. Then they discard one more bat and approach the batter's box confidently holding the ultimate bat for the ultimate encounter. Why do they have such an elaborate routine? Perhaps they saw a great hitter use that routine. Perhaps they once hit a home run following the implementation of the routine. Does the routine have any positive correlation with success at batting? Probably not. Similarly, with stock trading it is possible to carry out ineffectual routines mindlessly because others do or because it once appeared to produce desired results. There must be a commitment to test whether any given routine or trading system leads to successful results under appropriate conditions, and to abandon or refine unsuccessful systems.

GOAL-ORIENTED BEHAVIOR

Although an elaborate theory may not be necessary, appropriate measurable goals are always in order. One needs to specify parameters of success in order to know whether or not one is succeeding. The goal of trading is not just to make money, but to make more money than one could expect by other legal means. For example, it is possible to invest all of one's available capital in a good stock index fund. In this way one could reasonably expect to match overall market appreciation over a period of years. Because U.S. equity markets have historically yielded about 7 percent per year on average, one could hope that this level of return would continue. Unfortunately, annualized inflation has also averaged around 2 percent to 4 percent, with some upward variation. This means that we could expect our index-fund investments to give us back somewhat less than a 3 percent annualized yield in real purchasing power at the end of our investment period. Bank certificates of deposit may not even keep pace with inflation. For me, this level of yield is not acceptable. One needs appropriate measurable goals to attain threshold levels of success and to know when they have been attained at stock trading as with any other endeavor.

Trading, like farming, fishing, and designing race cars, is time-consuming and stressful, albeit enjoyable, labor. It is reasonable to expect to profit from that labor over and above the profits attainable through a bank CD or an index fund, where no labor is expended. Based on reading and prior experience, I have come to set earnings goals from the activity of trading at 10 percent of traded capital per month. Some months earnings will be less than 10 percent, and some months they will exceed that goal, so this is an expectation of 10 percent per month on average. If, for any reason, earnings should fall short of that goal consistently, then it is time to back off and examine the trading system to see if adjustments are needed, or to see if it is time to adopt a new system. I have found in my own trading experience, for example, that market trends can dictate whether stock selection should be weighted more heavily towards momentum and growth or towards value and earnings. This in turn can dictate what kind of trading system will be most effective.

TIMING

Timing is always a critical issue in trading—when to buy, when to sell, how long to hold, and when to be out of the market altogether. It is as the writer of Ecclesiastes has said, "To everything there is a season, a time for every purpose under heaven: . . . a time to gain, and a time to lose; a time to keep and a time to throw away." The trading window is a defining concern for stock trading. There are day traders who may hold positions for only a few seconds or a few hours, but who always close all positions before the close of trading each day. There are swing traders who tend to hold positions from one or two days to about one or two months. And there are investors who tend to hold the same positions from several months to many years. The first two categories of traders are often called speculators instead of investors. I find myself to be clearly in the middle category because I tend to hold positions from about three days to three months, depending on market conditions and individual stock price fluctuations.

My choice of such a short-term window is related to the concept of fractals that are involved in all natural measurements. To illustrate this point I might ask you the length of the State of California from the northern border of Mexico to the southern boundary of Oregon. If you consulted an atlas, you might reply that it is approximately 850 statute miles. But if you were to measure the coastal distance using fractals, you might conclude that it was a much greater distance—perhaps even rivaling the distance from the earth to the moon. I cannot be sure of the exact distance because no one has ever attempted such a measurement. To do so, one would need a flexible measuring tape or string of great length. One would need to hold all of the waves and tides constant long enough to trace the waterline for the entire length of the coast. One would need to go in and around San Francisco Bay, and all other inlets. One would need some decision rule to consider all rivers and other coastal tributaries. Although the presumed prevailing direction of measurement would be from south to north, many times the actual measurement would proceed from east to west or from west to east—or even from north to south. The point is that the true fractal distance would be many times greater than 850 statute miles.

The situation is very similar with the price movement of stocks. Consider for example a stock that has moved upward in price from 10 dollars to 15 dollars a share over the course of one year. An investor may be pleased with this 50 percent gain. However, a speculator like me might look at the chart and say, "Wait a minute! This stock actually went from 10 dollars to 8 dollars to 12 dollars to 11 dollars to 17 dollars to 14 dollars to 15 dollars." We can see that its actual price movement was much greater than the 5 dollar gain realized by the investor. What if he had bought at 8, sold at 12, bought again at 11, sold at 17, and bought again at 14? His gain would then be 11 dollars or 137.5 percent instead of 50 percent. This illustration may be oversimplified, but it explains why my own trading window is so narrow, and why I may frequently repurchase stocks without apology that I have sold only a few short weeks earlier.

Another related concern about timing is the observation that there are periods when it is advantageous to be fully invested in stocks, and there are times when it is best to be out of the market altogether. This opinion is brought home convincingly in Figure 10.1 of Chapter 10. There we can see that equity markets go through predictable cycles reflected in periods that are clearly advantageous or clearly disadvantageous for investing. I did not always believe that it was necessary or even possible to time the markets, but you will see later in this book why my views on this matter have changed dramatically.

STOCKS VERSUS COMMODITIES, OPTIONS, MUTUAL FUNDS, AND BONDS

Early on I traded in nearly every market to which I had access where I thought gains were available. I remember buying heating oil futures in the fall, thinking that prices had to go up in winter—only to discover that the reality was much more complex. Similarly, I bought orange juice futures when Florida experienced a hard freeze, not considering imports from Brazil. I bought precious metal futures as a hedge against inflation, only to see them retreat when worker productivity climbed. This pattern persisted for me in a variety of different commodities until one day I came across a web site where the profits of all major commodities trading firms were reported. I was astounded to discover that the best of the firms were averaging monthly returns of only about 1 percent and this in spite of all of their resources, professional research, and trading experience. That was when I gave up on commodities; although I still do trade exchange-traded funds and stocks that deal in a variety of commodities and other financial instruments.

Next, I discovered that options trading had one great advantage over stock trading; namely, options were much less expensive than their underlying stocks, so that when the price moved up, the percentage gain from options was potentially much greater than with stocks. Eventually, I traded OEX Index options to take advantage of the greater trading volume and liquidity than was available with most individual stocks. Certainly option trading is not a boring pursuit. I can remember the exhilaration of riding a call to its peak, exchanging it for the associated put option, and reaping the benefit as the underlying equity value declined. But then I made two disconcerting discoveries. The first was that options expire after a specified period, and if they are not exercised before expiration, the owner is left with nothing. I learned also that the majority of options did actually expire unexercised, so that most options traders were losing the battle. It was no great consolation that options were cheaper than stocks when the prospect of losing one's entire investment was ever present. The second discovery that was even more disconcerting was that options values do not always move in tandem with the underlying stock or index. Because options pricing is determined by supply and demand, it happened too often that the underlying stock or index would move up, but the option price would be unaffected. Eventually, these two considerations led me to abandon options as viable investments for me personally. I realized that I could alternatively choose to sell options on my stock holdings, effectively "renting out" my stocks in order to benefit from the premiums and the expiration phenomenon, but the potential returns from that activity appeared to be less than my avowed goals.

My next foray was into the arena of mutual funds trading. This was at a time when I was working at a full-time job as a university professor, and I did not have time to monitor my holdings throughout each trading day. It was also at a time when equities were in a long-term bull market and the Fidelity Funds imposed no penalty on short-term trading of their sector funds. These circumstances changed, and so did my attitude towards the trading of mutual funds. It concerned me that mutual funds were usually available for trading only once each day at the close of trading—meaning that there was not sufficient liquidity to deal with intraday news developments. It also troubled me that I had no control over the individual stock holdings in my funds, and the reported holdings were often six months or more outdated. Also, I had a growing conviction that I could pick stocks better than most of the mutual fund managers, so my only logical recourse was to select my own individual stocks. In addition, after I read the valuable book by Gary Smith on mutual funds trading that is referenced in Table 2.2, I realized that success in mutual funds trading depends a lot on one's skill as a market timer. Lacking that skill, I decided to stick with individual stocks. I have subsequently learned the hard lesson, however, that even when the focus is on the trading of individual stocks, a successful trader will learn the rudiments of market timing. William O'Neil (1995) was right when he asserted that general market trends are important concerns for those who trade individual stocks.

Bonds were never a great temptation for me. Bonds lacked the level of annualized return I sought. They seemed to be attractive only in bear markets, which fortunately are less frequent than bull markets. Also, with all due respect, bond traders appear to me to be the morticians of the market. They get excited only when there is some major calamity in the world and investors flee to bonds for safety. Of course, it is helpful that such a refuge exists, if only to preserve capital for reinvestment in stocks when the storms pass. I do recognize that there are many profitable trading arenas, and bond trading can be one of them, but just as fishermen seem predisposed to particular methods of fishing, I find the trading of stocks to be far more satisfying. Recently, a variety of exchange-traded funds (ETFs) have been created that deal in bonds and other financial instruments. Thus, the safety of bonds can be available while at the same time it is possible to maintain the liquidity of stocks, and in this way the distinctions among bonds and stocks and commodities have become blurred. That is probably the only way in which I personally ever invest in bonds.

SHORT TRADING

A word is in order about short trading. In every market trend, whether positive or negative, there are always individual stocks that are rising in price and those that are falling in price. Even during the negative time of the September 11, 2001 terrorist attacks, airport security stocks had a big run. Similarly, during the strongest of bull markets there are companies that fall into scandal and go bankrupt. Therefore, it appears that maximum earnings potential is found in those portfolios that hold both long and short positions simultaneously, and there is some research evidence to support that view. However, fortunately, equities markets have an upward bias over time.

If, as some advocate, the Fibonacci ratio, 0.618, holds in market trends as it does in other natural events, then the overall odds of success with random long positions compared to random short positions would be approximately 5 to 3. Thus, over time it is more difficult to succeed with short positions than with long positions, and a trader who exclusively trades short is swimming upstream. Furthermore, just as intensive long-position acquisition tends to drive share prices higher, intensive short-position acquisition tends to work in reverse and causes companies to lose capitalization.

Although it can be argued that short trading enhances liquidity for some stocks, it can also be shown that short trading of individual stocks may require additional capital—usually $25,000—in one's account that is essentially tied up to ensure against risk, and thus it can limit trading reach. However, my chief personal objection to shorting individual stocks is that seeking to benefit from the losses of others has little socially redeeming value. It distresses me that some hedge fund managers have been permitted to buy naked shorts with little collateral and thereby to play havoc with our equity markets. Unless serious controls are imposed on shorting activity, such as enforcement of the uptick rule or suspension of margin availability, massive hedge fund shorting can seriously destabilize equity markets—to say nothing of the potential that shorting has to destroy individual companies wrongfully. Shorting also provides motivation for dishonorable individuals to spread false rumors about companies in order to drive their share prices down. This to me is like shouting "Fire!" in a crowded theater.

All things considered, my own philosophy of trading has been to trade long almost exclusively. So far, this has worked for me to such an extent that I see no need to change and go short individual stocks. For me to succeed over the long haul, I must believe that what I do is noble and beneficial for humanity. When I short individual companies and cause them to lose capitalization, I lose that very confidence that gives me a competitive advantage. It is worth mentioning, however, that the function of hedging positions through shorting stocks can also be achieved through the purchase of index put options and leveraged bear funds, if anyone is so inclined. In addition, as I note in Chapters 10 and 11 of this book, with appropriate use of market-timing indicators, we can identify periods when the overall equity market can be expected to turn down and enter a bearish trend. During such negative periods it may be appropriate to own shares in an exchange-traded inverse index fund such as any one of dozens of such funds that have been created in the past decade.

USE OF MARGIN

Brokerages will usually lend money against your current account holdings to permit you to leverage additional purchases. The limitations are such that IRA accounts are ineligible, stocks priced under $4 or $5 are usually ineligible, and no more than 50 percent leveraging is permitted. Thus, for a $10,000 account of the right kind, you might be allowed to leverage and purchase up to $20,000 of acceptable stocks in return for whatever margin interest rate your brokerage might assess. The good news here is that, if you are fully margined and your stock holdings rise in value 10 percent, you have then earned a 20 percent gain on your original investment, minus the margin interest fees.

This sounds terrific. But wait! The bad news is that, if your stock holdings fall in value 10 percent, you have then lost 20 percent on your original investment, plus the cost of the margin interest. If, in this way, the capital remaining in your account drops below 35 percent of your holdings, you will receive a dreaded margin call. This will require you either to deposit more funds to restore 50 percent capitalization, or to liquidate sufficient stock at the rate of two for one in order to satisfy the call. And this does not take into consideration the cost of commissions and losses due to spread at the time of the transaction, i.e., the distance between the bid and ask price, which are also leveraged. If market conditions are strongly biased in your favor, and if the particular equity holdings in your account are nearly guaranteed to rise in value quickly, then you stand a chance of success. Otherwise, it is best to avoid the temptation to trade on margin. In my personal experience, my best success with margin was in trading mutual funds in a bull market. Interestingly, for some brokerages, their greatest earnings come from margin interest charges.

TRADING AND GAMBLING

For many years I was unwilling to attempt to trade for a living. My reluctance was due to my belief that stock trading was a form of gambling, which is contrary to my values system. The more I reflected on this problem, however, the more I realized that trading is no more gambling than farming is. When a farmer plants his crops, he has no guarantee of a harvest, much less of a market for his harvest. Yet he is taking on huge risk by investing in seeds and cultivation. Nevertheless, farming is considered a noble pursuit because it feeds the masses by relying on a combination of hard work, learned skill, and trust in Providence. However, to the extent that the farmer does not accompany obvious risk with hard work, appropriate learning, and trust in Providence, his efforts may indeed amount to a form of gambling, just as can be the case with many other pursuits. Through appropriate learning he can manage risk in such a way that the odds of success are greatly in his favor. Through appropriate planning he can distribute risk in such a way that one year of drought will not necessarily destroy his enterprise. Through hard work he can enhance his productivity.

The trading of equities is very similar. It can supply needed capital to promising new businesses and thereby provide jobs and goods and services. Through appropriate learning, you can manage risk so that the odds of success are ultimately in your favor. Through hard work, you can locate and capitalize on the most appropriate investments at any given time. Thus, trading need not be gambling. The decision to become a stock trader may not even be motivated by the desire to get rich, although it often is. This decision may come about as a logical consideration of the best alternative for appropriate stewardship of resources already accumulated. In other words, at some point it may be cost effective to take time off other work to manage your stock portfolio rather than to leave this responsibility to others while you work another job. You may find that it is more productive to make your own trading decisions than it is to let some fund manager make those decisions for you.

Recently I have had occasion to reflect on the fact that writing books on stock trading might also be considered a form of gambling because such books can represent an enormous investment of time, at the same time that there is no guarantee that anyone will buy them or read them. Fortunately the value of articulating one's beliefs and procedures in this area includes inherent compensation that mitigates risk.

People of conscience have never condoned gambling. Perhaps this is because gambling losses are wasteful, and gambling gains come at the expense of others. But trading in long positions is an entirely different category of behavior that can be as noble as farming or fishing or book writing because it does not produce zero-sum gains. To be strictly consistent, one could argue that stock trading is a vastly more noble pursuit than safely putting money in the bank to draw interest, because the Bible is a guide to moral conduct in many places (for example, Psalm 15:5; Proverbs 28:8; Ezekiel 18:8) speaks critically of the receiving of interest on some kinds of investments, at the same time that it speaks of rewards given for successful trading (Luke 19:15–17). In this connection, I welcomed the comments of Warren Buffett during a recent severe market downturn. He said that "cash is trash" and everyone should buy stock in order to help the economy.

BOLD PASSION

It is a matter of supreme importance that stock traders have a passion for trading. Trading should be an exercise of sheer delight, and not one of painful drudgery. Here I am mindful of the words of a championship college basketball coach who repeatedly told his players that he wanted them to have fun every time they were on the court, no matter who their opponents were and no matter what the consequences of the game might be. Of course, it is always more fun when you are winning. However, there is still the competitive thrill that comes from pushing oneself to the limit of one's endurance and exercising all of the reserve of one's hitherto undiscovered talent in the great rhythmic dance. It is a supreme learning opportunity where one can both learn how to play better and can reach new limits of self discovery. It would make no sense to tell athletes that that they would not be allowed to participate in a sport unless and until they were guaranteed that they would be number one in that sport. Imagine telling people that they would not be allowed to play golf unless their name was Tiger Woods.

Nevertheless, without the necessary passion, the trader will not only fail to face the opposition and overcome temporary defeats, but will also avoid bold new moves that spark success. In this motivational struggle, I am often reminded of the words of Jesus, "Actively trade until I come" (Luke 19:13, original Greek). This implies a need to be active and aggressive, and a need to persevere. Without a bold passion for trading, no trader can actively persevere in the face of those setbacks that will certainly come.

SUMMARY

In summary, the process of trading stocks may be best understood through the consideration of various analogies. The particular philosophical approach to trading advocated in this book is pragmatic. Such an approach works to produce desired results even if the underlying theoretical explanation of outcomes is not fully understood. If this approach consistently fails to produce earnings of 10 percent per month, then it is time to pause, reexamine, adjust, or replace the trading system.

There will be a lot of time and effort involved in implementation of a successful trading system, but the rewards should more than compensate for this. Many different approaches to stock trading can lead to successful outcomes. The trading systems advanced here do not usually involve taking short positions in equities, nor do they lead to long term buy-and-hold strategies, nor can they be labeled day trading. It is acknowledged from the outset that trading is a dangerous endeavor that is not for the faint of heart, but it can and should become a passionately enjoyable activity. Also, maintaining the necessary passion for trading is helped by maintaining a posture that does not bring harm to others. And it must ultimately be acknowledged that many of the variables at play in stock trading will always be beyond one's personal control.

CHAPTER 2

Tools of
the Trade

The opportunities for success in stock trading are truly mind-boggling. I recently witnessed a biotechnology stock jump 224 percent in value in one day on the heels of the announcement of the successful preliminary testing of a cure for arthritis. I suppose these opportunities have always been present, but today's technology can bring them instantly to our doorstep. In order to take advantage of these opportunities, we have need of several kinds of tools for stock trading. No carpenter, mechanic, physician, farmer, fisherman, or stock trader can expect to succeed without the right kinds and qualities of tools. At the same time it has been said that a poor carpenter always blames his tools, so it must be recognized that possession of the right tools is a necessary but insufficient condition for success in trading. There must also be good judgment and skill in using the tools. Here then are some necessary tools for success in trading.

ONLINE ACCESS

Although it seems that most people today already have high-speed Internet access, such access is so crucial that it bears emphasis here. Today's stock trader needs high-speed computer access to the Internet. A good computer with updated security protection is essential. High-speed connectivity to the Internet is absolutely essential, and is well worth the expense. Small, infrequently traded accounts can be managed with dial-up connections through Internet service providers. However, managing large accounts and several portfolios simultaneously requires broadband or other high-speed access to the Internet. Implicit in this access is the need for a high-speed computer with sufficient storage capacity to maintain and access trading software and data base management software at the same time that you are actively engaged in trading.

A RELIABLE BROKERAGE ACCOUNT

It is not my purpose to recommend any particular brokerage house. Suffice to say that I found that I reduced trading overhead expenses by 30 percent when I moved my primary trading portfolios from one discount brokerage that charges ten dollars a trade to another discount brokerage that charges only seven dollars a trade, regardless of whether trades are on market or limit orders. That is a big deal when you average between 10 and 20 trades per day as I do. In time it is likely that competitive trading commissions will become lower still, and it is best to take advantage of this trend. In fact, it is probably best to have more than one brokerage account. Recently, one of my brokerage accounts went down because of an ice storm in the area of the central trading office of the brokerage house. Its web site became unresponsive. It was not even possible for them to execute trades or monitor stock prices for several hours that morning. I was happy for my secondary brokerage account, where I could still monitor my holdings in real time.

In addition to the cost savings they may provide on commissions, some brokerages offer software trading platforms at their websites. This can be highly useful for stock analysis and account management. It is also beneficial if your brokerage has an office nearby. It is comforting to be able to look your broker or trading representative in the eye from time to time. Cultivating a positive relationship with your local brokerage staff can be a mutually rewarding endeavor, and it can be especially beneficial when you need special services such as wiring fund transfers. Also, the record-keeping benefits of a brokerage are not inconsequential for tax reporting purposes. In choosing a brokerage it is worthwhile to consider whether it employs tax-reporting software that allows you to prepare income tax reports with ease. It may also be useful for you to maintain a personal checking account through your brokerage if that is available.

In choosing a brokerage, therefore, there are a variety of considerations. Commissions should be competitive. Service should be prompt and courteous. On-line executions should be fast and accurate. The services provided and the cost structures should be compatible with the style of trading you maintain. For example, if you trade options frequently, the trading representatives should be fully informed about the nuances of such trading, they should be supportive of the strategies you wish to employ, and the commissions for option contracts should be competitive. Having the brokerage office nearby your home or work will be a definite plus. The on-line trading platforms should be state of the art. Also, there should be soft-ware available for income tax preparation purposes, such as Gainskeeper software.

INFORMATION

It is really not possible to trade successfully without many kinds of infor-mation. For example, one must know the share price of any stock of inter-est at the very instant that a buy or sell order is being contemplated. One must also know the bid and ask prices. Beyond that, the trader needs tech-nical information regarding how the stock has been trending over the past days and weeks, what the proximity is to its 52-week high, and what the trading volume has been. Of course, many kinds of fundamental informa-tion are also needed, such as earnings per share, cash flow and free cash flow per share, price/earnings ratio, price/sales ratio, debt per share, and forward earnings estimates.

Just as it is not possible to wage war successfully without intelligence information, so it is that successful stock trading requires a lot of timely information. Most of this information is available free of charge over the Internet. Thus, a collection of frequently visited websites is vital. Table 2.1 summarizes alphabetically several of my own most frequently visited web-sites, and some of the free information available at each.

Every trader should develop a unique collection of frequently visited websites. Over time these sites will change as different kinds of infor-mation become available in different locations and as some sites become outdated.

In addition to the abundant and timely information available on the In-ternet, other media also provide helpful resources. CNBC and Bloomberg TV provide useful information each day, so that many traders also watch them constantly during market hours in order to get timely insights. Print media also provide essential information. A trader should make it a prac-tice to read widely in order to gain appreciation of strategies and targets. It is especially useful to read interviews with successful traders. This will help identify approaches to trading that are best suited to individual tem-peraments, and it will help the trader establish reasonable expectations re-garding each approach. Table 2.2 lists those authors and publications that have been most helpful and influential in the development of my own trad-ing style.

TABLE 2.1 Stock Trading Websites

Websites	Information Available
http://Americanbulls.com	Individual stock signals and buy/sell recommendations
http://barchart.com	Technical analysis, stock signals, stock ratings
http://bigcharts.marketwatch.com	Interactive charting of EPS/PE discrepancies
http://www.cboe.com	Data on put/call ratios, and volatility index movement for market timing
http://cbsmarketwatch.com/tools/ quotes/profile	Fundamental data, cash flow, valuation ratios
http://clearstation.etrade.com	Fundamental ratios, cash flow and free cash flow per share ratios, futures prices
http://finance.google.com	Basic stock information, delayed quotes
http://finance.yahoo.com	Portfolio management, delayed quotes, key statistics, stock message boards
http://www.ino.com/exchanges/ futboard	Equity index futures, commodity futures
http://moneycentral.msn.com	Stock Scouter ratings, portfolio management, basic stock analysis
http://ragingbull.quote.com	Penny stock bulletin boards
http://stockcharts.com	Stock charting, money flow, technical ratings, new highs data
http://vectorvest.com	Limited free stock analysis

There are also several helpful periodicals which you may elect to obtain, such as *Investors' Business Daily*, the *Wall Street Journal*, and *Barrons*. However, much of their most useful information is now available over the Internet. The interview collections in Table 2.2 by Schwager, Tanous, and Train are a good place to start your reading. They are a tremendous help to beginners who are seeking to find their trading styles and to set appropriate expectations. I regularly go back and reread them from time to time. I try also to make it a practice to read at least one new trading book each month. This is an excellent way to keep abreast of new developments and successful strategies in trading.

FORMAL STUDY

For those who have the opportunity to pursue higher education courses, there are many outstanding programs of study, but few of them actually

TABLE 2.2 Foundational Readings

Binnewies, R. *The Options Course: A Winning Program for Investors and Traders.* New York: Irwin Professional Publishing, 1995.

Frost, A.J. & Prechter, R.R. *Elliott Wave Principle.* Gainsville, GA: New Classics Library, 1990.

Fullman, S.H. *Options: A Personal Seminar.* New York: New York Institute of Finance/ Simon & Schuster, 1992.

Graham, B. *The Intelligent Investor: A Book of Practical Counsel.* New York: Harper Collins, 2003.

Harnett, D.L. and J.F. Horrell. *Data, Statistics, and Decision Models with Excel.* New York: John Wiley & Sons, 1998.

Jurik, M., ed. *Computerized Trading: Maximizing Day Trading and Overnight Profits.* New York: New York Institute of Finance, 1999.

LeFevre, E. *Reminiscences of a Stock Operator.* New York: John Wiley & Sons, 1994.

Lynch, P. *One Up on Wall Street: How to Use What You Already Know to Make Money in the Market.* New York: Penguin Books, 1989.

Markman, J.D. *Swing Trading: Power Strategies to Cut Risk and Boost Profits.* Hoboken, NJ: John Wiley & Sons, 2003.

Maturi, R.J. *Divining the Dow: 100 of the World's Most Widely Followed Stock Market Prediction Systems.* Chicago: Probus Publishing Company, 1993.

Maturi, R.J. *Stock Picking: The 11 Best Tactics for Beating the Market.* New York: McGraw-Hill, 1993.

Nassar, D.S. *Rules of the Trade: Indispensable Insights for Online Profits.* New York: McGraw-Hill, 2001.

O'Neil, W.J. *How to Make Money in Stocks: A Winning System in Good Times or Bad.* New York: McGraw-Hill, 1995.

Peters, E.E. *Chaos and Order in the Capital Markets: A New View of Cycles, Prices, and Market Volatility.* New York: John Wiley & Sons, 1991.

Schwager, J.D. *Market Wizards: Interviews with Top Traders.* New York: Harper & Row, 1990.

Schwager, J.D. *The New Market Wizards: Conversations with America's Top Traders.* New York: Harper Collins, 1992.

Schwager, J.D. *Getting Started in Technical Analysis.* New York: John Wiley & Sons, 1999.

Schwager, J.D. *Stock Market Wizards: Revised and Updated.* New York: Harper Collins, 2003.

Smith, G. *How I Trade for a Living.* New York: John Wiley & Sons, 2000.

Sperandeo, V. *Trader Vic: Methods of a Wall Street Master.* New York: John Wiley & Sons, 1993.

Sperandeo, V. *Trader Vic II: Principles of Professional Speculation.* New York: John Wiley & Sons, 1994.

Tanous, P.J. *Investment Gurus: A Road Map to Wealth from the World's Best Money Managers.* New York: New York Institute of Finance, 1997.

Train, J. *The Money Masters: Nine Great Investors: Their Winning Strategies and How You Can Apply Them.* New York: Harper & Row, 1980.

Zweig, M. *Winning on Wall Street: How to Spot Market Trends Early, Which Stocks to Pick, When to Buy and Sell for Peak Profits and Minimum Risk.* New York: Warner Books, Inc., 1990.

train traders in approaches to the trading of equities. Critical in the choice of a degree program are factors such as (1) adequate trading facilities with hardware and software access on campus, (2) the availability of strong econometric and statistical courses to cultivate necessary research skills, (3) the presence of faculty with trading experience and knowledge of the workings of equity markets, (4) the availability of practical courses such as portfolio management and the associated analysis of equity derivatives, and (5) training in auditing and analysis of corporate financials. Although it is not my purpose to recommend any one program, programs such as those of the Smeal College of Business at Pennsylvania State University, the Graduate School of Business at the University of Chicago, and Wharton School of Finance at the University of Pennsylvania are well known programs of excellence.

I must hasten to point out, however, that my own higher education experience was not in finance, but was in psychometrics, educational psychology, and applied linguistics, so I believe it is possible to succeed as an equities trader without the benefit of the usual formal programs of study. For some of us, trading is a form of intellectual arbitrage in that we are taking information and skills acquired in other disciplines and applying them to trading. This implies that formal training in quantitative research methods will definitely be beneficial, even if those methods were not learned in a business school environment. One trader whom I respect once commented that there may even be a correlation between the ability to play chess well and the ability to succeed in a trading milieu. Certainly both activities require analytical skills, the ability to anticipate threats to success, the memorization of opening strategies, and familiarity with the variety and situational appropriateness of the moves that can be made.

ANALYSIS SOFTWARE

Traders with their own unique methods of database management and stock analysis usually rely on software packages as tools. As you will see as we proceed to examine my personal trading systems, I rely heavily on Microsoft Excel to maintain stock data and carry out mathematical computations. This enables me to rank all stocks in the universe of available candidate stocks in terms of their relative merits for buying or selling according to my own selection algorithm. There are also several other suitable database management software packages. Platforms like Microsoft Office are ideal in that they provide both widely used word processing software and database management software in the same package. Having Microsoft PowerPoint included is an added bonus when it comes to explaining what we do in a public forum. Some traders also invest heavily in commercial trading platforms that offer buy and sell signals. Personally, I tend to believe that most of the benefits of those packages are available elsewhere at no cost. In Chapter 15 instructions are provided in the use of an accompanying CD with Excel spreadsheets that may be used to implement the trading systems described elsewhere in this book.

PROTECTED WORKSPACE

It is difficult to overstate the need for a quietworkplace devoid of distractions. This need came home to me again recently as I was visiting with family in another city. On a particular day I could see that one of my stocks was moving up rapidly in a rally. I had a target sell order in at around 15 dollars, and I wanted to move it up to 18. However, in the next two minutes some family members came through to say hello and ask how things were going. In that brief time my sell order was executed at 15. I watched in disbelief from the sidelines as the stock rapidly climbed to 19 and then fell back. Although I was delighted to speak with family members, those two minutes cost several thousand dollars in missed opportunity.

The point is that every active trader needs a workplace that is protected from distractions during specified market hours. Even the distraction of a telephone call during market hours can cost a trader many thousands of dollars. Of course, this need not always be the case. In this regard, trading is a little like swimming breaststroke. You need to pause for air at regular intervals. It takes practice to time those intervals correctly.

MATHEMATICAL TRADING SYSTEMS

Another tool for success that is a special focus of this book is a mathematical trading system. By this I mean a set of mathematical procedures for identifying stocks for purchase or sale. It is a kind of algorithm that takes into consideration all of the known important measurable variables that determine stock performance and combines these variables with appropriate weightings to provide precise and reliable recommendations for dealing with every stock in the available trading universe. The advantages of such a tool are profound. It can eliminate much of the guessing and emotional anxiety from the task of stock picking. It can also rank order any subset of stocks for purchase or sale. Of course, no such system will be perfect because there will always be factors outside of the realm of prediction and control. Also, it must be acknowledged that appropriate stock selection is only one important activity involved in successful stock trading; but it is, after all, one of the most important activities.

It is possible also to subscribe to a service that provides the results of some mathematical trading analysis for decision-making purposes. This is precisely what happens when you subscribe to *Investors' Business Daily* or *Vector Vest* or some similar service. However, the focus of this book is on the development of your own independent trading system. There are many ways to approach the construction of mathematical trading systems. Neural networking is another example of mathematical analysis that can provide a basis for stock selection that is not explored in this book. The next chapters of this book are dedicated to the description of several mathematical trading systems. The nature of the activity and the extent of time and space available will limit any possibility of providing an exhaustive treatment of this important subject, but it is hoped that enough details will be available for you to copy and refine or develop your own mathematical trading system.

MARKET TIMING INDICATORS

Originally, I did not believe that it was either possible or necessary to time the general market. After all, I was buying individual stocks and some of them even had zero or negative betas, suggesting that they did not move historically with general market trends. However, in one market downtrend it became painfully obvious to me that nearly all of my stock positions moved down together with the general market. This happened in spite of the fact those stocks had been selected with due diligence and careful scrutiny of individual stock fundamental and technical indicators. It happened even though I was fully diversified across economic sectors and capitalization sizes. It was then that I learned that William O'Neil was correct when he asserted in his book *How to Make Money in Stocks* (1995) that determining general market trends is important for successful investing in individual stocks. But I was still not convinced that market timing was possible. Subsequently, I have found some helpful timing indicators that do indeed serve as guidelines for deciding when to be in or out of the general stock market. These will be discussed in Chapters 3, 10, and 11.

SUMMARY

It is critical to success that any stock market trader should have the tools necessary for success. These include high-speed Internet access, an appropriate discount brokerage account, access to many different kinds of timely information, formal education if possible, suitable analysis software, a workplace that is protected from distractions, one or more mathematical trading systems, and, ideally, some tools for timing the overall market.

CHAPTER 3

Constructing Mathematical Models for Stock Selection

Possibly the single most important activity in stock trading is identification and selection of the appropriate stocks to acquire. There are many different approaches to this important task. It is possible to group the different approaches under three broad rubrics: technical approaches, fundamental approaches, and hybrid technical-fundamental approaches. In this chapter, I share why I have increasingly moved from a strictly value-based approach to a hybrid approach. It is also critical for traders to decide the extent to which stock selection should be guided by mathematical formulations as opposed to mere intuition or professional recommendations. In the process of quantifying the stock selection process, we also need to be aware of common mistakes that should be avoided.

TECHNICAL APPROACHES TO STOCK SELECTION

Technical traders are most concerned with share price, momentum, volume, rate of ascent or descent in price, patterns of price movement, and proximity of price to new highs or lows. A true technician will usually claim that everything important about a stock is reflected in the price movement. If the stock is moving up, the claim is made that buyer sentiment is positive, and this in turn reflects all that is important and knowable about earnings, prospects for the future, management quality, sector strength, insider buying, sales, and so forth. In fact, some technicians may even claim that the fundamental data about a company are usually dated and inaccurate and not worth the time to consider, since everything is already reflected in the price. Or they may claim that the cost of any valid fundamental information that might provide a trading advantage washes out any advantage that may be obtained thereby.

Technicians are therefore highly concerned about price movement and have developed elaborate systems for the interpretation of charts and graphs of price fluctuation. Some have even been called "chartists" because of this focus. If the focus is largely on rate of share price increase and accompanying trading volume, these technicians may also be called "growth" or "momentum" investors; although fundamental traders may also be concerned with certain kinds of growth. Many successful investors apply technical approaches to the selection of stocks. Also, traders who trade options on major equity indexes must constantly rely on technical indicators for timing information. Elaborate technical schemes such as the Elliot Wave Principle referenced in Table 2.2 have evolved to assist traders in the interpretation and timing of market trends. As we shall see, there are websites that provide free technical information on all stocks that have been traded publicly for several months or long enough so that technical profiles are possible.

FUNDAMENTAL APPROACHES TO STOCK SELECTION

Fundamental traders are concerned most about value. Many different formulas have been developed for the promulgation of value, but most of these require some estimates of earnings, assets, and liabilities of the company in relation to share price and capitalization. Fundamental traders are often most concerned with price/earnings ratios, price/sales ratios, cash flow, and long-term debt of the company. The prevailing belief here is that by purchasing stocks that are undervalued, the trader will eventually realize gains in share price. The identification of undervalued stocks is therefore the primary focus, even though it often means holding undervalued stocks for a long time in the hope that their value will eventually be recognized in the marketplace. Investors that adopt this approach are often called "value" investors. Historically, many value investors have been highly successful as traders. These would include such notables as Benjamin Graham and Warren Buffett, whose writings are referenced in Table 2.2. Several of the websites listed in Table 2.1 provide fundamental data that facilitate this approach to trading. As an interesting aside, extreme random-walk theorists would maintain that there are no undervalued stocks in the marketplace, but that all stocks quickly reach equilibrium—a state where they are appropriately priced by the market according to their perceived value at any given time. The best argument against this extreme position is to note the many successful traders who capitalize on equity disequilibrium every day.

HYBRID APPROACHES TO STOCK SELECTION

In the considered opinion of this author, the most successful approaches to trading may ultimately require a combination of technical and fundamental strategies—a hybrid approach. In this way, fundamental data can help us identify the best values among stocks and technical data can inform us about the best timing for buying and selling those stocks. Most traders focus on one or two variables of interest, whether technical or fundamental, to the exclusion of all others. Although such a limited focus can lead to some success in trading, it may not permit optimal success. To return to the race car analogy mentioned in Chapter 1, if in designing the best possible race car we limit our focus to aerodynamic improvements, we will miss additional improvements possible through engine efficiencies or tire tread modifications. Thus, I believe that to call oneself a technical trader or a value trader to the exclusion of other defining variables is to limit potential in the same way. Examples of hybrid approaches to stock selection can be found in *Investors' Business Daily* and *Vector Vest*.

THE NATURE OF THE STOCK SELECTION CHALLENGE

In my view, stock selection can be reduced to an analysis of variance problem. By this I mean that the task is to find those variables that together explain the most variation in performance and combine them with the best possible weightings in order to maximize success in predicting future performance. There are many variables that deserve consideration in the process of constructing a model for predicting stock performance. Many of those variables, like high earnings and low debt, overlap like overlapping circles in a Venn diagram. Some of the variables, like chart patterns, are difficult to quantify and measure in a manner that is amenable to incorporation in a mathematical model. Choosing the right variables and weighting them appropriately is therefore a huge challenge.

Although statistical methods can be very helpful in this process, stock selection system design has ultimately posed challenges for even the keenest statistical minds. Many conventional statistical methods require normal distributions in the population targeted for generalization. This assumption has been questioned with stock market data because the variance observed often exceeds expectation. Most statistical methods assume independence of distribution. However, many stocks seem interrelated in the sense that they rise and fall together with undulations in the overall market. Using analysis of covariance to control for overall market variation becomes problematic because of the non-uniformity of component betas. Quite apart from these statistical challenges, a number of other mistakes are commonly made in the process of system design.

COMMON MISTAKES IN SYSTEM DESIGN FOR DECISION MAKING

In the process of designing mathematical systems for stock selection, the choice of variables to enter the models is a critical concern. Often the models employ too few variables, insufficiently diverse variables, invalid variables, or too many variables. I call these mistakes respectively under-specification, narrow specification, inaccurate specification, and over-specification.

Under-Specification

The first mistake some traders make is to rely on too few variables in selecting stocks for acquisition. For example, a value investor might screen stocks based on book value and PE ratio and leave it at that. Or a chartist might purchase a stock based solely on a double-bottom pattern or a cup-and-handle pattern in the performance chart and rush off to buy the stock. Those can be important indicators and often do lead to success, but over time they are inadequate in themselves as sole determiners of which stocks to buy and when to buy them. We could say that they are useful, but insufficient, bases for important stock-selection decisions.

Narrow Specification

A second mistake in stock selection appears when sufficient numbers of variables are employed, but the variables are all in the same category. For example, if you were to go to Barchart.Com for a quote on any U.S.-traded stock and to seek an opinion about the viability of that stock for acquisition, you would get valuable short-term, medium-term, long-term, and composite ratings based on thirteen useful variables of interest. However, all of those variables are technical variables, and none are fundamental. Although I rely on those same variables daily as timing indicators, I believe them to be too ephemeral to serve as the entire basis for ideal stock selection. Of course a strictly technical trader would disagree, believing that technical indicators incorporate and reflect all useful fundamental information.

Inaccurate Specification

A third common mistake is to rely on a variety of variables for stock selection, but to choose the wrong variables, immeasurable variables, or redundant variables. For example, in William O'Neil's excellent book *How to Make Money in Stocks* (1995), we find that he has identified seven key variables for stock selection according to his C-A-N S-L-I-M method. These variables include both fundamental variables such as current quarterly earnings per share and technical or timing variables such as new highs in share price. This is a vast improvement over systems that rely on only one or two variables, or even on several variables that are all in the same category, and this helps to explain why O'Neil and *Investors' Business Daily* have been so successful in stock picking. However, the "N" of his method refers to "New Products, New Management, and New Highs." Although I do not doubt that these are all important considerations, when it comes to establishing mathematical models for stock selection, it should be apparent that products, management, and share-price highs are qualitatively different component variables that are not additive as part of the same unified measurement construct. They are thus immeasurable as a unified construct. Furthermore, "New Management" is not always an improvement, and thus it may sometimes have an adverse effect on share price. In fairness, O'Neil's approach has doubtless undergone many further refinements since the publication of his fine book, and I find that many of my own independent stock selections do parallel those of *Investors' Business Daily* that was founded by O'Neil and makes use of his approach. My point overall is that optimal stock selection requires attention to a variety of non-redundant, measurable, and highly predictive variables that can inform both value and timing concerns.

Over-Specification

It is also possible to employ too many variables for stock selection. It needs to be recognized also that there is an observable principle of diminishing returns or a possibility of "measurement overkill" when ordering variables for stock selection. As with the construction of any performance prediction model, we will find that with the inclusion of every new explanatory variable, there is less variance in performance left to be explained. Therefore, after we have identified a handful of key technical variables and a handful of key fundamental variables, there is no variable of interest left that will add any new predictive power to our model.

This same phenomenon is observable in the construction of models to predict student academic success in college. Thus, after we have included high-school grade-point averages, Scholastic Aptitude Test scores, parental education and income levels, and possibly some attitude-towards-study inventory scores, there may be no other variable left that can enhance the prediction of success. Even such important variables as well-established study habits and student work ethic may already be encompassed in high school grade-point average, so that including these new variables is inviting redundancy that adds nothing to prediction accuracy.

When we use a statistical procedure such as stepwise multiple regression analysis, these redundancies become readily apparent. Each of these statistical methods identifies and even quantifies errors of measurement and estimation, so that we do not blindly pass over the possibility of variable-selection mistakes. But again, these statistical methods assume normal and independent distributions, so we can use them only as a preliminary or partial step in decision making. The point here is that, even if we discover variables that are highly predictive of share-price gain, it is possible to include too many of them in our prediction model, and thereby we invite redundancies and excessive labor.

EARLY BEGINNING APPROACHES

I began my quest for an optimal trading system with a value-investing approach. I used a multiple regression statistical method to backtest a number of fundamental variables to find which ones were best predictors of share-price gain. I found several key variables that were important criteria for stock selection. These included a weighted combination of cash-flow-per-share ratios and free-cash-flow-per-share ratios, proximity to new 52-week highs, earnings per share and earnings-per-share growth, low debt, and share price (there was a slight advantage for penny stocks, which tended also to be micro-cap stocks, over large-cap, higher share–priced stocks). I used this value-based approach successfully for several years, but eventually became somewhat disenchanted with it.

The three problems I found with a strictly value-based approach were as follows:

1. Many undervalued stocks remained unrecognized in the marketplace for months and years at a time. When I bought and held positions in those stocks, there was no price appreciation. I was forfeiting legitimate gains in other stocks as I dutifully held my ground with undervalued stocks.

2. Much of the variance in overall price appreciation remained unexplained. By this I mean that many other stocks saw share-price gains for reasons other than earnings per share. For example, the entire biotech sector was inaccessible to me because most of those stocks have negative PE ratios, and yet in some periods biotech and pharmaceutical stocks have outperformed all other sectors.

3. There are many different methods for estimating value, and some of them are not reliable. They depend on fundamental data released by the companies, and there are still ways in which companies can inflate earnings estimates. Thus, some of my value estimations were cases of "garbage in and garbage out" because I was relying on unreliable data.

Fortunately, I continued to incorporate proximity to new 52-week highs as a selection variable of interest. My rationale for using proximity to new 52-week highs as a selection criterion is as follows:

- It is reasonable to expect that any good stock will eventually make new highs in price. If there is little prospect of making new highs, the stock should be avoided.
- It is precisely at the time of making new highs that the stock attracts the most attention and becomes most interesting as an acquisition target.
- Stocks that are priced far below their 52-week highs have an overhang problem. By this I mean that a lot of persons bought the stock at higher-than-present prices and they are waiting for an opportunity to unload the stock at minimal loss. Therefore, although the stock may increase in price, the rate of increase can be expected to be slower than that of other stocks without this overhang problem.

In practice, I have defined "proximity to new 52-week highs" as a price range from zero to 3 percent of the last intraday-posted 52-week high for any given stock. This has been shown by experience to circumvent the overhang problem successfully. However, it should be noted that my mathematical algorithms for stock selection incorporate the percentage lag from the 52-week high at its precise value regardless of how far the current stock price may be below the high. This is important to remember because some stocks, especially highly volatile stocks, may be viable acquisitions even when their prices lag more than 3 percent below their 52-week highs. In order to better understand how these various technical, fundamental, and hybrid approaches to stock selection system design can be implemented, it is useful to consider some examples. These will be presented in Chapters 4, 5, and 6.

ADVANTAGES AND DISADVANTAGES OF MATHEMATIZATION

The discussion of the design of mathematical models for stock selection would not be complete without some mention of the advantages and disadvantages of such approaches. It should be readily apparent that reliance on mathematical models can make the process of stock selection more consistent and can take away guesswork and the harmful tendency to chase tips. If the models are successful, it can greatly enhance profitability and thereby build trading confidence. I find it greatly encouraging when the stocks identified by my models as acquisition targets subsequently appreciate rapidly in share price, and when the stocks identified as selling targets fall in share price. This encouragement is so reinforcing that I will never return to haphazard "finger-to-the-wind" approaches to stock selection.

At the same time, there may be justifiable limits to the degree of mathematization or automation of the process. At one extreme end of the continuum would be a kind of programmed trading in which the decisions of what to buy or sell, when to buy or sell, how much to buy or sell, and the actual trade executions are all made by a computer program without any human intervention. At the other end of the continuum would be an approach that places no reliance whatsoever in any mathematical model for decision making. What I propose in this book is something between those two extremes. Here we are inviting the computer to rank order all stocks for desirability based on the best available data, and we leave it to the individual trader to decide what to do with this information. I suppose that this compromise is not unlike that faced by scientists in the NASA space program. How much of the decision making will be left to the pilot of the spacecraft or the supervising ground crew, and how much will be controlled by the computer? Certainly there is an optimal blend in which the speed, accuracy, and efficiency of the computer is harnessed, all the while that human values and purposes are never circumvented. Hopefully this blend will capitalize on the advantages and limit the weaknesses of exclusivity in either direction, so that trading will not become blindly devoid of all human sentiment and experience, and at the same time will not be dominated by ego and anxiety.

SUMMARY

Most trading systems can be characterized as technical, fundamental, or hybrid technical-fundamental systems, depending on whether they address timing concerns, value concerns, or a combination of timing and value concerns. Statistical procedures such as analysis of variance and multiple regression analysis can help us identify and organize optimal combinations of variables for the prediction of future share-price gain in stocks in spite of weaknesses that arise when the data observed fail to satisfy the assumptions underlying use of those methods. Stocks can then be rank-ordered in terms of the likelihood of share-price gain. This process will usually lead to the construction of hybrid trading systems in preference to either strictly technical or strictly value-based trading systems. The advantages of such mathematical trading systems can be profound. They can eliminate much of the guesswork and anxiety associated with stock selection. In general, trading systems also do well to incorporate proximity to new 52-week highs as a variable of interest because this will increase the probability of future gains.

CHAPTER 4

Stock Selection: A Technical-Momentum System

During one bull-market trend, I found that growth and momentum stocks were outperforming value stocks. Being a pragmatist, I temporarily abandoned my value-based approach in favor of a technical momentum-based approach. During that bull-market period, I was able to average gains of about 20 percent per month. But, alas, bull markets do not last forever. Nevertheless, I need to describe that approach more clearly because it represents a preliminary step in my current stock selection methodology.

QUALIFYING VARIABLES

Regardless of the trading system adopted, there will be certain qualifying variables established before its implementation. These three qualifying variables serve to delimit the field of stocks meriting further analysis.

1. *Sufficient Rate of Gain.* Because my goal in developing a trading system is to generate earnings in excess of 10 percent per month, the first qualifying variable is the realization of 30 percent gain over the past three months by any candidate stock, and to accept only those stocks that have at least doubled in share price over the past 52 weeks. Admittedly, this will eliminate some stocks from consideration that will eventually become winners, but hopefully those stocks will be identified and included at some point in their ascendancy.

2. *Sufficiently High Share Price.* Another delimiter that has been ironed out on the anvil of experience is to consider only stocks with a share price exceeding 5 dollars. This latter qualification stems not from the observation that handsome profits cannot be made with penny stocks, but it grows out of personal experiences that lead me to the conclusion that risks can exceed rewards with such stocks. Perhaps this is because those stocks can more easily be manipulated due to their low share prices, or because the underlying companies are often new and unestablished and have greater performance uncertainties. In any case, my own research has indicated that I have done better with higher-priced stocks.

3. *Sufficient Trading Volume.* And finally, the system requires that ideally only those stocks with an average daily trading volume exceeding 10,000 shares traded should be considered. This restriction is imposed because of the potential difficulty of unloading such stocks in a timely way without depressing share price or losing money due to excessively wide spreads. Once these qualifications are imposed, we can effectively delimit the field of candidate stocks to less than 200, and we can proceed with the implementation of the system.

Table 4.1 illustrates how a technical trading system can be implemented.

In Table 4.1, data are presented for 10 stocks that were of interest at the time this analysis was conducted. The first column on the left side provides the stock symbol. The next column shows the share price as of January 1, 2008. Only those stocks priced above five dollars a share are

TABLE 4.1 A Growth-Momentum Strategy for Stock Selection (1/2008)

Symbol	Price ($)	High ($)	Low ($)	Mltp	%Lag	Inv Value	3-Mo Gain	Rank	Tally
QSC	5.77	6.49	0.21	27.47	0.11	371.50	815.87	0.14	+++ B
EMDH	8.00	10.00	0.90	8.88	0.20	66.66	233.33	0.52	++ H
TWRT	14.30	4.50	1.76	8.12	0.01	883.59	164.81	0.67	++++ SB
DGLY	7.30	7.65	1.45	5.03	0.04	165.05	114.70	1.13	+++ B
MELI	73.88	81.17	22.00	3.35	0.08	56.08	103.75	1.44	++ H
STP	82.32	88.65	31.41	2.62	0.07	55.05	106.31	1.41	++ H
TRA	47.76	51.15	11.08	4.31	0.06	97.55	52.78	2.04	
MA	215.20	227.18	95.30	2.25	0.05	64.23	45.43	2.46	
DECK	155.06	166.50	55.99	2.76	0.06	60.46	41.22	3.25	
RIG	143.15	149.62	72.47	1.97	0.04	68.51	26.62	3.90	

included because penny stocks tend to be subject to price manipulation and "pump-and-dump" schemes, and they are often not amenable to trading on margin if that is of interest to you. The next column gives the 52-week high price for the 12 months preceding January 1, 2008. Similarly, the fourth column shows the 52-week low price for each stock during the same period. The fifth column provides the 52-week multiple; that is, it shows how many times the share price has multiplied from its low to its current price over that period. This is computed simply as Price divided by Low. Note that, according to this strategy, only those stocks with a multiple value above two are initially included in the first screening. Here the rationale is that, because our goal is to realize gains of at least 10 percent per month, stocks that have not at least doubled over the past year do not show a rate of ascent that is likely to help us reach our goal. In practice, this step allows us to narrow our list of stocks from about 8,000 to less than 200. The sixth column is labeled "% Lag." Multiplying the value in this column by 100 gives the percentage that current share price lags below the 52-week high. The values in this column are obtained by simply subtracting current price from the 52-week high and dividing the remainder by the 52-week high. For stock-selection purposes, the smaller the percent lag, the better. Three percent has been found to be a critical point for most stocks. Above 3 percent the overhang problem begins to come into play. Note that, if current price is identical to the 52-week high, the computation involves dividing zero, which is not possible. In those cases, I arbitrarily subtract 2 cents from current share price before entering it into the table and the formula.

So far the steps have been very simple, employing simple arithmetic with data to be found free of charge at any number of internet web sites. But now the computations become a bit more complicated. The seventh column is labeled "Inv Value" for investment value. The numbers in this column are obtained by dividing a weighted rate-of-ascent value, as reflected in the price multiple, by a weighted percent lag value. The formula is as follows:

$$\text{Inv Value} = (3 * \text{Mltp})/(2 * \%\,\text{Lag})$$

You can see that the computation of investment value in this column rewards higher price multiples and lower percentage lags. Thus the higher the investment value obtained, the better. For stock selection purposes, investment values above 100 are preferable to those below that critical value. Initially, the method stopped here, and selection was made from those stocks with the highest investment values. However, it was soon determined that the price multiple can be influenced by irregularities in price movement. For example, it sometimes happens that a stock will double in the first month of the year and show no further gains in the rest of the year.

Sometimes share price can dip in the middle of the year and quickly return to its pre-dip value and go no higher from that point. There needed to be a way to smooth the price-ascent curve and give priority to stocks that were continuing to show gains in the latter part of the year just as they had done earlier in the year. In essence, a way was needed to do some curve fitting so that the selection of stocks could be made on the basis of optimal patterns of ascending share price.

The columns labeled "3-Mo Gain" and "Rank" show how this was accomplished. First, the percentage gain over the past three months was computed by simply subtracting intraday share-price low during the three-month period prior to current share price from current share price, and dividing the remainder by the same three-month share-price low, and multiplying this result by 100. The following formula summarizes this calculation:

$$3\text{-Mo Gain} = (\text{Price} - 3\text{m Low Price})/3\text{m Low Price} * 100$$

The end result of this calculation is entered for each stock in the "3-Mo Gain" column. This percentage gain over the past three months is also highly important as a screening criterion. Because our goal is to realize gains of at least 10 percent each month, it is useful to eliminate all stocks that did not gain at least 30 percent over the past three months. This will further reduce the number of stocks in our list to approximately 75 to 150, depending on market conditions. It is easy to find the share-price low over the past three months. You can go to http://finance.yahoo.com and request a quote for any stock. Then you click on the chart function and go to the "three months" interactive chart. By moving the cursor from the beginning of this chart at the far left side, you can see at the top what the share-price low for that stock was during this period. Other sites such as http://bigcharts.com also provide this information with interactive charting.

The column in Table 4.1 labeled "Rank" is the most important column for decision-making purposes according to this strategy for stock selection. All of the preceding information is involved in the calculation of the data in this column. What happens in this step is that the investment value data from column seven is rank ordered and smoothed using the Excel RANK function, and the result for each stock is divided by three-month percentage gain in order to give priority to stocks that are continuing their share-price ascent in the most recent quarter of the year. The Excel formula is expressed as follows:

$$\text{Rank} = (\text{RANK(G2, G2:G50,0)} * 2 + 100)/\text{H2}$$

where   RANK is the Excel RANK function

           G2 is the first data cell in the investment value column (Inv V)

           G2:G50 is the designation of range for the RANK function (A 50-stock range is designated here even though it is known that the database will often exceed 100 stocks. This mid-range specification appears to work best to insure separability and thus reliability in the ranking of stocks.)

           0 signifies that the rank statistic will be expressed in ascending order

           H2 is the first data cell in the three-month percentage gain column.

Once a complete table has been generated like that shown in Table 4.1, it is possible to make a selection tally and actually rank order the stocks for acquisition. In this process, one point is awarded for each stock with percent lag at 3 percent or lower, one point is awarded for each stock with investment value (Inv V) at 100 or above, one point is awarded for each stock with three-month percentage gain above 100 percent, and one point is awarded for each stock with a rank value below 1.50. The maximum of four points for a stock is interpreted as a "strong buy" (SB). A stock with three points is considered a "buy" (B). And a stock with two points is considered a "hold" (H). In Table 4.1 we can see that TWRT, a wind-energy stock, was rated a strong buy at that particular time. QSC and DGLY were both rated buys. And EMDH, MELI, and STP were each rated holds. None of the other stocks were considered to be appropriate acquisitions at the time these data were assembled. As you can see, by this approach it is possible to get a numerical ranking of all viable publicly traded stocks on any given day. Bear in mind that these patterns regularly change for any subset of stocks, so that over a one-month period the acquisition orderings for the stocks may be radically altered.

SAMPLE RECOMMENDATION SUMMARY TABLE

Once the computations have been completed through use of data base management software as illustrated in Table 4.1, it is desirable to rank-order recommendations, as shown in Table 4.2.

By this method, only those three stocks listed as "strong buy" or "buy" would be acquisition targets. Stocks are also arranged from left to right in descending order of relative strength for acquisition. Stocks listed as "hold" recommendations may be kept in one's portfolio if they have already been

TABLE 4.2   Growth-Momentum Selection
Recommendations Summary (1/2008)

Rank	Recommendation	Symbols
+6	Strong Buy	TWRT
+5	Buy	QSC, DGLY
+4	Hold	EMDH, MELI, STP

acquired, but they should normally not be newly acquired unless they move higher on the scale. Stocks that are in one's portfolio, but do not qualify for a recommendation of strong buy, buy, or hold are prospective candidates for sale, as indicated under question 3 below.

QUESTIONS AND ANSWERS

People often have questions about the implementation of this growth-momentum strategy. Here are eight common questions with answers.

1. How frequently is it necessary to perform these calculations?

    It is important to do these calculations at the close of trading each day. Sometimes I even perform intra-day calculations to consider the status of particular stocks of interest. Volatile stocks can quickly move in or out of viability as investment opportunities. Such stocks often have viable investment life spans as short as two or three days before they must be sold. If you maintain an Excel spreadsheet with all stocks that have doubled in price in the past 52 weeks, it is not onerous to enter new share prices and run the calculations each day. This database will normally include approximately 75 to 150 stocks. Each day several stocks may be added or removed from the database according to their changing qualifications. Of course, if you cannot do the calculations for a few days, you can always resume where you left off with no loss of vital information.

2. How many stocks do you need to hold in your portfolio to maintain adequate diversification by this method?

    Interestingly, technical data appears to be more ephemeral and changeable than fundamental data, and this implies that more stocks are needed to maintain adequate diversification and minimize risk in a technical approach. In my experience, a value-based approach may require as few as five stocks to minimize risk; whereas, a growth-momentum technical approach appears to require at least twice as many stocks—at least 10 to 12 stocks, depending on market conditions. Of course, the decision of how many stocks to hold will also depend on the amount of available trading capital, on overall market conditions, and on the availability of viable stocks to acquire.

3. This method indicates when stocks can be acquired, but how do you know when to sell those stocks?

Because all stocks are rank-ordered for viability as investments by this method, the goal is to hold only those stocks that are at the top of the list. In practice, all stocks that fall below the "hold" rating are candidates for sale. However, this decision needs to be tempered by the consideration that the unwinding of low-volume positions needs to be done with care over time. Also, stocks that remain near their 52-week highs are not to be dropped quickly even if they fail on other criteria. Finally, the decision to sell a stock can be reinforced if there are clearly better positions identified and available.

4. Can this methodology be applied in reverse for the selection of stocks to be shorted?

This is an empirical question that is worthy of research. Because the taking of short positions on individual stocks is not a strategy that is advocated here, this research has not yet been done by me. I suspect that a number of modifications would be needed for such an application. For example, this approach targets stocks near their 52-week highs for acquisition as long positions. Choosing stocks near their 52-week lows for acquisition as short positions could backfire, because many of those stocks could be oversold and nearing a price bottom from which they could quickly rebound. One possibility for further investigation would be to take the individual stock data in the *Rank* column in Table 4.1 and multiply them by the data in the three-month percentage gain column or in the 52-week multiple gain column to identify stocks that are candidates for shorting. In this way, stocks with weak overall rankings, but which have had rapid gains, would be the stocks most likely to experience corrections and decline in value, and those stocks would have the highest products from this multiplication process. Of course, this idea needs research corroboration before implementation.

5. Does this growth-momentum technical approach work equally well in both bull and bear market conditions?

Not always. Stocks that have had a good run in a bull market are often particularly vulnerable when that market turns south. Over time, however, this problem seems to correct itself. For example, during a recent market downturn I witnessed a real estate exchange-traded bear fund actually rise toward the top of the list after the downturn became established for more than one month. This was a fund that specialized in short-position real estate instruments in order to benefit from a downturn in the real estate market. A similar pattern emerged with a financial sector bear fund during the recent downturn of financials. I can report that the method has been tested under both bull market and bear market conditions and it has held up in both environments; however, it is definitely more profitable in bull market conditions. It should be apparent that, if you are following a system like this that has you selling declining stocks and buying rising stocks, you will always be in the best stocks. However, in market downtrends you may need to trade more frequently and see less benefit from those trades. Meanwhile, it helps to blunt any bear-market vulnerability by choosing stocks that have strong earnings fundamentals to complement their technical strengths. This is the approach advocated in Chapter 6 with a hybrid technical-fundamental stock-selection algorithm.

6. Why did you choose a three-month window for the smoothing of the 52-week growth curve?

This was admittedly somewhat arbitrary because of the easy availability of the data and because earnings are often reported on a quarterly basis. Other windows would probably also work. It is analogous to the use of stochastics, where the user has the choice of slow and fast periods for the drawing of the comparative curves. In reality I suppose that some stocks have different cycles than others, so the use of one window to fit all may be a little misleading. But the greater utility of the ability to rank-order all stocks with the same metric appeared to me to outweigh this concern.

7. What are some of the major strengths and weaknesses of this method?

The greatest strength is that it will identify all of the stocks priced above five dollars that are currently moving to new highs and that have a history of rapid share-price growth. This is particularly useful because of the human tendency toward continuing expectations of growth or self-fulfilling prophecy for stocks that have regular ascending price charts. It also helps one avoid stocks that have temporary price surges based on rumors or other passing events, but which often quickly reverse and give back share-price gains. Another advantage of mathematical models like this is that they actually rank-order stocks in a way that eliminates much of the emotional stress and guesswork usually associated with stock picking. At the very least, this process may allow a trader to focus on the best stocks for further research inquiry. Also, I have found that careful examination of those stocks with lowest percent lag that may not yet have attained most advantageous investment rank can sometimes help identify great stocks in advance of their ascendancy. Furthermore, one can infer comparative sector strength at any given time from the patterns of stocks that are ascendant each day.

On the other side of the coin, purchasing stocks that have had a history of rapid growth always has the potential of loss due to panic selling in a rapid downturn as investors seek to preserve their gains. Often the stocks with most rapid growth in share price are also the most volatile stocks, so they are subject to wild swings in price. Because the focus is on share-price growth rather than on underlying fundamentals, it is easy to become too involved with stocks that may not have real earnings growth potential. Such stocks may be making new highs based merely on speculative rumors with no real fundamental support. This is another argument for the use of hybrid models that complement technical information with critical fundamental information.

8. In application, have you made any subsequent refinements to this method?

Yes. I have found it useful to add two additional screens in order to refine judgments still further. The first is to perform Point-and-Figure Analysis for each remaining stock, as described in Chapter 6, using the charting facility at http://stockcharts.com. Here I am looking for positive breakout signals and bullish price objectives. Often this analysis only serves to add additional weight to the percent lag column in Table 4.1 because the results are highly correlated with percent lag. However, unlike most other technical indicators, Point-and-Figure Analysis will identify stocks that are overextended, even though they may still be near their 52-week highs.

The second screen is to consider consistent growth in average trading volume. In physics, momentum is equal to mass times acceleration. It would be difficult to imagine a momentum trading model that does not in some way consider acceleration in trading volume. For this latter refinement, I look at the three-month average daily trading volume and the 10-day average trading volume as reported at http://Finance.Yahoo.com. Dividing the 10-day by the three-month volume average, I look for a ratio exceeding 1.25 as a positive indicator of volume growth. I am constantly looking for refinements, but so far these are the only ones I have implemented regularly. Of course, because I have moved towards a hybrid model as described in a subsequent chapter, I have found it valuable to incorporate cash flow and free cash flow ratios to ensure that the stocks chosen are truly winners and not just flash-in-the-pan stocks; however, these are fundamental variables that are best left out of the discussion at this point.

SUMMARY

In this chapter we have seen how one particular technical stock-selection system can be implemented in a way that provides a mathematical rank-ordering of all viable stocks. It has been suggested that such a growth-momentum approach may not be appropriate under every kind of market condition, and the trader should be prepared to employ a fundamental-value approach when market conditions are more favorable to that approach, or a hybrid system to encompass the benefits of both technical and value approaches. Several questions were asked and answered concerning the precise implementation of the technical trading system described in this chapter.

CHAPTER 5

Stock Selection: A Fundamental-Value System

I n the previous chapter, we saw how a technical-momentum approach can be applied to stock selection in a way that permits a mathematical ranking of stocks and thereby minimizes much of the emotion and guesswork associated with appropriate stock picking. This time, we need to consider how a fundamental-value approach can be applied to stock selection for the same purposes.

In seasons when value stocks with strong earnings are outperforming technical-momentum stocks that may be overvalued by traditional methods of valuation, a pragmatic trader will have a value-based strategy to fall back on. Similarly, a value-oriented trader may reference a technical-momentum strategy like the preceding example in times when value-based strategies are not working. The following fundamental example identifies 10 criterion variables for stock selection. Three of these are qualifying variables as in the example of Chapter 4 which means that their requirements must first be met before any stock can be considered for further analysis. The seven remaining variables are fundamental variables.

QUALIFYING VARIABLES

Initial screening according to these three variables should limit the field of viable stock selections from around 8,000 to only around 200 stocks. You will want to create a watch list for those remaining 200 stocks. These are the same qualifying variables that were introduced in the construction of the technical trading system in Chapter 4.

Share Price

Share price should ideally exceed five dollars to minimize price manipulation and pump-and-dump strategies. Some adventurous traders will want to set this criterion much lower in particular trading seasons or in consideration of particular stocks. However, a selection criterion of five dollars per share is not unreasonable. This higher criterion may also permit trading on margin for those so inclined, and it will make one less susceptible to price manipulation problems than would be the case with lower-priced stocks. I have personally moved to limit purchases to stocks priced over five dollars per share based on my experience of making more consistent gains with such stocks. Perhaps this experience is related to the fact that, as stocks pass key price thresholds such as five dollars, ten dollars, and fifteen dollars, there is more institutional involvement and the buying volume in terms of total investment capital increases.

Volume

It is best to limit purchases to stocks with an average daily volume of at least 10,000 shares. One should also consider whether recent volume shows a regular pattern of increase over trading volume in the past month or so. Otherwise, low volume trading may prevent you from eventually selling your position without driving the price down and losing your investment gains. Of course, if you have recognized value before the crowd has found it, you can expect the volume to increase dramatically in the future. However, getting caught with a large position in a low volume stock is like being grounded in a boat in shallow water when the tide is out. When you wish to sell a low-volume stock, all you can do is wait for volume to pick up and sell your position a little at a time. Dumping large positions in low-volume stocks with market sell orders is foolish and harmful. It leads to unnecessary losses. It is like fishing in a small pond using dynamite. It destroys the habitat for many creatures that depend on the pond, and it means that no one can return to that pond later with any expectation of success in fishing.

One-Year Gain and Three-Month Gain

As noted earlier, because of my goal of realizing 10 percent trading gains each month, it has become necessary to limit my acquisitions to stocks with appropriate ascending price curves that are suggestive of reaching such a goal. Therefore, I accept only those stocks that have at least doubled in the past 52 weeks, and only those stocks that have registered gains of at least 30 percent over the past three months. This restriction is implemented in constructing the initial watch list from which the subsequent formal analysis procedures may proceed. Admittedly, this criterion may exclude some stocks whose growth rates will accelerate later, but those stocks will eventually qualify for inclusion into the model.

FUNDAMENTAL VARIABLES

These are the variables that together help define a stock as a great value. They are also variables that emerged as positive predictors of share-price gain when backtesting studies were conducted using multiple regression analysis. For each variable it is necessary to set a selection criterion for decision-making purposes.

Earnings

Strong earnings performance is the hallmark of any value-based approach. Here we are looking for stocks with earnings per share that equal or exceed 10 percent of share price. This is tantamount to saying that we want only those stocks with a price-to-earnings (PE) ratio of 10 or less. Because of the tendency for some companies to inflate earnings reports, some traders prefer to consider price-to-sales ratios (PSRs) instead of PE ratios. Setting such a stringent PE criterion is anathema to technical traders who would argue that good stocks will support much higher PE ratios. To be fair, one must acknowledge that such a stringent earnings criterion will eliminate many good stocks such as biotech stocks that may indeed show great future price appreciation. At the same time, stocks with such great earnings are much less likely to tank when the market goes south. Happily, as you can see, this is not the only criterion considered, so that a stock may fail to score high on this criterion and still qualify for selection. For purposes of quantification, a PE ratio of 5.0 or less is valued at 2 points. A PE ratio ranging from 5.0 to 12.0 is valued at 1 point. A PE ratio ranging from 12.0 to 25.0 is valued at zero points. And a PE ratio above 25.0 or that is negative is valued at −1 point.

Earnings Growth

It is not enough to find stocks with great earnings; ideally, one is also looking for stocks with consistent growth in earnings from quarter to quarter. One can therefore examine quarterly earnings history and also look at future earnings estimates. This is a way to get a more reliable picture of earnings than by merely looking at the most recent quarterly earnings.

Companies sometimes inflate earnings reports, but it is difficult to persist in such deception over several quarters. Furthermore, just as some analysts prefer price-to-sales ratios over price-to-earnings ratios, it is also possible to focus on revenue growth rather than on earnings growth. Year-over-year quarterly growth in income is reported at the Yahoo Finance key statistics web page.

Another approach to the measurement of earnings growth is to compare current actual earnings with future estimated earnings. I have personally had greater success with earnings-growth statistics that include future earnings estimates than with statistics that focus only on growth in the present over the past. An easy and effective way to consider earnings growth related to future expectations is simply to compare the current PE ratio with the estimated future PE ratio. Here one is looking for a future estimated PE ratio that is substantially lower than the current PE ratio and lower than the average PE ratio for the industry and for the S&P 500 Index average. For purposes of obtaining a measurement to incorporate into our model, a future estimated PE ratio that is lower than the present PE ratio and is lower than the S&P 500 Index average PE ratio is rated 1.0. A future estimated PE ratio that is equal to or lower than the current PE ratio but is still higher than the S&P 500 Index average is rated zero. A future estimated PE ratio that is higher than the current PE ratio and is higher than the S&P 500 Index average, or that is negative, is rated −1.0. In cases where PE estimates are not available, one is forced to infer a rating from cash flow, past earnings growth, or analyst expectations. However, if no data are available, a zero rating is given.

Book Value

Doubtless there are hundreds of ways to estimate value, and book value is only one of them. Earnings ratios and sales ratios and cash-flow ratios may also be considered indicators of value, and all of those indicators deserve a place at the table. But book value is more closely related to liquidation value of the company, and it is therefore important as a safety concern. I would never consider buying a used car without first consulting the estimated book value of that car. Here we are looking for book value per share and setting ratings of acceptability as follows: price-to-book ratios less than 2.0 are rated 1.0; price-to-book ratios greater than 2.0 but less than 4.0 are rated zero; and price-to-book ratios above 4.0 are rated −1.0.

Low Debt

Companies that are saddled with a lot of long-term debt are not as likely as debt-free companies to show rapid price appreciation. Too much of their revenue income goes to service their debt. Here we look at the ratio of debt to equity and seek a level of debt that is less than 10 percent of equity. It must be understood that some companies, like mortgage lenders, acquire debt in order to lend to others. Debt does not have the same meaning for every company. In some exceptional cases, the ability to assume debt is a measure of the health of the company. Some of these differences may be addressed in the presentation of free cash flow considered next. Again, for purposes of implementation of our model the following ratings apply: a debt-to-equity ratio of zero to 0.10 is rated 1.0; from 0.10 to 0.50 is rated zero; and above 0.50 is rated −1.0.

Cash Flow and Free Cash Flow

Possibly the best overall predictor of future price growth is cash flow. "Cash flow" is the net money flowing into or out from the company from operations, and that is different from "money flow," which is the net money flowing into or out from the company from investors. Companies usually report both "cash flow" and "free cash flow." "Free cash flow" is cash flow that is unencumbered by operational expenses, and it is the more desirable of the two kinds of cash flow. However, because there is often a big discrepancy between these two statistics, it is best to consider them both. It is rather like statistical means and standard deviations; they should be considered together to get the most accurate picture. By this method we consider both the cash-flow-per-share ratio and the free-cash-flow-per-share ratio. These ratios are like PE ratios in that the smaller they are the better as a reflection of value. The rigid criterion observed is that the sum of these two ratios should not exceed 10. In practice, I have moved to averaging these two ratios and weighting the result as follows: under 12.5 is rated 1.0; from 12.5 and 25 is rated zero; over 25 or with either ratio being negative is rated −1.0. One website where this information is readily available through the inspection of individual stock ratios is http://clearstation.etrade.com.

EPS/PE Divergence

Another of the most telling leading indicators of future performance is a positive divergence between rolling earnings per share and the price-earnings ratio. This occurs when there is a sudden bump upwards in earnings that is not yet reflected in the PE ratio or when there is a share buy-back that results in greater earnings per share that is not yet reflected in the stated PE ratio. This information is available through the interactive charting facility at http://bigcharts.com and specifying rolling earnings per share and PE ratio as variables of interest. If any stock is found to show a

TABLE 5.1 One Year EPS and PE Divergence for DMND (2007–2008)

	Nov	Dec	08	Feb	Mar	Apr	May	Jun	Jul	Aug	Sep	Oct
Share Price	21.9	20.2	21.4	19.0	16.6	19.0	20.6	21.0	22.7	24.2	25.3	29.7
EPS	.53	.53	.44	.44	.44	.48	.48	.48	.79	.79	.79	.91
PE	41.4	38.1	48.7	43.2	37.8	39.6	42.8	43.8	29.2	30.7	32.0	32.6
Sign			Sell				Buy		Buy			Buy
Rated	0.0	0.0	−1.0	−1.0	0.0	1.0	0.0	0.0	1.0	1.0	1.0	1.0

jump in earnings per share not yet accompanied by a jump in PE ratio or a jump in share price, that stock qualifies for acquisition by this variable. Obviously, an increase in earnings per share should by definition cause the PE ratio to fall. However, investors tend to buy into stocks with positive earnings reports, and this ultimately drives the PE ratio upward. The object is to find stocks with recent positive earnings reports that have not yet ascended in share price and PE ratio. Table 5.1 illustrates how this variable is applied for decision making.

Notice in Table 5.1 that the rolling earnings per share for Diamond Foods, Inc (DMND) saw a decrease in January, 2008, followed by increases in April, July and October. At the time of the January decrease, the PE ratio actually rose from 38.1 to 48.7, and there was no accompanying drop in share price. The share price actually rose slightly from 20.2 to 21.4. This combination of a drop in earnings per share, a rise in PE ratio, and an unchanging or rising share price provided a strong "sell" signal in January. You can see that the share price subsequently tumbled to the 16-dollar range by March. At the time of the next earnings report in April, earnings rose slightly to .48 per share. At the exact time of that report, share price was in the 18-dollar range, and the PE ratio at 39.6 was still below levels seen earlier when EPS was higher. This composite configuration provided a weak "buy" signal. The weakness of the signal was due to the fact that the earnings-per-share increase was only slight, and there had already been some gain in share price. Subsequently, you can see that by the time of the next earnings report in July, the share price had risen from 19.0 to 22.7 and EPS rose sharply to .79. This sharp rise in earnings was accompanied by a sharp drop in the PE ratio from 43.8 to 29.2, and a very modest rise in share price from 21.0 to 22.7. This new PE ratio was much lower than previous PE ratios that were accompanied by comparable share prices. This composite configuration provided a strong "buy" signal in July. You can see that from July until the next earnings report in October, the share price rose from 22.7 to 29.7, a 30.8 percent increase. This was all the more remarkable when you consider that this was a period during which the S&P 500 Index fell more than 30 percent. The monthly ratings for divergence on a scale of 1.0 to −1.0 are also given in the table. Ratings on divergence can be determined as follows: ascending rolling earnings per share with level or descending PE ratio and with share price not yet above earlier levels seen with lower rolling earnings per share is rated 1.0; ascending earnings per share with accompanying rises in share price and PE ratios to levels above market averages or with negative or unavailable PE ratios is rated zero; and falling rolling earnings per share regardless of share price and PE ratio changes is rated −1.0.

Money Flow

Money flow is also a matter of great concern. Unlike cash flow which is an indication of revenue from operations, money flow is a reflection of investment money flowing into or out of a company. Chaikin's Money Flow (CMF) is shown in graphic form at http://stockcharts.com in the gallery view section. There, red charting shows money outflow and green charting depicts money inflow. In this case we are looking for stocks with ascending money flow in the green direction. Often the flow of money into a stock is a leading indicator of future growth in share price. For measurement purposes, any ascending trend in money flow is rated 1.0; any level or unestablished trend is rated zero; and any descending trend is rated −1.0. It is sometimes difficult to see established trends because movement on this variable is often so closely tied to short-term movement in share price.

Table 5.2 shows how this fundamental-value trading system may be implemented with an arbitrary sample of ten qualifying stocks.

where   SYM = Stock Symbol
        ER = Earnings
        EG = Earnings Growth
        LD = Low Debt
        CF = Cash Flow
        DV = EPS/PE Divergence
        MF = Money Flow
      SUM = Total Outcome, the sum of the variable ratings for each stock.
      PCG = Percentage Gain, the share-price percentage gain or loss for each stock over the six-month observation period.

TABLE 5.2 A Preliminary Fundamental-Value Selection Strategy for Stocks (August, 2008)

SYM	ER	EG	BV	LD	CF	DV	MF	SUM	PCG
BTM	1	0	1	−1	1	0	1	3	20
CALM	1	1	0	0	−1	1	−1	1	45
CNRD	1	1	1	0	0	−1	0	2	−12
DRYS	1	0	1	−1	0	1	0	2	−14
DYII	1	0	1	1	1	0	1	5	−10
FSIN	0	1	0	0	0	1	0	2	−20
GGB	0	1	0	−1	0	1	0	1	40
GHM	0	0	−1	1	−1	1	1	1	180
MCF	1	1	−1	1	0	0	0	2	30
OI	1	0	0	−1	1	1	−1	1	−30

For purposes of decision making according to this system, any stock with a summary rating of 5 or above is considered a strong buy. Any stock with a summary rating of 4 is considered a buy. Any stock with a rating of 3 is considered a hold. Stocks with ratings below 3 are candidates for sale. The final recommendations by this system for the stocks listed in Table 5.2 are summarized in Table 5.3.

As we can see from Table 5.3, DYII was rated as a "Strong Buy" by this system, BTM was rated as a "Hold," and the rest of the stocks were candidates for sale. Unfortunately, although these fundamental-value ratings tended to be highly consistent over the past six months, the sum of them can be shown to have had an insignificant correlation with share-price gain during that period. So it was that DYII actually ranked eighth out of the ten stocks in comparative performance despite its high ranking on value. Still worse—GHM was first in share-price performance but was tied for last place in value rating. What can we conclude from these findings? Three conclusions can be drawn from this: value and gain are unrelated over brief time intervals, variables may have been incorrectly chosen to

TABLE 5.3 Preliminary Stock Selection Recommendations According to a Fundamental-Value System

Rank	Recommendation	Symbols
+6	Strong Buy	DYII
+5	Buy	—
+4	Hold	BTM

represent value, or the stocks selected were insufficiently representative of the total population of stocks. Each alternative conclusion is explained in more detail in the following list.

1. Value as measured here and in most traditional formulations is not related to share-price gain over periods as short as six months. A longer interval of observation is needed in order to detect a positive relationship between value and share-price gain. However, this interpretation is not intuitively satisfying because stocks that are undervalued in the marketplace should increase in share price to achieve equilibrium—even over very short periods. Certainly there was significant share-price fluctuation over the period considered, and it is logical to expect that this fluctuation was in part related to the underlying value of those stocks.

2. Alternatively, perhaps some of the fundamental variables chosen to represent value in Table 5.2 were not sufficiently related to the underlying value construct or to share-price performance. That is to say, perhaps some variables as measured lacked construct validity as measures of value. To examine this problem the author conducted another correlation study with a random sample of qualifying stocks that had been stratified on investment rank as has been defined for Table 4.1 in the preceding chapter. Results suggested that the variables low debt (LD) and money flow (MF) as measured were unrelated to value and to share-price performance. When those two variables were removed, the revised total score for value did show a significant correlation with share-price performance, and DYII ceased to be a strong-buy recommendation.

3. Yet another explanation of the unanticipated results stems from the fact that the ten stocks in Table 5.2 were disproportionately high on the earnings variable. Seven of the ten stocks had PE ratios below ten. Since they were not a random representation of all stocks, and since they were not stratified on past performance, results therefore cannot be generalized. Seven of the ten stocks had PE ratios below ten. That is another reason for the replication of the correlation study that was subsequently conducted with a much larger stratified random sample.

The revised fundamental-value selection strategy is presented in Table 5.4 for the same ten stocks listed in Table 5.2. Note that the variables low debt (LD) and money flow (MF) have been removed from the table and from the selection strategy.

TABLE 5.4 A Revised Fundamental-Value Selection Strategy for Stocks (August, 2008)

SYM	ER	EG	BV	CF	DV	SUM	PCG
BTM	1	0	1	1	0	3	20
CALM	1	1	0	−1	1	2	45
CNRD	1	1	1	0	−1	2	−12
DRYS	1	0	1	0	1	3	−14
DYII	1	0	1	1	0	3	−10
FSIN	0	1	0	0	1	2	−20
GGB	0	1	0	0	1	2	40
GHM	0	0	−1	−1	1	−1	180
MCF	1	1	−1	0	0	1	30
OI	1	0	0	1	1	3	−30

Symbols used in Table 5.4 have identical interpretations as those employed in Table 5.2. Stock selection recommendations by this revised method are presented in Table 5.5.

Notice that, when the two questionable variables were removed, the stock selection recommendations changed dramatically. You can see that there were no strong buy or buy recommendations by this revised fundamental-value approach from among the ten stocks listed in Tables 5.2 and 5.4. Parenthetically, this occurred in spite of the fact that many of the stocks in the tables had PE ratios below 10. Interestingly, the recommendations were now much more closely aligned with actual share-price performance during the six-month period of observation, although GHM was still not selected for acquisition by any variable except divergence, as measured.

As was the case with the technical-momentum system described in the preceding chapter, there are often questions that arise concerning the implementation of such systems.

TABLE 5.5 Revised Summary Stock Selection Recommendations According to a Fundamental-Value System

Rank	Recommendation	Symbols
+6	Strong Buy	—
+5	Buy	—
+4	Hold	BTM, DRYS, DYII, OI

QUESTIONS AND ANSWERS

1. In the case of the technical-momentum system, it was claimed earlier that the analysis needs to be repeated at the close of each day of trading. How often do you need to carry out the analysis with this fundamental-value system?

    Obviously, fundamental data on stocks do not change as frequently as technical data. In some cases earnings-per-share data may be reported only once a quarter; whereas, technical data on breakouts, overextensions, and other price patterns can occur daily and even intraday. Therefore, it is normally not necessary to update fundamental data more frequently than once every two weeks. However, there will always be new data to be entered for those stocks newly qualifying to be added to the watch list by virtue of their rising above five dollars in share price, increasing in daily trading volume to more than 10,000 shares, doubling in price over a 52-week period, or gaining more than 30 percent in three months. Also, as individual earnings reports and financial statements are reported, changes should be incorporated.

2. How can you be sure that the five fundamental variables you have chosen are the best ones for entry into your stock-selection algorithm?

    These final five fundamental variables were determined as the result of three separate correlation studies conducted with different samples of stocks, at different times, and under different market conditions. I do acknowledge possible problems with application of these statistical methods to market data where the assumptions underlying the methods may not be fully satisfied in the data. Also, I am continually searching for new fundamental variables of interest, such as the divergence measure that is described in this chapter. It is also possible that certain variables may change in explanatory power with changing market conditions. That is all to say that these are the best variables I could find at present. I am definitely open to suggestions concerning other candidate variables.

3. Given that someone may have limited time to examine all stocks on all variables, which one or two variables emerged from research as the best predictors of share-price performance?

    That's a very important question, but the answer is not as straightforward as the question. In short, the best variables appeared to be a partial function of market conditions. In bull-market conditions, it appeared that cash flow and divergence as measured were the best predictors of share-price performance from among these variables. However, in bear-market conditions it appeared that book value and earnings as measured by PE ratio were superior predictors of performance. On reflection, this outcome seems intuitively satisfying to me; nevertheless, it deserves replication study with much larger samples under controlled market conditions.

4. Earlier there was mention of weighting the variables differently according to their explanatory power, but in implementation of the strategy it appears that all variables were weighted equally by the assignment of 1.0, −1.0, or zero values for each. Why were they assigned the same weight?

Part of the answer to this question is in the answer to the preceding question. The actual regression weights assigned to variables were found to vary depending on market conditions. Therefore, since market conditions were in flux, rather than assigning constant values as weights when the weights were not in fact constant, it seemed wiser to weight everything the same. It turned out to be much easier to proceed in this fashion as well. This is by no means a unique approach to this problem. William Eckhardt in Jack D. Schwager's book *The New Market Wizards* cited earlier in Table 2.2 points out a concern that market data may not be normally distributed, and therefore may not satisfy this underlying assumption for the application of statistical methods that make the assumption. He argues therefore that it is better to proceed categorically and weight variables equally as one or zero, depending on whether the measured characteristics are present or not.

5. What do you believe to be the strengths and weaknesses of this fundamental-value system by comparison with the strengths and weaknesses of the technical-momentum system described in the preceding chapter?

Both systems effectively serve to identify stocks that are likely to gain in share price based on information available on past performance and future estimated performance, and therefore both systems increase the statistical odds of success by taking advantage of what is known in order to minimize emotion and guesswork in the stock selection process. However, because the two systems rely on totally different underlying variables to achieve these purposes, the systems perform differently under different market conditions. In the best of worlds, traders will view these two systems as complementary, and will approach their implementation with an attitude describable as *both/and* rather than *either/or*. It must also be remembered that what we have seen so far is analogous to developing two different methods for designing a faster race car, where each method focuses on different design variables. Both methods can be used to develop fast cars. However, winning the race will ultimately depend not only on having the best car for the given race conditions, but also on having the best driver who has the most skill at driving in those conditions. Skill at trade execution and portfolio management will be considered in subsequent chapters.

SUMMARY

In this chapter we have examined the implementation of a fundamental-value strategy for the selection of stocks. Information was given about the variables used in the stock-selection algorithm—how they were measured and why they were chosen. In the end several questions were asked and answered concerning the implementation of this approach.

CHAPTER 6

Stock Selection: A Technical-Fundamental Hybrid Approach

S o far we have seen examples of mathematical model construction for the selection of stocks based on technical-momentum considerations, and again on the basis of fundamental-value considerations. At this point we want to examine a hybrid model that relies on both technical and fundamental information for stock selection. To return to the race car analogy yet again, in developing the fastest car we want to consider all of the relevant variables—not just technical variables and not just fundamental variables. The fundamental variables can supply value information and the technical variables can give us timing information.

Once again, we will use a set of qualifying variables or criterion variables in the implementation of this system. These variables are exactly the same ones that we observed in the implementation of prior systems.

QUALIFYING VARIABLES

Initial screening according to these three variables should limit the field of viable stock selections from around 8,000 to only around 200 stocks. You will want to create a watch list for those remaining 200 stocks. Use of these particular variables for screening stocks is a judgment call. Different traders will have different thresholds of tolerance for the stocks they admit to final consideration.

Share Price

Share price should ideally exceed five dollars to minimize price manipulation and pump-and-dump strategies. Some adventurous traders will want to set this criterion much lower in particular trading seasons or in consideration of particular stocks. However, a selection criterion of five dollars per share is not unreasonable. This higher criterion may also permit trading on margin for those so inclined, and it will make one less susceptible to price manipulation problems than would be the case with lower-priced stocks. I have personally moved to limit purchases to stocks priced over five dollars per share based on my experience of making more consistent gains with such stocks. Perhaps this experience is related to the fact that, as stocks pass key price thresholds such as five dollars, ten dollars, and fifteen dollars, there is more institutional involvement and the buying volume in terms of total investment capital increases.

Volume

It is best to limit purchases to stocks with an average daily volume of at least 10,000 shares. One should also consider whether recent volume shows a regular pattern of increase over trading volume in the past month or so. Otherwise, low volume trading may prevent you from eventually selling your position without driving the price down and losing your investment gains. Of course, if you have recognized value before the crowd has found it, you can expect the volume to increase dramatically in the future. However, getting caught with a large position in a low volume stock is like being grounded in a boat in shallow water when the tide is out. When you wish to sell a low-volume stock, all you can do is wait for volume to pick up and sell your position a little at a time. Dumping large positions in low-volume stocks with market sell orders is foolish and harmful. It leads to unnecessary losses. It is like fishing in a small pond using dynamite. It destroys the habitat for many creatures that depend on the pond, and it means that no one can return to that pond later with any expectation of success in fishing.

One-Year Gain and Three-Month Gain

As noted earlier, because of my goal of realizing 10 percent trading gains each month, it has become necessary to limit my acquisitions to stocks with appropriate ascending price curves that are suggestive of reaching such a goal. Therefore, I accept only those stocks that have at least doubled in the past 52 weeks, and only those stocks that have registered gains of at least 30 percent over the past three months. This restriction is

TABLE 6.1   Phase One of a Technical-Fundamental Hybrid Stock Selection System

Symbol	Price	High	Low	Mltp	% Lag	Inv Value	3-Mo % Gain	Inv Rank
HIRE	19.69	20.23	8.00	2.46	0.027	138.31	122.98	0.829
FSYS	53.58	59.64	9.80	5.47	0.102	80.71	138.13	0.825
STAA	5.42	5.96	2.00	2.71	0.091	44.87	113.39	0.970
PARL	6.48	6.50	2.83	2.29	0.003	1116.25	98.17	1.039
ALTH	9.69	10.19	4.36	2.22	0.049	67.94	98.16	1.100
AFAM	40.21	44.44	15.09	2.66	0.095	41.99	89.76	1.248
LDG	71.99	72.19	36.65	1.96	0.003	1063.50	82.25	1.240
ECPG	11.76	13.00	6.10	1.93	0.095	30.32	44.47	2.294
CALM	45.83	46.92	14.60	3.14	0.023	202.68	65.33	1.561
IKN	15.52	16.00	16.73	2.31	0.030	115.30	43.97	2.320

All values are based on August 15, 2008, data.

implemented in constructing the initial watch list from which the subsequent formal analysis procedures may proceed.

We are now ready to begin to implement this hybrid stock selection system with stocks that qualify according to the criterion variables just cited. In Table 6.1 you can see how the first phase of implementation proceeds with a random sample of ten qualified stocks selected on August 15, 2008. Notice that this first step is identical to the first step in implementation of the technical-momentum system we saw in Chapter 4. In combining technical and fundamental concerns in the design of stock selection systems, I prefer to begin with technical information because that is a more restrictive procedure and it causes a trader to focus immediately on stocks that are under accumulation.

In Table 6.1, prices quoted were the prices on August 15, 2008, and the highs and lows reported were for the 52-week period preceding that date. The values in the "Multiple" column were obtained by dividing the then-current price by the 52-week low. "% Lag" is obtained as the quotient of the difference of "High" minus "Price," divided by "Price." As explained in Chapter 4, the seventh column is labeled "Inv Value" for investment value. The numbers in this column are obtained by dividing a weighted rate-of-ascent value, as reflected in the price multiple, by a weighted percent lag value. The formula is as follows:

$$\text{Inv Value} = (3 * \text{Mltp})/(2 * \%\,\text{Lag})$$

You can see that the computation of investment value in this column rewards higher price multiples and lower percentage lags. Thus the higher the investment value obtained the better. For stock selection purposes, investment values above 100 are preferable to those below that critical value. Initially, the method stopped here, and selection was made from those stocks with the highest investment values. However, it was soon determined that the price multiple can be influenced by irregularities in price movement. For example, it sometimes happens that a stock will double in the first month of the year and show no further gains in the rest of the year. Sometimes also share price can dip in the middle of the year and quickly return to its pre-dip value and go no higher from that point. There needed to be a way to smooth the price-ascent curve and give priority to stocks that were continuing to show gains in the latter part of the year just as they had done earlier in the year. In essence, some curve fitting was needed so that the selection of stocks could be made on the basis of optimal patterns of ascending share price.

The columns labeled "3-Mo % Gain" and "Inv Rank" show how this was accomplished. First, the percentage gain over the past three months was computed by simply subtracting intraday share-price low during the three-month period prior to current share price from current share price, and dividing the remainder by the same 3-month share-price low, and multiplying this result by 100. The following formula summarizes this calculation:

$$3\text{-Mo \% Gain} = \{(\text{Price} - 3\text{-Mo Low Price})/3\text{-Mo Low Price}\} * 100$$

The end result of this calculation is entered for each stock in the "3-Mo % Gain" column. This percentage gain over the past three months is also highly important as a screening criterion. Because our goal is to realize gains of at least 10 percent each month, it is useful to eliminate all stocks that did not gain at least 30 percent over the past 3 months. This will further reduce the number of stocks in our list to approximately 75 to 150, depending on market conditions. Three-month low prices are easily available at websites such as http://finance.yahoo.com and http://bigcharts.com.

The final column in Table 6.1 labeled "Inv Rank" is the most important column for decision-making purposes according to this technical phase of the stock-selection system. All of the preceding information is involved in the calculation of the data in this column. What happens in this step is that the investment value data from column seven is rank ordered and smoothed using the Excel "RANK" function, and the result for each stock is divided by 3-month percentage gain in order to give priority to stocks that are continuing their share-price ascent in the most recent quarter of the year. The Excel formula is expressed as follows:

$$\text{Rank} = (\text{RANK}(G2, \ G2:G50,0) * 2 + 100)/H2$$

where   RANK is the Excel rank function

           G2 is the first data cell in the investment value column (Inv V)

           G2:G50 is the designation of range for the RANK function. (A 50-stock range is designated here, even though it is known that the database will often exceed 100 stocks. This mid-range specification appears to work best to insure separability and thus reliability in the ranking of stocks.)

           0 signifies that the rank statistic will be expressed in ascending order

           H2 is the first data cell in the 3-month percentage gain column.

Now that we have completed phase one of this hybrid stock-selection system, we are ready to move on to phase two. Phase two is a technical consolidation phase that is summarized in Table 6.2.

Notice in Table 6.2 that points have been awarded or subtracted from each of ten randomly selected candidate stocks reported in Table 6.1 in accordance with scores attained on six technical indicators. First, in the "% Lag" column one point was awarded to stocks whose current share prices were within 3.5 percent of their 52-week highs. Not reflected in this table is a further guideline that any stock whose share price drops below 50 percent of its 52-week high is automatically dropped from consideration, except possibly in severe bear-market conditions where many good stocks suffer large corrections in share price. Next, you can see in Table 6.2 that one point is awarded in the "Inv Value" column to stocks whose Investment Value reading in Table 6.1 exceeded 100. An additional point is awarded in the "3-Mo Gain" column to any stock whose percentage gain over the past three months has exceeded 100 percent. Another point is awarded in the

TABLE 6.2 Phase Two of a Technical-Fundamental Hybrid Stock Selection System

Symbol	% Lag	Inv Value	3-Mo Gain	Inv Rank	P&F	Tech Rating	Tech Total
HIRE	1	1	1	1	−1	0	3
FSYS	0	0	1	1	0	1	3
STAA	0	0	1	1	1	1	4
PARL	1	1	0	1	1	0	4
ALTH	0	0	0	1	1	1	3
AFAM	0	0	0	1	−1	0	0
LDG	1	1	0	1	1	1	5
ECPG	0	0	0	0	0	0	0
CALM	1	1	0	0	1	1	4
IKN	1	1	0	0	1	1	4

"Inv Rank" column to those stocks whose investment rank as reported in Table 6.1 is less than 1.5.

All of this summative information so far has been derived from Table 6.1, but now it is important to add two additional technical indicators that have not yet been considered.

POINT-AND-FIGURE ANALYSIS

Point-and-figure analysis is another valuable tool for the interpretation of price movement in stocks. This analysis, originally attributed to Charles Dow, is a terrific tool to provide a further guideline concerning the timing of stock purchases and sales. It provides signals such as "triple-top breakouts" and "long-pole reversals" to guide buying and selling decisions. The method tracks share-price increases using Xs and share-price declines using Os. Unit of price movement is registered in a vertical column in an upward direction as an X if the price has increased, or in a downward direction as an O if the price has decreased. A reversal of price direction results in the creation of a new column in the chart. Fortunately, the task of description and explanation of this procedure is greatly minimized by referencing again to http://stockcharts.com. If you visit that site and click on the P & F charts lead, the program will construct a point-and-finger analysis chart for any stock of interest. Here you should be most attentive to the signal provided along with each chart, where green signals suggest a possible buying opportunity and red signals indicate a sell. Also, the bullish price objective posted with the charts provides some indication of where the analysis suggests the stock price is headed. I find this particular method of technical analysis especially useful because, unlike many other technical indicators that give uniformly positive signals as long as a stock price continues to climb, point-and-figure analysis will provide bearish signals if a stock is overextended, even if it is still climbing to new highs. In Table 6.2, this technical information has been incorporated in the "P & F" column by awarding one point to every stock with a bullish green point-and-figure analysis signal; by awarding a zero when no new signal is provided; and by awarding a −1 point whenever a bearish red signal is given. This is a way to overcome the challenge of providing consistent mathematical scores for technical charting patterns.

TECHNICAL RATINGS

It is possible to gather summative technical ratings on every stock that has a long enough history of trading, such as those with at least six months. One good site where this is easily possible is http://barchart.com. There, if you submit any stock symbol for a quote and then click on "Opinion," you will get short-term, medium-term, and long-term estimates of the viability of the stock over each of 13 technical indicators, including a trend spotter, an average directional indicator, the moving average hilo channel, the MACD oscillator, Bollinger bands, the parabolic time/price indicator, and an average volume indicator. Overall ratings are provided across all of these indicators individually and as a composite. Because explanations of each of these technical indicators are provided at that website and in references already cited, treatment of each one of these indicators is not repeated here. For example, I have not provided a separate discussion on average daily volume because this information is provided at that website; however, it should be apparent that stocks that are regularly increasing in daily trading volume are often desirable acquisitions. Volume trending information is also available at http://finance.yahoo.com under the key statistics page for individual stock quotes. In order to provide an overall mathematical rating of the viability of each stock listed in Table 6.2, we can proceed as follows: any stock with an overall average rating of *96% Buy* to *100% Buy* is awarded one point in the *Technical Rating* column; any stock with an overall average rating of *25% Buy* to *95% Buy* is awarded a zero in that same column; and any stock with a rating below *25% Buy* is awarded a −1 in that column.

Oddly, some persons have objected that this technical information is all from the past, and it can therefore at best serve only as a lagging indicator with little bearing on future performance. My response to them is that, in a sense, all technical and fundamental decisions are necessarily based on data gathered from the past. This is not necessarily a limitation. We expect that the sun will rise tomorrow morning based on information gathered in the past. We expect that, in temperate zones, spring will follow winter, and summer will precede fall. Our expectations about sunrise and seasons are seldom if ever disappointed, because our data are highly reliable. In the same way, our task in using technical ratings is to make our decisions based on the most reliable data we can find and to use the composite of several kinds of indicators when available in order to make the most accurate estimates concerning future price movement that we can. That is why this procedure employs both point-and-figure analysis and a composite of technical ratings as shown in Table 6.2.

OTHER TECHNICAL INDICATORS

There are many other technical indicators that are beyond the scope of this book to examine. The Elliott Wave Principle and stochastics are two noteworthy approaches that come to mind. These and other techniques

TABLE 6.3 Phase Three of a Technical-Fundamental Hybrid Stock Selection System

Symbol	PE	Book Value	Growth	Divergence	Cash Flow	Fundamental Total
HIRE	0	−1	0	1	0	0
FSYS	−1	0	1	1	1	2
STAA	−1	0	−1	−1	−1	−4
PARL	0	1	1	1	1	4
ALTH	−1	−1	−1	−1	−1	−5
AFAM	0	−1	1	1	0	1
LDG	0	1	1	1	1	4
ECPG	1	1	1	0	1	4
CALM	0	1	0	1	0	2
IKN	1	1	1	1	1	5

are explained in several of the superb resources that were cited earlier in Table 2.2. Jack Schwager's book on technical analysis is an excellent resource. It will become apparent from that work that a detailed examination of all charting patterns is beyond the possible scope of this book. Rather than revisit the esoteric literature on cup-and-handle patterns and head-and-shoulder patterns and the myriads of other patterns that guide technical decision making, I am here limiting focus to a finite number of quantifiable indicators. Remember also the variance-explanatory principle of diminishing returns. Adding more technical variables than those already introduced in Table 6.2 would be to invite redundancy. So now we can move on to phase three and incorporate fundamental data into our hybrid system as reported in Table 6.3.

Notice in Table 6.3 that points have been awarded or subtracted based on ratings of fundamental variables such as PE, book value, growth, divergence, and cash flow, as was described in detail in Chapter 5.

PRICE-TO-EARNINGS (PE) RATIO

Strong earnings performance is the hallmark of any value-based approach and is the focus of the first column of Table 6.3. Here we are looking for stocks with earnings per share that attain the highest possible percentage of share price. This is tantamount to saying that we prefer those stocks with a price-to-earnings (PE) ratio of 10 or less. Because of the tendency for some companies to inflate earnings reports, some traders prefer to consider price-to-sales ratios (PSRs) instead of PE ratios. Setting such a stringent PE criterion is anathema to technical traders who would argue that good stocks will support much higher PE ratios. To be fair, one must acknowledge that such a stringent earnings criterion will eliminate many good stocks such as biotech stocks that may indeed show great future price appreciation. At the same time, stocks with such great earnings are much less likely to tank when the market goes south. Happily, as you can see, this is not the only criterion considered, so that a stock may fail to score high on this criterion and still qualify for selection. For purposes of quantification, a PE ratio ranging from zero to 12.0 is valued at 1 point. A PE ratio ranging from 12.0 to 25.0 is valued at zero points. And a PE ratio above 25.0 or that is negative is valued at a −1 point.

BOOK VALUE

Doubtless there are hundreds of ways to estimate value, and book value is only one of them. Earnings ratios and sales ratios and cash-flow ratios may also be considered indicators of value, and all of those indicators deserve a place at the table. But book value is more closely related to liquidation value of the company, and it is therefore important as a safety concern. I would never consider buying a used car without first consulting the estimated book value of that car. Here we are looking for book value per share and setting ratings of acceptability as follows: price-to-book ratios less than 2.0 are rated 1.0; price-to-book ratios greater than 2.0 but less than 4.0 are rated zero; and price-to-book ratios above 4.0 are rated −1.0. These points are placed column labeled *Book Value* in Table 6.3 and in the row opposite each stock.

EARNINGS GROWTH

It is not enough to find stocks with great earnings, as recorded in the *PE* column of Table 6.3, but ideally we are also looking for stocks with consistent growth in earnings from quarter to quarter. We can therefore examine quarterly earnings history and also look at future earnings estimates. This is a way to get a more reliable picture of earnings than by merely looking at the most recent quarterly earnings. Companies sometimes inflate earnings reports, but it is difficult to persist in such deception over several quarters. Furthermore, just as some analysts prefer price-to-sales ratios over price-to-earnings ratios, it is also possible to focus on revenue growth rather than on earnings growth. Year-over-year quarterly growth in income is reported at the key statistics page at http://finance.yahoo.com.

Another approach to the measurement of earnings growth is to compare current actual earnings with future estimated earnings. I have personally had greater success with earnings growth statistics that include future earnings estimates than with statistics that focus only on growth in the present over the past. This is probably due to the fact that investment sentiment has greater focus on future expectations than on past accomplishments. An easy and effective way to consider earnings growth related to future expectations is simply to compare the current PE ratio with the estimated future PE ratio. Here one is looking for a future estimated PE ratio that is substantially lower than the current PE ratio and lower than the average PE ratio for the industry and for the S&P 500 Index average. For purposes of obtaining a measurement to incorporate into our model, a future estimated PE ratio that is lower than the present PE ratio and is lower than the S&P 500 Index average PE ratio is rated 1.0. A future estimated PE ratio that is equal to or lower than the current PE ratio but is still higher than the S&P 500 Index average is rated zero. A future estimated PE ratio that is higher than the current PE ratio and is higher than the S&P 500 Index average, or that is negative, is rated −1.0. In cases where PE estimates are not available, one is forced to infer a rating from cash flow, or past earnings growth, or analyst expectations. However, if no data are available, a zero rating is given. These ratings are then entered in the "Growth" column of Table 6.3.

EPS/PE DIVERGENCE

Another of the most telling leading indicators of future performance is a positive divergence between rolling earnings per share and the price-earnings ratio. This occurs when there is a sudden bump upwards in earnings that is not yet reflected in the PE ratio or when there is a share buyback that results in greater earnings per share that is not yet reflected in the stated PE ratio. This information is available through using the interactive charting facility at http://bigcharts.com and it indicates that rolling earnings per share and PE ratio are variables of interest. If any stock is found to show a jump in earnings per share not yet accompanied by a jump in PE ratio or in share price, that stock qualifies for acquisition by this variable. Obviously, an increase in earnings per share should by definition cause the PE ratio to fall. However, investors tend to buy into stocks with positive earnings reports, and this ultimately drives the PE ratio upward. The object is to find stocks with recent positive earnings-per-share reports that have not yet ascended in share price and PE ratio. Figure 5.1 in Chapter 5 illustrates how this variable is applied for decision making.

Notice in Figure 5.1 that the rolling earnings per share for GENC saw increases in August, December and February. At the time of the August increase, the PE ratio actually fell from 8 to 5.5, and there was no accompanying rise in share price. This provided an initial alert that this stock deserved further attention. The December EPS increase was very slight; although, again it was accompanied by no increase in PE ratio and a very slight increase in share price. In February the rolling earnings per share nearly doubled, from 1.8 to 3.2; although, the PE ratio rose only to 7 and fell back to 4.5—eventually climbing to 6.0. At the same time the share price shot up from 10 to 14, and eventually doubled to 21. Several excellent points of entry were suggested by the EPS/PE divergence in August, December, and February. Ratings on divergence can be determined as follows: ascending rolling earnings per share with level or descending PE ratio and with share price not yet above earlier levels seen with lower rolling earnings per share is rated 1.0; ascending earnings per share with accompanying rises in share price and PE ratios to levels above market averages or with negative or unavailable PE ratios is rated zero; and falling rolling earnings per share regardless of share price and PE ratio changes is rated −1.0.

CASH FLOW AND FREE CASH FLOW

Possibly the best overall predictor of future price growth is cash flow. "Cash flow" is the net money flowing into or out from the company from operations, and this is different from "money flow" that is the net money flowing into or out from the company from investors. Companies usually report both "cash flow" and "free cash flow." "Free cash flow" is that cash flow that is unencumbered by operational expenses, and it is the more desirable of the two kinds of cash flow. However, because there is often a big discrepancy between these two statistics, it is best to consider them both. It is rather like statistical means and standard deviations; they should be considered together to get the most accurate picture. By this method we consider both the cash-flow-per-share ratio and the free-cash-flow-per-share ratio. These ratios are like PE ratios in that the smaller they are the better as a reflection of value. The rigid criterion observed is that the sum of these two ratios should not exceed 10. In practice, I have moved to averaging these two ratios and weighting the result as follows: under 12.5 is rated 1.0; from 12.5 to 25 is rated 0.0; and over 25 or with either ratio being negative = −1.0. One website where this information is readily available through the inspection of individual stock ratios is http://clearstation .etrade.com.

OTHER FUNDAMENTAL INDICATORS

As indicated in Chapter 4, there are many other fundamental variables worthy consideration. There we looked at money flow from investors into stocks as shown at http://stockcharts.com. We also considered debt per share from the perspective that low debt is desirable due to the loss of growth potential when a high percentage of revenue goes to service debt. I am always looking for better fundamental variables to incorporate into my mathematical stock-selection system. However, there is also the redundancy concern mentioned earlier as well. With the five fundamental variables already incorporated into this hybrid system, as reported in Table 6.3, we have now covered all of the explanatory variance we can based on our own research conducted up to this point.

It is now time to move to the fourth and final phase of implementation of this hybrid stock-selection system. This phase consists simply of combining the technical total rating from Table 6.2 with the fundamental total rating from Table 6.3 to come up with a grand total rating and a formal recommendation as demonstrated in Table 6.4.

In Table 6.4 we can see how final recommendations are derived from this hybrid technical-fundamental stock-selection system. Because there are six technical indicators shown in Table 6.2 and five fundamental indicators shown in Table 6.3, thus making eleven total variables considered, in theory, scores for any stock could range from +11.0 to −11.0. In practice, however, since we routinely eliminate stocks from our watch list with percentage lag greater than 50 percent and with three-month gain less than 30 percent, minus scores are not usually awarded for those variables. The

TABLE 6.4   Phase Four of a Technical-Fundamental Hybrid Stock-Selection System

Symbol	Technical Total	Fundamental Total	Grand Total	Recommendation
HIRE	3	0	3	Sell
FSYS	3	2	5	Weak Hold
STAA	4	−4	0	Very Strong Sell
PARL	4	4	8	Strong Buy
ALTH	3	−5	−2	Very Strong Sell
AFAM	0	1	1	Very Strong Sell
LDG	5	4	9	Very Strong Buy
ECPG	0	4	4	Weak Sell
CALM	4	2	6	Hold
IKN	4	5	9	Very Strong Buy

Short-term recommendations as of 8/18/08.

final recommendations reported in Table 6.4 are drawn from the grand total scores as follows: 9–11 = Very Strong Buy; 8 = Strong Buy; 7 = Buy; 6 = Hold; 5 = Weak Hold; 4 = Weak Sell; 3 = Sell; 2 = Strong Sell; 1 and below = Very Strong Sell.

It is important to emphasize that these recommendations are highly temporary in nature and are not to be taken as permanent guidelines. The only way I can underscore this is to point out that, as I write this sentence, it is two weeks after I performed the computations and derived the recommendations in Table 6.4. Although AFAM was then recommended as a *Very Strong Sell*, it subsequently moved to a *Buy* recommendation, and it is currently a *Hold*, and I do now own shares in this stock. It is also useful to point out that, in bear market seasons, there may be few if any stocks rated as *Buy* or above. If you maintain a guideline that you will never invest more than 10 percent of available capital in any one stock, this may enable you to be totally out of stocks when market conditions are weakest.

QUESTIONS AND ANSWERS

Here are some common questions and answers regarding the implementation of this hybrid system.

1. How long does it take to gather data and conduct analyses required for this system, and how often is it necessary to do this work?

    Initially it could take a whole day to conduct the necessary research and narrow down a list of candidate stocks and then to gather data on each of them and enter this information into database management software. But once a watch list has been established including all qualifying stocks with requisite technical and fundamental information, each day's analysis can be completed within an hour. It is preferable to gather data at the close of trading each day. This is less important for the fundamental variables that change infrequently, but technical data often change each day and need updating to maintain an accurate picture. Of course, if you are unable to update each day, you can leave it for a few days and resume again where you left off. However, decision-making with outdated information has its own dangers.

2. As you indicated previously, there are hundreds of technical and fundamental variables. How can you justify limiting the field to just six technical and five fundamental variables in this system?

    Obviously, to make any mathematical system functional, you must deal with a finite number of variables. There are time and cost constraints associated with updating all stocks on all variables regularly.

Happily, research has shown that many of the possible variables are redundant and overlapping in the performance variation they explain. As with any performance prediction model, after you have entered a reasonably small number of reliably measured variables, you reach a point of diminishing returns, so that prediction accuracy does not increase by adding new variables. The example I gave earlier concerned models used to predict successful college performance on the part of high school seniors. It turns out that, after including high school grade-point average, Scholastic Aptitude Test scores, parents' socioeconomic status, possible character references, and some possible motivation indicator, little or nothing is added to the prediction model by adding any new variables because they are already indirectly covered. For example, adding a measure of study habits or work ethic may already be reflected in GPA. In the same way with stocks, if you already have measures of earnings, earnings growth, and cash flow, including an additional measure of long-term debt may be redundant because it is already reflected in earnings and free cash flow. If anything, I am probably guilty of measurement overkill with this system because I employ eleven variables, and one of the technical variables labeled *Technical Rating* is really the sum of 13 other underlying technical variables.

3. If there is insufficient time to gather all of the data indicated, which of these variables are most important for decision-making purposes?

   In order to make the best possible predictions of share-price gain, I believe it is necessary to incorporate both technical and fundamental indicators. The technical variables provide timing information and the fundamental variables supply value information. I would rank percentage lag, point-and-figure analysis, and the summative technical rating variable as explained in this chapter among the most important technical indicators. Fundamental variables are a little more difficult to rank because it appears that their predictive power may vary with market conditions. For example, cash flow, free cash flow and growth variables appear to work well as predictors in a bull market scenario, but book value and price-to-earnings ratios seem to work well when the overall market is trending downward. For researchers, there are many exciting areas here for further investigation.

4. What do you do in cases where stocks may have solid fundamental data but weak technical data, and in cases where technical data are strong but fundamental data are weak?

   Perhaps a good example of a stock with good fundamentals but weak technicals is found by considering ECPG in Table 6.4. At the time of that analysis the stock had strong fundamentals and weak technicals. My posture in such a case would be to wait for the technicals to improve before purchasing the stock. Very often the technicals do improve if the fundamentals are strong. Coincidentally, two weeks after the computations completed earlier for Table 6.4, ECPG has risen from a *Weak Sell* to a *Buy* recommendation, and I have acquired that stock. Conversely, if the technicals are strong and the fundamentals are weak, as was the case with STAA in Table 6.4, it may help to take a closer look at the fundamentals. Perhaps there is a news development that suggests that earnings will greatly improve in the near future. Perhaps there is word of a pending acquisition of the stock. However, it is always dangerous to buy stocks that have no supporting fundamentals, even though the technicals may be superb. Accordingly, I see that, two weeks after the initial computations, the technical data for STAA have moved down to coincide with the fundamental data. Persons with an inclination to short stocks, and I am certainly not one of them, might do well to look for stocks with strong technicals and weak fundamentals as shorting candidates. This whole question of the comparative performances of stocks with strong technicals *versus* stocks with strong fundamentals is one of the most exciting and possibly most productive areas of research inquiry.

5. Aren't you worried that by disclosing your trading systems you are giving away trading secrets that could compromise your future trading success?

Not really. My approach to trading does not produce zero-sum gains. If other people end up chasing the same stocks that I am chasing, that will only drive their prices higher. Thus it could be argued that the more persons there are who adopt these trading systems, the better it will be for me and for them.

6. At various points you have indicated that you make a living by trading stocks. How much investment capital does it require for someone to live off their trading proceeds in this way?

Obviously there is no single answer to this question. Answers will ultimately depend on how much income is required, and on the ratio of income to principal, that is, on how much a trader is able to make with any specified amount of trading capital. That is why I prefer to speak in terms of percentage gain over specific intervals. So, for example, a person with $100,000.00 of investment capital who is able to realize gains of 10 percent per month on average will be able to make $10,000.00 per month on average. Is that enough income to live on? For some persons it will be more than enough and for some other persons it will not be enough. A more important question, one that I have tried to address in this book, is how a person can be enabled to realize average gains of 10 percent per month. I have found that to be possible through the design of appropriate trading systems and through the skillful implementation of those systems.

SUMMARY

In this chapter, we have considered a sample trading system that is a hybrid technical-fundamental that takes into consideration several technical indicators to provide timing information along with several fundamental variables to provide value information. The variables involved in implementation of this system were explained and criterion values were set for decision making. Finally, several common questions were asked and answered about the use of this trading system.

CHAPTER 7

Buying Stocks

It should be acknowledged from the outset that, although appropriate stock selection is among the most important concerns of any successful stock trader, it is only about one-fourth or less of the total effort involved in trading. Another equally valid focus needs to be on the actual purchase of those stocks that have been selected. Decisions about when to buy, the exact price entry point, whether to buy at market or by using a limit order, and whether to buy all in one trade or by using a series of smaller trades are all-important concerns that can determine success or failure. To borrow the race car analogy again, even if you manage to design the perfect race car that is far superior to the competition, unless it is driven with skill in the race, there is little chance of winning. Therefore, even if you develop the perfect stock-selection algorithm, unless you execute trades with expertise, the system alone will not guarantee success. The following procedures can help in this challenging process of driving the race car.

PREPARING THE SLATE OF CANDIDATES

On the evening before trading, a list of candidate buy orders is made on the basis of a thorough screening of the entire universe of publicly traded stocks. This may involve up-to-date analysis of all stocks in a large watch list by using one or more of the analysis techniques described in Chapters 4, 5, and 6. Normally, this will yield only four or five candidate stocks for purchase, depending on market conditions, and some of these may already be present in your portfolio. Barring some unforeseen developments affecting other top-rated stocks in the watch list, buy orders throughout the trading day should be limited to this slate of candidate stocks. On some days there are no qualifying candidate stocks for acquisition. On those days no purchases are made. It is critical to maintain this discipline and not go off on tangents to purchase stocks based on tips or other whims.

The first step is to prepare the list of candidate buy orders, and this usually happens in the evening prior to trading. If use is made of the trading system contained in the CD accompanying this book, as explained in Chapter 19, the derivation of the slate of candidates will involve inputting a considerable amount of technical and fundamental data for each stock, and then generating a ranking of all possible candidate acquisitions.

GATHERING INTEL

In the morning, prior to the market open, it is important to gather the latest information on the candidate stocks as well as on any other stocks currently held. This process can be greatly facilitated by constructing a watch list at http://finance.yahoo.com or at your brokerage account, or elsewhere. There the news should automatically be posted for any stocks in your list as the news becomes available. You will want to know any current details about surprising or disappointing earnings, takeover speculations, insider transactions, analyst upgrades or downgrades, and so forth. On the one hand, positive news that has not yet been reflected in the share price can be an encouragement to pull the trigger and actually purchase the stock if it is on the candidate buy list. On the other hand, if this positive news has already prompted a large run up in share price, it may not suggest a purchase. If there is any news of a pending takeover or acquisition of your target stock, and if it has already stimulated a run up to a price approaching the rumored takeover price, the stock should usually be avoided. Of course, any negative news may guide you to avoid new acquisitions of affected stocks on your list altogether, or at least to wait until after a price correction has taken place. Negative news can also prompt you to consider selling stocks that you already hold in your portfolio.

Another part of the intel needed prior to the market open consists of the bid and ask prices and the sizes of the bid and ask for each of the candidate stocks. This information can often presage price movement for the day. If there is a trade imbalance such that the bid size is massively larger than the ask size, it can be highly rewarding to buy at the open. It is also important to consider the actual sectors reflected by each of the candidate stocks. In this way you can be careful to maintain appropriate diversification. You do not want a preponderance of your holdings to be within any one sector. Sometimes it can also be helpful to scan the message boards of any candidate stocks. Occasionally traders may share insights that exceed the information easily available elsewhere.

DEMANDING SUPPLY

Some traders wisely refuse to make any purchases until after the market has been open for at least 30 minutes. That way they don't often get caught in any artificial opening surges that often become reversals a few minutes later. Heaviest trading usually tends to be in the first 30 minutes and the last 30 minutes of each trading day. Around noon there seems to be a lull in the action, and prices tend to retrace slightly. To the extent that this observation holds, the opening and closing 30 minutes are best for selling, and midday is the best time for buying stocks. Of course, if you can get in early on a price surge at the open, that is fine. What you do not want to do, however, is to chase a run up. The trader's calling is to demand supply and to supply demand. What you are doing when you chase a run up is to demand the demand, and that usually means that you will pay too much for the stock. Minimally, I make it a rule never to buy at the high price of the day, and never to sell at the low. If a stock has already gained 10 percent or more on the day, it is *usually* best to look for greener pastures. Alternatively, if your analysis suggests that you must acquire the stock, you can set a limit buy order at least 3 percent below the daily high.

The best days for buying stocks are often days when the major averages are down. On those days most persons are selling and pessimism is prevailing. Some may even be selling to cover margin calls on their holdings. There is an excess supply of stocks, and your purchase can be perceived as a service aimed at restoring equilibrium. With regard to the purchase of individual stocks, many wise traders wait until there is a moderate retracement in their target stocks before they buy. One popular technique is to wait for the candidate stock to decline and bounce off its 50-day moving average. Unfortunately, many great stocks do not make such declines until it is too late and the stock is no longer of interest.

COST AVERAGING

It is often wise to buy a stock in increments instead of buying all at once. For example, if the ask price is $15 and you have $10,000 to invest in that stock, why not buy 333 shares at $15 for $5,000 and wait a few hours or days to buy the rest when the price comes down? If you are later able to purchase 345 shares of that stock at $14.50 for $5,000, you have then lowered your cost basis to just below $14.75 plus commissions, and you have acquired 678 shares instead of only 666 shares had you bought the shares all at once. Implicit in this process is the fact that you must always compute your cost basis with every new purchase. Many online brokerage accounts will do this computation for you automatically. Also implicit here is that you have been watching price movement for a few days or weeks, and you have reason to believe from patterns of fluctuation that the price will soon come down.

This process of lowering your cost basis through successive purchases of a stock at lower prices is called "averaging down." Many experts caution against it because you may become saddled with an ever-increasing position in a stock that is in decline. I advocate this procedure only when your prior analysis suggests that the underlying stock is a "must buy" based on a variety of fundamental and technical factors. There is also a process known as "averaging up" that consists of buying increments in a position in a stock at successively higher prices as the price moves up, and thereby raising your cost basis in that stock. There is nothing inherently wrong with averaging up—as long as you do not violate diversification rules by acquiring too many shares of any one stock. The subject of diversification is explored in Chapter 9. Averaging up can be especially beneficial if purchases are made using the proceeds from the sales of less tenable positions in your portfolio. By contrast, some traders mistakenly sell their best stocks as soon as they show a profit, and they keep their "dogs" in hope that they will eventually turn a profit so they can sell them above purchase price. This is a compound error because it fails to keep the winners and ride them up, and it also encumbers your portfolio with losers. It is better to cut your losses and buy winners.

LIMIT AND MARKET ORDERS

Should you make your purchase by using a limit order at a pre-specified price, or by using a market order that will hopefully get you whatever the current market ask price may be? This is an important question, but it is by no means easy to answer. The answer depends on many other factors such as average daily trading volume in the stock, momentum direction and strength, magnitude of the spread (i.e., the distance between the bid price and the ask price), bid and ask sizes, commissions for limit and market orders, and general market conditions. Rather than give a pat answer that will invariably have many exceptions to the rule, let me share some anecdotal examples that may ultimately provide a better answer.

First, imagine a low volume stock (averaging less than 10,000 shares a day) that last traded at $10 with a bid price of $10 and an ask price of $10.50. On closer inspection you see that the bid size is 200 shares and the ask size is also 200 shares. Over the past three months the stock has moved up from $7.50 per share, and the 52-week high is $10.75. Imagine that your analysis indicates that this is a stock that has excellent fundamentals and should move higher. You have decided to acquire 1,000 shares. You are mindful of the fact that you have at least three great adversaries in this venture. First, your broker will ask a commission for the trade. Hopefully, you have found a broker that charges the same low rate ($7 or less) whether the trade is a market order or a limit order. In this way, the commission will be such a tiny fraction of 1 percent of the transaction that it will no longer be a consideration—even when you realize that the commission will be assessed again at the time of sale, or that you may need to buy and sell in increments.

Next, there is the market maker or specialist who makes his living on the spread, which in this case is a whopping 5 percent or about $500 with the trade you are contemplating. When you consider that you may face this same cost again at the time of sale, this is a truly formidable expense. Finally, the U.S. government may expect around 20 percent of your proceeds in the form of capital gains taxes. To some extent you may be able to mitigate this most serious consideration by trading stocks in your IRA account so that you don't need to settle that obligation until you withdraw the cash. Or you may have capital losses that will offset capital gains, so that the gains will not be an issue.

Now consider that the bid and ask prices are being set by the specialist or market maker rather than by some independent buyer and seller. This is likely because the spread is so great, the bid and ask are equal in size, and it is a low-volume stock. This means that, if you enter a limit order to buy 1,000 shares at $10, the market maker will have no incentive to fill your order. He or she is even likely to raise the bid to exclude your offer from the market. Technically speaking, the market is the region bounded by the bid and the ask prices, so if your offer to buy falls below the official bid, you are no longer in the market. What is worse, some independent buyer may see your 1,000-share purchase order and recognize a disparity between the bid and ask sizes and become motivated to buy at $10.50 and take out the ask. Then, you have only succeeded in moving both the bid and ask prices higher by announcing your intention to make a comparatively large purchase.

What can you do? Your alternatives are limited. One alternative is to place a limit order for 1,000 shares at $10.50. That way you can purchase at least 200 shares before the price moves up, and you stimulate buying so that trading volume increases, the spread narrows, and you realize gains. In this case, you definitely do not want to place a market order because, after the initial 200 shares are filled at $10.50, your remaining order could get filled at $11 or $12, and then the market could immediately fall back to the original bid and ask prices, and you will suffer loss. Another alternative, if you are patient, is to "split the difference." By this alternative you reduce the size of your offer to parallel the current bid and ask sizes, and you make a good-till-cancelled bid to buy 200 shares at $10.25. By narrowing the spread in this way, you have potentially reduced the profit of the market maker, and you have made future transactions in the stock more attractive to buyers and sellers. And, most importantly, you have potentially lowered the cost of your purchase by reducing the spread. However, this does not guarantee that you will get an execution any time soon. In a sense, you have become the market maker. If you do get an execution, you have reserved the capacity to follow the market with your next purchase of the stock and possibly even reduce your cost basis. Your decision whether to employ one of those two alternatives or to move on to another stock altogether will be influenced by factors such as the strength of that particular stock, your need to diversify into that particular sector, your limits of patience, and general market conditions.

Now let's imagine another example. Consider a high-volume stock averaging over two million shares per day that last traded for $25. The bid price is $24.98 and the ask price is $25.04, with a bid size of 1200 and an ask size of 200. The market has only been open ten minutes and the stock is already up 2 percent over yesterday's close. The previous all-time high for the stock was $24.50, but that has already been exceeded in today's trading. Your analysis indicates that the stock has strong fundamentals and a lot of room to move higher. You have decided to acquire 1,000 shares of the stock. Should you place a limit order for 1,000 shares under $25 and wait for the stock price to come to your offer, or should you place a market order for 1,000 shares and take what you can get at whatever price is available? If you see from your study of intraday price movement that the stock regularly shows high volatility, you may choose yet a third alternative. You could buy 500 shares at market, and then wait for the price to decline to such a point that your next purchase of 500 shares would lower your cost basis overall. In this buying example liquidity is clearly not a problem, so that your small order at the market price is not in danger of being filled at a much higher price, and market makers do not pose a threat because there is large trading volume. Clearly the stock is moving up fast, so the biggest threat may be that it could get away from you if you do not buy in quickly. Therefore, I would most likely enter a market order for the full 1,000 shares immediately. If the stock had already moved, say 5 percent on the day, then the third alternative may be the most advisable and you make two smaller purchases and lower your cost basis.

These are two very different examples. In both cases the decision to buy was made tentatively on the basis of analysis prior to the day of purchase. However, deciding when and how to pull the trigger and make the actual purchase is a decision with a different basis in each case, and is directed more by experience than by textbook. You could conclude that the original decision to buy was all science, but the actual execution of the purchase was art.

Now let's consider yet a third example. Imagine that you have five stocks on your candidate buy list, and they are all exceptionally strong in every way. After gathering pre-market intel, you find that three of the five are set to open much lower than the previous closing price, and the other two are about to open much higher, as you can see from the current bid and ask prices. On closer examination you see that two of the three stocks that are set to open lower have just reported very disappointing earnings, and their current growth cycles appear to have ended. The third of these decliners has just been downgraded by an analyst and has reported a large proposed quantity of insider selling. All three of these decliners will at the open fall far below the 3 percent criterion lag from their 52-week highs reached earlier in the week. You immediately scratch all three from your candidate buy list, and breathe a sigh of relief that you didn't buy them earlier. Next you examine the two remaining stocks that are bid higher at the open. The first is a pharmaceutical stock that has just received a takeover tender offer at $45 a share from a larger company. The stock closed at $35 the day before, but is now bid to open at $43 a share. News reports suggest that the board of directors of the company will accept the offer and the company will be acquired at the offered price. Reluctantly, you scratch this stock from your candidate buy list as well because you realize that the potential 28 percent takeover gain is already practically built into the opening price, and the stock will not go higher from that point.

Also, you know from experience that, if you hold the stock as it goes through the mechanics of takeover, your funds may be tied up for several months before you are compensated, and the payment may be in the form of stock from the acquiring company, and your analysis suggests that is not an attractive candidate for purchase. The final stock on your list is a gold mining stock, and it is bid to open at around $18 a share from the previous day's close of $15.50. You see that the London spot gold futures contract hit an all-time high overnight, and you suspect that there is panic buying.

As you study the charts, you see that this has happened before, and it has always been followed by a sharp decline in the commodity price to near-previous levels. You reason that, if you already hold the stock, it would be a great time to sell, but it is definitely not a great time to buy. You remember that your goal is to demand supply and to supply demand, and so you cross this final stock off your candidate buy list. Having now eliminated all of your candidate buy stocks from contention, you look carefully at your existing holdings to see if there are any compelling reasons to add to your current positions or lighten them. Once you are satisfied that there is nothing further to be done that day, you decide that the best possible investment of your time will be to take your children fishing.

AVOIDING PURCHASES WITH UNSETTLED FUNDS

Although this topic is discussed more thoroughly in Chapter 14, it is useful to point out here that using unsettled funds to buy new stock positions can be hazardous. It is perfectly legitimate and highly tempting to trade with unsettled funds; however, if you purchase a stock with unsettled funds, you must wait until the funds settle before you can sell that stock. Normally it takes three days for funds to settle from a sale. Three days can be an eternity in stock trading. It is ample time for an analyst to downgrade the stock, for a CEO to resign, for an earnings report to disappoint, and even for a company to announce bankruptcy proceedings. I have learned the hard way that it is often best to wait for funds to settle before reinvesting them in other stocks. However, it is only fair to point out from a more balanced perspective that there is something really nice about purchases with unsettled funds. It is that, during the three-day period while you are waiting for the funds to settle, you are not assessed any interest for the funds you have used for purchases. If you are constantly selling stock and using the proceeds for immediate purchases, it is possible that you may continually be using thousands of dollars in unsettled funds that you do not yet actually have for making those purchases, and you are not being charged interest for this privilege. This is one more thing to be thankful about. However, another possible argument in favor of not using unsettled funds to make purchases is the fact that it is often a good idea to wait at least three days before selling any new acquisitions anyway. There can often be a slight price decline immediately after the purchase of a volatile stock that has been moving up in price, and this decline should not necessarily become a basis for the immediate sale of that stock.

SUMMARY

In this chapter we have considered several guiding principles involved in the successful purchasing of stocks. These include preparing a slate of candidate stocks the evening before making any purchase and limiting purchases to those stocks, gathering intel on candidate stocks before the market opens, demanding supply as an approach to making purchases, the use of cost averaging, the appropriate use of limit and market orders, and avoiding the use of unsettled funds for the purchase of stocks.

CHAPTER 8

Selling Stocks

M ost traders will agree that the most difficult trading decision is not what to buy, but when to sell. It is not difficult to find good stocks, especially in bull-market seasons. But it is possible to hold those stocks too long and never manage to sell for a gain. It is equally possible not to hold the stocks long enough to realize an appropriate gain and thus to sell a potential winner too soon. I find the decision to sell a stock every bit as challenging and rewarding as the decision to buy a stock. Perhaps this is because selling is the ultimate way to make gains and avoid losses, and because gains are never actually realized until a stock has been sold. And selling a stock is an excellent way to free up capital for future investments.

It is just as important to minimize losses as it is to lock in gains. I am reminded that Tiger Woods says that he often gets more of a rush from saving par than from making a birdie or an eagle. In the same way, getting out of some purchases with your shirt still on your back can be every bit as satisfying as making huge gains. There are few things more satisfying to a stock trader than selling a complete position in a stock based on prior analysis, and then watching the share price of the stock plummet dramatically below the sale price. The remainder of this chapter is devoted to the discussion of strategies for selling. It is likely that it will be appropriate to consider more than one possible approach in any given selling decision.

SETTING TARGETS

Many successful traders set a specific selling price target at the time they purchase each stock. This has several advantages. First of all, if you enter a limit sell order at a target price above where you bought the stock, it may ultimately be more profitable than a stop-loss sell order because you will be selling when the stock is climbing to new highs rather than when it is falling to previous lows. This is consistent with the calling to supply demand and to demand supply. Also, placing limit sell orders on your holdings has the added advantage of removing the stock from short sellers who could otherwise borrow the shares from your broker to sell them short. In other words, it limits the supply of stocks available for shorting. This is a useful consideration if you are holding a long position on any low-volume stock. Placing realistic limit sell orders is also a discipline that enables patient traders to hold on through seasons of volatility. Furthermore, this practice can reduce the number of trades you make, and thereby cut losses due to commissions and spreads. But how can you identify a realistic selling price? Some traders use the price targets offered by point-and-figure analysis at http://stockcharts.com. Other traders find those targets too generous and tend to place limit sell orders at somewhat lower prices. The higher your price objectives, the more infrequent your trading executions will be.

At the same time, it is important to recognize that targets must be flexible. For example, if a company comes out with a surprisingly positive earnings report, it may be appropriate to adjust the selling target higher in order to avoid needlessly discarding a winner too soon. In the same way, if you have been holding the same stock for several months and it has made no movement towards the selling target price, it may be appropriate to lower the target price, or sell at market. It is always useful to have selling price targets both above and below current share price, even if these are only mental targets that you record in your daily log of market activity.

SETTING PARTIAL TARGETS

Related to the strategy of setting selling targets in advance, many successful traders set targets for partial sale of their holdings. For example, if a stock increases 20 percent in value, some traders may automatically sell 20 percent or more of their holdings in that stock. There are many different strategies for setting partial-sell benchmarks. I like to maintain holdings in any given stock in $5,000 units. When the value of that holding reaches $6,000, I routinely consider selling $1,000 worth of the stock to maintain the unit and take profits. However, decisions about selling should depend on more information than just percentage gains in your holdings.

USING STOP-LOSS ORDERS

Placing stop-loss sell orders is a way of protecting your investments against sudden, unpredicted downturns during panic selling episodes. This procedure is especially useful when a trader is traveling or otherwise unable to monitor holdings during the trading day. Most traders will set stop-loss orders somewhere between 3 percent and 5 percent below current bid price, and will adjust the orders upwards as the stock price rises, depending on factors such as spread and daily volatility. Because the stop-loss sell order is triggered as a market order when the price of the stock falls to the target price, the actual sale transaction may take place at a price much lower than the specified sale price. Therefore, for some low-volume stocks in panic selling episodes, even if the stop-loss price is set at 5 percent below current stock price, the actual sale may take place at 10 percent or more below the specified price. For this reason, many traders use stop-loss limit orders. These orders are like regular stop-loss orders in that they are triggered when the share price falls to the specified level, but they are unlike regular stop-loss orders in that they will not be executed if the bid price falls below the specified limit price. I have a distinct memory of setting a stop-loss limit order to be triggered at 5 percent below current share price, but with a floor or limit set at 10 percent below current share price. The amazing thing that happened was that the share price quickly fell below my specified trigger price without a sell execution, and then the price fell below my specified limit price where an execution was not allowed. Later in the day, the price rebounded above the limit price and then above the original trigger sell price–still without an execution. At the end of the day, the share price closed higher than on the previous day's close and I still owned all of my shares.

Stop-loss orders are not without their own hazards. The chief hazard is that all such orders are visible to the market makers or specialists maintaining the market for the stock. When a large number of such orders accumulate just below the current share price, it often becomes financially advantageous for these specialists to move the share price down temporarily in order to "take out the stops." Afterwards the price quickly rebounds to previous levels and continues its upward movement, but with the important difference that you no longer own any shares. Because of this real hazard by which I have been burned many times, I often prefer to monitor my holdings closely and place sell orders only when conditions indicate that the stock has reached my pre-specified limits for selling, rather than to place stop-loss orders.

Another hazard is that, because the triggered sell order is usually a market order, it is possible that the execution of the sell order will take place at a price much lower than intended, and it may in fact take place at the low for the day. Although I try to avoid placing stop-loss orders, there are notable exceptions that dictate their use. One is when a stock has experienced a rapid run up beyond sustainable limits of value. Such stocks are usually ripe for retracements, and stop-loss orders may be useful to preserve gains. The other is when the trader is traveling or is otherwise unable to monitor intraday price movement.

CULLING OUT LOSERS

In the same way that it is important to discover candidate buy orders in the evening before the market opens, it is also important to find candidate sell orders from among the stocks in your portfolio beforehand as well. This is a process very similar to that of a gardener who prunes the dead branches from a shrub or tree in order to promote more healthy growth. Here a losing stock is defined as one that has retreated in share price to a point that you have specified at which you must sell in order to prevent further loss. This may be 5 percent or more below the price at which you bought the stock, depending on features that may be unique to that stock. If you have held a stock for several weeks and there has been no upward price movement, this may also indicate that the stock is a loser that should be eliminated. Using the trading systems described in Chapters 4, 5 and 6, you may simply define a loser as any stock that has fallen below a "hold" rating after daily analysis. That process is described under "Rank Indicators" below.

Many persons make the mistake of holding their losers in order to wait for them to register a gain. At the same time these same traders may compound their mistake by selling their winners as soon as they realize a gain of 10 percent or so. The key problem introduced by this behavior is "lost opportunity." When you have identified stocks that are moving up with solid fundamentals and good technicals, it makes little sense to hold on to losers. Nor is it ever a good strategy to throw away winners. It is true, however, that today's loser may become tomorrow's winner, and we need to have sufficient humility to be willing to reacquire a stock we sold earlier if conditions so dictate.

RANK INDICATORS

Another good way to determine when to sell a stock is to consider the ratings produced by the trading systems described in Chapters 4, 5, and 6. By this approach, whenever a stock falls below the rating of "hold," it becomes a candidate for sale. In this way a lot of the emotion is removed from the decision to sell. Because this rating is ascertained after the market close, it is not usually possible to make the sale until the market opens on the following day, unless you have an after-hours account that has other disadvantages such as low trading volume that may prevent you from getting the best price. However, on the following day when the market opens, the stock may also rebound in share price and no longer be a candidate for sale. It is important to be sensitive to this possibility and not to consider a stock that falls below the rating of "hold" to be an automatic sale.

Although using rank indicators is my own most common method for identifying stocks that are candidates for sale, it has a few disadvantages that can partially offset its advantages. One of the main disadvantages is that the sell indicator given by the trading system may not be triggered until the stock has already lost 3 percent or more of its value. Few technical sell indicators are triggered until a stock has fallen sufficiently to signal that it is in retreat. One possible exception to this generalization is the point-and-figure analysis mentioned earlier. It can be triggered when a stock is "overextended" to the upside. Another possible disadvantage is that stocks falling sufficiently to trigger a sell indicator may also be approaching an oversold limit, which will in turn initiate a bounce in the stock. For this reason it is important to inspect a recent trading chart of any stock you hold. This can help you recognize normal retracements and thereby avoid selling on every dip in price.

HOLDING LIMITS

As you wait for a stock in your portfolio to climb to its price objective, there are limits to the amount of patience that can be justified. In the rare event that a stock shows no movement up or down in the space of three weeks, I consider it a candidate for sale. On reflection, I think this parallels human food consumption. When we eat food, there is a time limit within which our bodies must assimilate nutrients and put them to good use. After that deadline, what is not productively assimilated is expelled.

With some embarrassment I admit that once or twice I have found that I was holding such a stagnant company in my portfolio. My embarrassment stems from the fact that the reason for its lack of price movement was that the company had actually agreed to be acquired by another company at or near the current trading price. Such stocks are readily apparent from the performance charts as well as from the news bulletins. They usually show a jump in price at the time of the acquisition announcement, and then the price remains practically unchanged until the acquisition is complete and the symbol disappears. It is almost never worthwhile to hold such stocks. Not only will the price not change, but also the payment for the company may be in shares of the acquiring company that are much less attractive than the acquired company. Also, there may be a holding period of several weeks or months during which time your shares are non-negotiable as the transaction is in process. Other stocks that do not move in price are often held in a narrow price range by some similar transaction arrangement that is not always easy to detect.

BREAKING THE 50-DAY MOVING AVERAGE

Because most stocks are constantly dipping and swelling in price like drift-wood bobbing in the ocean, many savvy investors wait for a stock to fall to its 50-day moving average and use that decline to signal a point of entry. The point here is that, if the stock breaks through its 50-day moving average line without bouncing, it could also be interpreted as a sell indicator. Of course, this indicator has the same disadvantage as the trading system rank indicator, namely, that a stock may give up too much of its value before it reaches its 50-day moving average line. However, selling on a breakdown of the 50-day moving average may help prevent the disappointment that comes from selling your position early only to discover that it bounces soon afterward and moves to new highs.

IDENTIFYING MARKET DOWNTURNS

One other sell indicator is a general market downturn. It has been said that a rising tide lifts all boats, and conversely, a falling tide lowers all boats. It is unusual to see much individual stock price appreciation during a bear market trend. Of course there are exceptions to this rule, and our own trading systems will help to identify such exceptions when they occur. However, as is noted in Chapter 10, we can often make more investment gain by being out of the market nearly 50 percent of the time based on fluctuations in the Chicago Board Options Exchange (CBOE) Volatility Index or some other indicator, than by being fully invested in long positions all of the time. By this rule we may choose to sell our holdings whenever our overall market timing indicator suggests we are headed for a downturn.

SUMMARY

In this chapter, we have considered a variety of approaches to the appropriate selling of stocks. These have included the setting of selling price targets at the time of purchase, the use of stop-loss orders, the process of culling out losers, the use of rank indicators from our trading systems, the setting of holding time limits on stocks with no price appreciation, looking for stocks that fall through their 50-day average price line, and identifying general market downturns as selling indicators. It was noted that more than one of these approaches may be useful in particular situations.

CHAPTER 9

Portfolio Management

Although in previous chapters we have considered a variety of approaches to the successful identification of stocks, purchase of stocks, and sale of stocks, there is still more that a successful trader needs to do. One important additional concern is the appropriate management of one's portfolio of stocks. Failure to manage one's portfolio properly can nullify a lot of good work.

There is a joke about a man who was carrying a basket of eggs on his head as he spied a banana peel in his path. Not wanting to slip and break the eggs, he set his basket of eggs on the ground and then proceeded to step on the banana peel. He slipped and fell, but then picked up his basket and walked away happily in the sure knowledge that he had saved his eggs. In this chapter, I hope to make the point, if only obliquely, that we should not put all of our eggs in one basket, and that we must proceed cautiously with our holdings.

DIVERSIFYING OVER STOCKS

In order to minimize and distribute risk, it is important to hold more than a few different stocks. It is inevitable that some companies whose stock you hold will announce unexpected bad news, such as disappointing earnings, analyst downgrades, CEO retirement, or even pending bankruptcies. It is a lot easier to absorb the related losses if you hold ten to twenty stocks in your portfolio than if you hold only one or two. In this connection, the analogy of the farmer and his crops is fitting. Most farmers do not know what the sales prices of their crops will be in advance of the harvest, nor do they know what kinds of blights or insect infestations may come. A wise farmer will have a diversity of crops with varying harvest times, depending on the limits of his or her land and resources to maintain those crops. In the same way, a wise investor will hold a variety of stocks, depending on the limits of his or her investment capital and ability to keep abreast of developments with each stock. Of course, the practice of diversification is built on the premise that stocks will not all move in the same direction at the same time and pace.

In the event of a global stock market crash, when nearly all of your stocks are moving down at the same rate, there would be no risk reduction through diversification of stocks. Economists would maintain that this kind of global risk or "systematic risk" is common to all stocks at any particular time to the extent that they tend to move together in response to market conditions. "Unsystematic risk" is risk that may be peculiar to any particular company irrespective of overall market conditions. Ultimately, appropriate diversification of stocks can minimize unsystematic risk, but it cannot limit systematic risk. Systematic risks can be minimized through diversification into other assets outside of equities.

In any discussion of diversification there is always a dynamic tension between potential losses due to excessive risk associated with holding too few stocks, and depressed gains due to excessive caution associated with holding too many stocks. When you hold too many stocks, you effectively become a kind of index fund and are unable to surpass the gains of the overall market. Earlier in this book I have argued that, if you are employing a value-earnings approach to stock selection, you need at least five or six stocks in your portfolio. And if you use a technical-momentum approach, you need at least ten or twelve stocks in your portfolio because momentum-based stocks are more ephemeral in their progress. This rule of thumb is based more on personal experience than on any empirical research. Optimal numbers of stocks held will certainly vary according to overall market conditions and in consideration of the limits of investment capital you have available. Also, because in bear market conditions there may not be more than two or three stocks worth holding, it is likely that a preponderance of one's available capital should then be moved into cash.

It is important to consider that the kind of diversification contemplated here is only limited diversification into the best stocks. If you are able to rank-order stocks according to some metric of desirability as we do with the trading systems described in Chapters 4, 5, and 6, you can readily understand that acquiring new stocks that are successively lower on our rankings will necessarily serve to dilute your portfolio. That explains why some professional traders have referred to the addition of excessive stock holdings as the "deworsification" of your portfolio. This also helps to clarify what

I meant earlier when I wrote about the dynamic tension between holding too few stocks and holding too many stocks in one's portfolio.

Capital limitations are a serious concern because of commission and spread costs attached to each transaction. Therefore, I tend to think roughly in $5,000 units, with each $5,000 allocated to a single stock. By this view, if you have only $15,000 to invest, you could be limited to approximately three stocks. However, if you have $50,000, you may consider ten stocks at $5,000 each by a technical-momentum approach or five stocks at $10,000 each by a value-earnings approach, or some combination or permutation thereof.

DIVERSIFYING OVER SECTORS

There is a strong tendency for stocks within sectors to move together. Thus, if crude oil prices are moving to new highs, many oil and oil-service stocks will also move higher at the same time. The same is true with most other sectors, including precious metals, retail stores, steel producers, restaurants, housing builders, solar energy stocks, defense contractors, health care service providers, transportation stocks, and so forth. When you use a mathematical stock-selection model such as those described in Chapters 4, 5, and 6, you will often find that the best stocks identified at any given time will all fall within the same out-performing sector. The temptation will be to maintain the requisite numbers of stocks in your portfolio, but to draw them all from the same leading sector. This is a mistake to be avoided. The problem is that, when the sector finally corrects, all of your stocks may go south at the same time. I try never to draw more than a third of my holdings from the same sector at any given time. To a more limited extent the same may be true for capitalization sizes of the stocks you hold. Therefore, it may be better not to hold all micro-cap or all large-cap stocks in your portfolio at the same time.

RECORD KEEPING

Most on-line brokerages nowadays keep very good records of all of your transactions, and with software programs such as Gainskeeper they allow you to file your income taxes accurately in record time. However, as you begin to trade more frequently and maintain additional portfolios, you will need even more thorough personal records.

I keep a college-ruled notebook for every portfolio I trade. In this notebook I record the date, buy or sell transaction type, number of shares, and symbol for every trade. If I am adding to an existing position, I will include the revised cost basis in parentheses. In addition, I usually will add other pertinent information such as target sell price, reason for buying, and lessons learned. In the space for lessons learned, I may record such comments as, "See what happens when you buy with unsettled funds," or, "I should have sold at the open." This helps me to benefit from my mistakes and to identify my most frequently recurring blunders.

PROPORTIONALITY OVER PORTFOLIOS

Most fund managers pool the funds invested and issue shares to investors that correspond to the size of their investments. However, in some cases it is also possible to leave individual investor portfolios intact and proceed to manage multiple portfolios. When you manage multiple portfolios as I do, and some of those portfolios belong to friends and family or clients, you are often faced with serious ethical dilemmas. One of these dilemmas is associated with the need to replicate holdings across portfolios. You may want to assure the owners of these portfolios that their holdings are identical to your own, so that, if there are any losses, you can say, "Yes, but I suffered the same percentage losses in my own portfolios." I have found that this assurance comes at great personal disadvantage. For example, suppose you own 1,000 shares of stock XYZ in your portfolio A and you have purchased 700 shares of that same stock in portfolio B and 1,300 shares in portfolio C, to correspond with proportional differences in the total capital available in each portfolio. Now suppose that the CFO of stock XYZ is indicted for fraud, and the stock suddenly gives up 15 percent of it value and moves from a "strong buy" to a "sell" rating in minutes. The question then arises, "Whose stock do you sell first?" For reasons explained earlier, I may be reluctant to place a stop-loss order and let the market maker decide sequence for each portfolio order, and if the purchase was made with unsettled funds, a stop-loss order is not possible until the funds settle. If I sell my personal holdings first, it may drive the stock price lower and the other portfolio holders will suffer in subsequent sales. So, I naturally tend to sell the others first and take greater losses myself. The same dilemma appears in reverse at the time of purchasing a stock. If the stock is moving up, the portfolio that gets first purchase gets the best price on the transaction. Again, I tend to buy for others first and make inferior subsequent purchases for my own portfolio. This sounds like a trivial concern, but it is not. It can play havoc with your trading performance.

More recently, I have approached this dilemma from an entirely different perspective with greater overall satisfaction. Instead of attempting to replicate holdings across portfolios, I use a sandlot team-selection approach. I rank order prospective stock purchases at any given time in accordance with my current mathematical stock-selection algorithm. Then, after randomizing portfolio sequence, I make the first purchase for the first portfolio, the second purchase of a different stock for the next portfolio, and so on. In this way, I tend never to hold the exact same positions in any given portfolio, diversification overall is increased, and the decision to buy or sell within a portfolio does not affect the share prices in any other portfolio. However, regardless of how one chooses to accommodate responsibility for multiple portfolios, having this additional responsibility will tend to limit performance somewhat. This limitation comes through the constraints due to timing of trade sequences. With the "team-selection" approach, the limitation comes through the necessary dilution entailed in acquiring additional stocks that are lower in system ranking.

PROPORTIONALITY OVER INDIVIDUAL STOCKS

Although, as mentioned in the preceding paragraph, I have abandoned the attempt to maintain proportionality of holdings across all portfolios I manage, there is a type of proportionality that I still find useful to maintain. That is proportionality over individual stocks. Imagine, for example, that in one of my portfolios I have purchased five stocks in equal $10,000 amounts, so that these holdings could be said to be proportionally balanced regardless of differing share prices. Now suppose that one of the stocks is with a company that announces fabulous earnings, and its share price doubles in a week. In that case, assuming nothing has changed about the positive prospects of each of my holdings, I am very likely to sell eight thousand dollars worth of that stock and plow the proceeds back into the other four stocks in 2,000-dollar amounts equally. In that way, I would now have twelve thousand invested in each of the original five stocks, and I would have taken back some of the profits from the stock with the sudden explosion in price. This scenario is more likely to take place in a bull market, however, because I have found that at other times it is often difficult to find five stocks that are all worth holding at the same time.

TURNOVER RATIO

One concern in managing any portfolio is the rate of turnover. In the space of one month, for example, what percentage of holdings have been sold and replaced in your portfolio? It is possible to exceed 100 percent turnover in one month if you find yourself selling and replacing stocks that are already replacements for stocks you held before. Because of the inherent transaction costs in commissions and spreads, it is desirable to keep the turnover ratio at a minimum without ever adopting a buy-and-hold strategy. It is difficult to pinpoint an optimal turnover ratio. Likely, optimal turnover ratios will vary with market conditions. One of the best stock mutual funds, CGM Focus Fund (CGMFX), that has averaged about 30 percent as a 5-year annualized return, has an annual turnover rate of about 384 percent compared to an average turnover rate of about 71 percent for other mutual funds in its category. The point is that, although there are overhead costs associated with the maintaining of a high turnover ratio, this does not necessarily mean that a reasonably high turnover rate will impede success in trading.

TIMING THE MARKET

Another significant consideration in the process of managing portfolios is timing the market. The idea here is that there are times when a trader should be fully invested, and there are other times when it is best to be completely out of the market, or to be short the market. Market timing is often not considered in a discussion of portfolio management because so many investors do not believe it is possible to time the market. Personally, I have come to view market timing as such an important consideration that the entire next chapter is devoted to that single concept.

SUMMARY

In this chapter we have considered several concerns related to successful portfolio management. Specifically, details were provided about diversifying over stocks, diversifying over sectors, record keeping, multiple portfolio maintenance, proportionality of holdings, turnover ratios, and market timing.

CHAPTER 10

Market Timing

There was once a time when I believed the same as many others that it was impossible to time the markets and to discover with any degree of certainty when one should be invested in the stock market and when one should be out of the market or be short the market. I even went so far as to believe that it was not important to time the market because there were always some stocks moving up, so the task of prudent investing essentially could be reduced to that of finding those stocks moving up and acquiring them and getting rid of the ones that were not moving up—or so I believed. But after surviving several bear markets and finding several reliable indicators of market trends, I have changed my views. Moreover, I have come to believe that market timing skill is an essential component of successful trading.

Perhaps this change of position was also influenced by the reading of books, such as those cited earlier in Table 2.2, by Maturi, O'Neil, Smith, and Zweig. Maturi purports to set forth 100 different prediction models used by economists and traders throughout history to predict market trends. Although this profusion of prediction systems indicates the historical importance that has been attached to market timing, many—perhaps most—of those systems he reported belong to the realm of mythology. In this chapter, I am ultimately limiting support to two methods of market timing for which I was able to find statistical evidence of success in my own quest for reliable market-timing indicators.

Extreme proponents of "random-walk" theory or "equilibrium" theory would maintain that it is not possible to predict market trends with any degree of accuracy, and therefore the best approach to the stock market is to buy shares in a stock index fund and wait for its price appreciation over time with a kind of "buy-and-hold" strategy. Although their arguments may seem persuasive, I cannot remember a year in which I did not outperform all of the index funds through timing strategies and capitalizing on "disequilibrium." One of the best supportive descriptions of random-walk theory is provided by Malkiel (1996) in his book *A Random Walk Down Wall Street*. One of the most scholarly refutations of that theory is given in Peters' (1991) book, *Chaos and Order in the Capital Markets*.

MYTHOLOGICAL INDICATORS

The study of market timing indicators is one of the most fascinating studies I have found. Many indicators have been proposed that have no logical connection to market fluctuations whatsoever. For example, in my inferential statistics courses I occasionally assigned students the task of computing the point-biserial correlation between the winner of the Super Bowl (with National Conference winners coded as 1.0 and American Conference winners coded as zero) and the eventual performance of the Dow Jones Industrial Average as percentage gain or loss for every Super Bowl year. Students were often astounded to see that, at the time, there was a high positive correlation between National Football Conference (NFC) team victory and subsequent market gains. If an American Football Conference (AFC) team won, the market would do poorly. I hasten to add that, following a series of AFC wins in recent years, the relationship is no longer that strong. This does not mean that I have ceased to support certain NFC teams during the Super Bowl.

Another supposed indicator of market trends is sunspot activity. It is believed by some prognosticators that heightened sunspot activity is a reliable indicator of an impending bear market. However, I cannot help but mention that 2008 has been one of the worst years on record for the global stock market, and it has also been a record year for low sunspot activity.

Yet another mythological indicator is known as the "bull markets and bare knees" theory. According to this theory, when popular fashion dictates that ladies' hemlines should rise above their knees, that is a bullish indicator for stocks. However, recent trends have not been supportive of this theory. It certainly gave no warning about the 1987 market crash. And I can think of several Middle Eastern countries that, according to this theory, will never experience a positive year for their economies.

QUASI-MYTHOLOGICAL INDICATORS

There are several market timing indicators that I choose to call quasi-mythological indicators. These are indicators for which there may be a logical basis for the belief that they are related to market trends, but they are very difficult to use for market timing with any degree of certainty.

One of these quasi-mythological indicators is presidential election year. It is believed by some commentators that the year preceding a presidential election will be a good year for stocks. There is some basis for this belief, both in logic and in experience. First, it is logical to believe that politicians will want to place their best foot forward by putting the economy in order during an election year. A rising stock market looks good for the incumbents. Also, it is clear that a lot of money will be spent on campaign advertising during an election year, and this may have some beneficial influence on the overall economy. In practice, however, when you consider that the stock market has a predisposition to rise on average each year, in recent elections there has been little advantage for election years over other years. Certainly the advantage, if any, is not sufficient to base an investment strategy upon it.

Another quasi-mythological indicator, in my opinion, is odd-lot volume. Advocates of this indicator maintain that buyers of odd lots of shares (i.e., any quantity less than a 100-share round lot) are smaller and less-sophisticated investors. When the volume of their trades increases relative to the overall volume of trades, it is taken by believers in this indicator that the ratio of "dumb" money to "smart" money in play has increased, and therefore the market is about to experience a decline. There may be some logic to this reasoning, but I cannot accept it for at least three reasons. First, it does not take into consideration whether the odd-lot traders are buying or selling their shares. If they are selling, it can be argued conversely that the "smart" money is buying the "dumb" money, and thus the market conditions are improving. Of course, one variation of this theory purports to compare odd-lot selling with odd-lot buying, and maintains that it is more positive for market conditions if odd-lot selling surpasses odd-lot buying. No matter that, unless lots are bundled by the market makers, every odd-lot sold must also be purchased as an equivalent odd-lot. Second, there is evidence that odd-lot volume as a percentage of total volume has historically diminished over time, so it has become difficult to set specific odd-lot volume criteria for decision making. And third, there is no evidence to support the theory that odd-lot traders are any dumber than round-lot traders. At least I can take umbrage because I almost always trade in some odd lots along with every round-lot trade.

My most controversial example of a quasi-mythological indicator is what is known as the Elliott Wave Principle (Frost 1990). These remarks will be controversial because this approach to market timing has as many ardent advocates as it does determined detractors. Ralph N. Elliott, a little known accountant, devised this theory in the early 1930s during a period of convalescence from a physical ailment. On observing stock market ripples, he concluded that investor sentiment appeared to pass through predictable waves reflected in gyrations of the stock market indices. In my personal opinion, this approach has some merit. Certainly, the stock market does appear to fluctuate in waves that are probably associated with investor sentiment. However, I am not convinced that the timing of these waves is as neatly predictable as the theory maintains. Here we could probably take a lesson from surfers who patiently await promising waves to ride towards shore. Some of them may time the distance between waves, but most do not take their plunge until a big wave actually hits—and even then there is an element of chance. And occasionally there is a tsunami that no one anticipated. My point is that the timing of waves is a skill that involves both science and art. It is definitely a worthwhile endeavor from the perspective of enhancing trading performance, but it is probably not bounded by parameters as tidy as we could wish.

RELIABLE INDICATORS

In spite of the many false and unreliable indicators of market direction, in this final section of the chapter, I want to present two timing indicators that I believe to be reliable in that they have both a logical basis for their relationship to market trends and are amenable to application for market timing. As it happens, both of these indicators are investor sentiment indicators. They reflect the prevailing mood of traders at any given time. Moreover, they are cyclical contrarian indicators, so that when investors exhibit a peak of heightened anxiety and fear, it often marks a bottom of a negative trend, and it signifies that the market is finally turning positive. When investor fear and anxiety diminish to a cyclical low or nadir, it usually indicates that bearish times are ahead for the stock market. The two indicators in question are the Chicago Board Options Exchange (CBOE) Volatility Index (VIX) and the put/call ratio, which is the ratio of put options to call options that also are traded at the Chicago Board Options Exchange.

Volatility-Index-Based Timing

One reliable approach to market timing involves analysis of the relationship between the Chicago Board Options Exchange (CBOE) Volatility Index (VIX) and the Dow Jones Industrial Average, as shown in Figure 10.1.

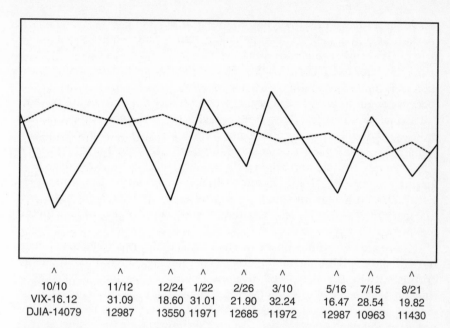

∧	∧	∧	∧	∧	∧	∧	∧	∧
10/10	11/12	12/24	1/22	2/26	3/10	5/16	7/15	8/21
VIX-16.12	31.09	18.60	31.01	21.90	32.24	16.47	28.54	19.82
DJIA-14079	12987	13550	11971	12685	11972	12987	10963	11430

FIGURE 10.1 The Relationship between the CBOE Volatility Index and the DJIA from October 2007 to November 2008

Notice in Figure 10.1 that the period extending from October 2007 to September 2008 was not a good time for investing in any stocks whose price movement was at all related to the performance of the Dow Jones Industrial Average, because that index lost about 20 percent of its value during that 12-month span. More importantly, notice the peaks and valleys of the CBOE Volatility Index in relationship to the movement of the DJIA. Whenever the Volatility Index reached a peak in the 29 to 32 range, it marked the beginning of a period of ascent for the DJIA. Conversely, whenever the Volatility Index hit a bottom in the 16 to 20 range, it marked the beginning of a period of decline for the DJIA. The implication for portfólio management is simply that, in spite of the overall bearish trend of the market, investment profit would have been realized if a portfolio manager had purchased stocks at the peaks and sold stocks at the bottoms of the CBOE Volatility Index cycles. In fact, the composite gains in the DJIA during the upward trending intervals amounted to a 21 percent increment over the value of the DJIA at the starting bottom of November 12, 2007, which exceeded in absolute magnitude the total 20 percent decline of that index over the 52-week span. Note also that the average time interval between tops and bottoms that year was about 40 days. Over the past five years that interval has averaged about 49 days. The conclusion I draw from Figure 10.1 is that an investor in a Dow stock index fund over that year would have turned a 20 percent loss into a 21 percent gain by being in the market for only about six months at the appropriate intervals instead of being in the market the entire year.

This relationship between the VIX and the DJIA and other major stock indices is analogous to the relationship between inches or centimeters of mercury as an index of barometric pressure, and the probability of rainfall. When pressure is falling from a high, the probability of rainfall increases, and when pressure is rising from a low, the probability of sunshine increases. Similarly, when volatility is falling from a high, the stock market tends to rise, and when volatility is rising from a low, the stock market tends to fall. I am not sure whether this relationship would persist if all fund managers sought to capitalize on it at the same time, but I suspect that it may be exacerbated by such popularizing of this timing technique.

There are two critical observations related to this relationship between the VIX and the DJIA and all the other major market indices that are highly correlated with the DJIA. The first observation is that this inverted relationship between the VIX and the stock market is real and dependable as an indication of market trends. The second observation is that there are practical and dependable ways to apply this information in trading.

Obviously I cannot say with certainty that every time the VIX drops to 16 it marks a bottom in that index cycle, nor can I affirm that every time the VIX rises to 30 it marks a top in that index cycle. For example, late in 2008, around the time of the presidential election, the VIX set an all-time high above 89, and the successive peaks and valleys reached higher levels than those reached earlier that year. There were actually valleys reached in the 40s and 50s at that time. So it has not been possible to set constant timing values bracketing the 16-to-30 range in the VIX in order to know when to buy and sell stocks. In practice, the implementation of the VIX as a timing indicator becomes a much more "hands-on" procedure that requires occasional recalibration. You gather confidence that a valley has been reached in the cycle as you begin the ascent on the other side of the valley by as much as 5 percent from the low, and you gather confidence that a peak has been reached as you begin the descent on the other side of the peak by as much as 5 percent from the high.

Another guide to this kind of decision making is the recognition that the peak-to-valley and valley-to-peak cycles have averaged approximately 49 days in length over the past five years. This means that, after about a month or so in any given short-term trend, you begin to expect a reversal—even if the reversal is not expected to take the index back to previous lows or highs. The good news here is that, because of the average length of the cycles, waiting a day or two to establish that a bottom or a top has been reached does not remove all chance for capitalization on a short-term trend, because there is usually always plenty of time left for the trend to run. If it becomes a concern that there is excessive "noise" or "Brownian movement" in the VIX for accurate decision making, it is possible to base decisions on the 5-day moving average of the VIX, rather than on the actual daily closing values. This procedure is followed in the next section with regard to use of the put/call ratio as a timing indicator. Notice that Table 10.1 reports the peaks and valleys for both the VIX and the put/call ratio in relation to the peaks and valleys of the S&P 500 Index over a one-year period.

Put/Call-Ratio-Based Timing

Much has been written about the use of the ratio of put options to call options as traded at the Chicago Board Options Exchange for purposes of market timing. Fortunately, these ratios have been calculated daily over many years and are available for each of the past five years free of charge at www.cboe.com. You can see from Table 10.1 that there is a strong relationship between peaks and valleys of the 5-day moving average of the put/call ratio and the peaks and valleys of both the CBOE Volatility Index (VIX) and the inverse peaks and valleys of the S&P 500 Index. The relationship is such that, when the put/call ratio and/or the VIX reach a peak, it usually signals a near-term bottom in the S&P 500 Index.

In Table 10.1 we can see the actual values of the 5-day moving average of the put/call ratio for the entire year extending from 11/10/07 through 11/14/08. We can easily see the peaks and valleys for the put/call ratio and how they relate to the peaks and valleys of the VIX and the S&P 500. You can see that the S&P 500 is inversely related to both the put/call ratio and the VIX. Thus, when the put/call ratio reaches a peak, it is usually close to or on the same day that the VIX reaches a peak. And when those two indicators reach their peaks, it usually corresponds very closely to the bottom of a valley in the S&P 500. You can see also that the put/call ratio tends to exhibit less variance than the VIX, inasmuch as the put/call ratio ranged only from 0.82 to 1.30 during that year, while the VIX ranged from 16.3 to 80, and actually reached nearly 90 intraday.

It is helpful to note that these two timing indicators appear to corroborate each other and to be equally reliable. Therefore, in timing equity markets, you may use either or both of these indicators with the same level of confidence and you may expect the length of the trending cycles to be about the same for either one. These are both what may be called "market sentiment" indicators. They represent the fear or anxiety levels of investors at any given time, and serve as contrarian indicators of future market direction. Use of the put/call ratio for decisions about market trends is the same as use of the VIX for such decisions. You gather confidence that a peak or

TABLE 10.1 Put/Call Ratio Signals and Volatility Index Signals versus the S&P 500 Index for One Year—Peaks and Valleys (11/10/07 through 11/14/08)

Date	P/C	VIX	S&P	Date	P/C	VIX	S&P	Date	P/C	VIX	S&P
11/10	1.06			3/17	1.27p	32.2p		7/17	1.05		
	1.10				1.24				1.00		
	1.07				1.26				0.95		
	1.09				1.24			7/22	0.90	21.2v	
	1.13				1.12				0.89v		
	1.17			3/25	1.02v		1353		0.93		
	1.15				1.03				0.95		
	1.21p				1.01				0.94		
	1.13				1.02			7/30	0.93		
11/26	1.07	28.9p	1407		1.06				0.91		
	1.01			4/1	1.05	22.7v			0.95		
	0.96				1.05				0.92		
	0.89v				1.04				0.91		
	0.93				1.05				0.92		
	0.90			4/7	1.03		1373		0.94		
	0.95				1.08				0.93		
	0.95				1.10				0.91v		
	0.93				1.09			8/11	0.97	20.1v	1305
12/10	0.96	20.7v	1516		1.11				0.98		
	0.97			4/14	1.11p	23.8p	1328		0.95		
	0.99				1.10				0.96		
	1.02				1.05				1.00		
	1.04				1.05				1.02		
12/7	1.07	24.5p	1445		0.95				1.00		
	1.05				0.94			8/22	1.02	18.8v	
	1.09p				0.94				1.00		
	1.01				0.94				1.01		
	0.91				0.94				0.98		
12/24	0.86	18.6v			0.95				0.95		
	0.86				0.96				0.92		
12/26	0.83v		1498		0.96				0.94		
	0.88				0.97				0.91		
	0.98				0.97				0.89v		
	1.03				0.95			9/4	0.94	24.0v	
	1.01				0.90				0.98		
	1.04				0.92				0.96		
	1.06				0.91				0.99		
1/8	1.12	25.4p			0.91				1.04		
	1.12				0.91				1.02		
	1.14p			5/15	0.90	16.3v			1.03		
	1.10				0.86				1.14		
	1.08				0.84				1.18		

TABLE 10.1 (*Continued*)

Date	P/C	VIX	S&P	Date	P/C	VIX	S&P	Date	P/C	VIX	S&P
1/14	1.06v	22.9v			0.82				1.23	36.2p	
	1.06			5/19	0.82v		1427	9/18	1.27p		
	1.17				0.88				1.23		
	1.25				0.95				1.13		
1/22	1.30p	31.0p	1311		0.99				1.08		
	1.28			5/23	1.03		1376		1.01		
	1.22				1.05p			9/25	0.94v	32.8v	
	1.12				1.00				0.97		
	1.04				0.93				1.06		
	0.98				0.90v				1.11		
	0.92				0.91				1.10		
	0.93				0.95			10/2	1.21		
2/1	0.88v	24.0v	1395	6/4	1.00		1377		1.23		
	0.89				1.03				1.26		
	0.94				1.09p				1.22		
2/6	0.99	29.0p	1325		1.06				1.25		
	1.03				1.02			10/10	1.27p	70.0p	899
	1.09p			6/11	1.03	24.1p			1.15		
	1.09				1.03				1.10		
	1.09				0.98				1.09		
	1.07				0.98				1.05		
	1.05				0.99				1.00		
	1.05				0.98				0.98		
	1.06				0.99			10/20	0.98v	53.0v	
	1.00				1.07				1.00		
	1.00				1.06				1.02		
	1.03			6/24	1.06				1.08		
	0.98v				1.01			10/27	1.15	80.0p	849
2/26	0.99	21.9v	1381		1.04				1.17p		
	1.04				1.00				1.09		
	1.10				1.04				1.00		
	1.12				1.05				0.94		
	1.18				1.09				0.91		
	1.21				1.10			11/4	0.90v	47.7v	1005
	1.22				1.12				0.93		
	1.22				1.10				1.04		
	1.22			7/9	1.10				1.04		
	1.27p				1.10				1.07		
3/10	1.25	29.4p	1273		1.09				1.10		
	1.24				1.08				1.15		
	1.23			7/15	1.11p	28.5p	1215		1.08		
	1.27				1.09			11/14	1.28p	64.4p	873

Where p = peak and v = valley

a valley in the put/call ratio has been reached when you begin the descent or ascent, respectively, on the other side. And you look for these reversals to occur on average about every month and a half.

SUMMARY

In this chapter, we have examined several unreliable or quasi-reliable market timing systems and two reliable market timing indicators, the CBOE Volatility Index (VIX) and the put/call ratio. We have seen how these two indicators are inversely related to movement of the stock market, and how they appear to corroborate each other. We have also seen examples of how they may be applied for decisions about when to be long or short the equity markets.

CHAPTER 11

A Performance Record

S everal friends and colleagues have mentioned that it would be beneficial if I could provide actual data on performance with the trading systems mentioned in this book. Earlier I mentioned that my overall performance objective has been to realize average gains of 10 percent per month. Specifying this objective became a necessary component in the stock-selection systems described in earlier chapters because gain objectives serve to delimit stocks selected by including only those with the requisite rate of ascent in expected growth. In some favorable market periods I have exceeded 20 percent gains per month, and at other times I have fallen somewhat short of my 10 percent monthly goal.

PERFORMANCE CAVEATS

In this chapter I attempt to report annualized performance over the past five years. I do so in the following paragraphs with certain caveats and hesitations. Those may be summarized as follows:

1. Past performance is no guarantee of future success. Just because I have experienced success with the trading systems described in this book does not ensure that I will always do so, or that others who seek to copy these methods will always succeed.

2. The trading systems presented in this book are tools for performance enhancement. These systems essentially provide mathematical estimates of the best stocks to acquire or sell at any given time, and they

supply tools for timing the market in order to know when to be in and when to be out of the market. Use of these tools cannot guarantee success any more than driving a perfect race car can guarantee a winning race, or using a perfect set of golf clubs will ensure that we will always beat Tiger Woods in golf tournaments. Skill at execution of buy and sell orders, market timing, and portfolio management also come into play, and the jury is still out regarding how much of this can be taught and how much must be learned by experience.

3. The trading systems described here are the result of years of refinement, and they are still subject to further refinements going forward. Thus, it must be said that what I do now is slightly different from what I did last year and the year before that, and it may well differ slightly from my approach next year and the year after that. In this context, it is a challenge to interpret definitive results because evaluation of the trading systems involves shooting at a moving target. Therefore, the only fair way to evaluate current systems presented in this book is to back test in order to see what performance would have been if the current systems had been employed over an extended period. My actual performance was comparable to the estimates reported in Table 11.1, but because my trading systems at that time were not exactly the same as those advocated in this book, it is not relevant to report them here.

With these caveats in mind, we can examine Table 11.1 to evaluate performance of the hybrid trading system described in Chapter 6 against the S&P 500 Index over the past five and three-quarters year period from January 1, 2003 to October 24, 2008.

Notice in the "S&P 500 % Change" column of Table 11.1 that the annual percentage gains or losses for the S&P 500 Index are reported for the years 2003 through three quarters of 2008. Next, the reported favorable investment periods are the time intervals from each major peak to valley cycle of the CBOE Volatility Index (VIX), as described in Chapter 10. You can see that there are regularly four of these cycles each year, and they have averaged about 49 days in length over this period. Recall that the trading systems advanced in this book advocate being fully invested only during these favorable periods, and being out of the market or in index short funds at all other times. In the "S&P 500 Adjusted % Gain" column, you can see what your gains would have been in an S&P 500 Index fund, not counting any fees, if you were fully invested only during the favorable periods. Note that for the year 2008, the data reported are annualized data because not all of the favorable time intervals for those entire years are yet available at the time of this writing.

In the column labeled "System % Gain Estimate" we can see the estimated gains using the hybrid technical-fundamental trading system

TABLE 11.1 Five-Year Trading System Gains (1/03–10/08)

Year	S&P 500 % Change	Favorable Investment Periods (VIX)	S&P 500 Adjusted % Gain	System % Gain Estimate	RYTPX Short % Between	Total % Gain
2008*	−30.0	1/22–2/11; 3/10–5/12; 7/7–8/18; 10/24–n.a.	+21.0*	+71.2*	+114.0	185.2
2007	+3.5	1/3–2/12; 3/5–4/16; 8/13–10/1; 11/5–12/24	+18.7	+74.2	+29.3	103.5
2006	+13.6	1/17–3/20; 5/22–6/26; 7/10–10/9; 11/6–12/26	+15.7	+105.0	+10.4	115.4
2005	+3.0	1/18–2/22; 4/11–7/5; 8/22–9/26; 10/17–12/19	+16.0	+92.3	+21.2	113.5
2004	+9.0	12/29–2/23; 3/15–4/19; 8/9–9/27; 11/8–12/20	+14.4	+75.8	+9.6	85.4
2003	+26.4	1/27–2/28; 3/11–5/15; 8/5–9/18; 9/30–12/18	+34.6	+73.0	+13.2	86.2

*Partial year data that has been annualized where indicated

111

described in Chapter 6. Again, for the year 2008, reported gains have been annualized to accommodate the fact that all four quarters of that year are not available in the table at the time of writing. The average estimated gain using this trading system over these years was 81.9 percent, including costs of commissions. However, it is important to note that, if I had put the trading proceeds in a leveraged short fund such as RYTPX during the three intervals between the favorable periods in the table, substantial additional gains would have been realized. In 2008, for example, a year in which the S&P 500 Index lost more than 30 percent, total gains would have been 71.2 percent from system trading plus an additional 114.0 percent from trading in an ultra-bear fund during unfavorable intervals, or a total of 185.2 percent. It would of course be more than that because this percentage total does not reflect the gains from compounding the gains from system trading.

What about our stated objective of reaching 10 percent gains on average per month? You can see that this goal was realized for the favorable periods when I was invested. Had I chosen to short the market with a bear fund such as RYTPX during the intervening three unfavorable periods, I would have regularly averaged total gains in excess of 100 percent per year. In the past two years, a large number of exchange-traded short funds (ETFs) have been created, such as SSG, SKK, AGA, EUM, EFZ, MYY, SIJ, EFU, DUG, EWV, RRZ, TWM, SMN, BGZ, MWN, TZA, ERY, FAZ, TYP, DPK, and EDZ,. Most of these ETFs actually pay dividends in addition to their price movements. Based on the evidence advanced in this chapter, I am currently giving serious consideration to acquiring one of more of these ETFs during the unfavorable periods.

HINDSIGHT IS 20/20

It is said that hindsight is 20/20. I can see clearly now in retrospect that, if I had simply held two Rydex exchange-traded ultra funds, RRY and RRZ, in the appropriate favorable and unfavorable periods, my gains would have approached 300 percent per year during the 5-year period considered. RRY seeks to realize two times the gains of the Russell 2000 Index, and RRZ is designed to appreciate by two times the inverse of the Russell 2000 Index. Presumably the fund company can maintain these funds profitably because they operate handsome spreads between the bid and ask prices, and because the two different funds offset gains and losses in bull and bear periods. A related conservative strategy would be to buy equal dollar amounts in both funds simultaneously, and then to sell half of whichever fund first realizes a 10 percent gain, plowing the proceeds back into the opposing fund while it is depressed. Of course, the fund companies anticipate such strategies, and the laws of supply and demand also influence the prices of such funds, and so it is that the share prices do not always move exactly in tandem with the market or the underlying index. Also it is appropriate to consider that investing in such index funds does not make capital directly available to the economy in the same way that buying stock in individual companies does. It is worth considering, however, that some of these funds also offer dividends.

A word is in order about the identification of the favorable periods reported in Table 11.1. This is the key to success for the achievements reported in this chapter. This process was explained in greater detail in Chapter 10 on market timing. In practice it will be difficult to pick the exact tops and bottoms of the CBOE Volatility Index going forward, as this method entails. But it is not difficult to come within 5 percent of these tops and bottoms if you keep two things in mind: (1) the average interval of 49 days from the cycle bottoms (sell signals) to the cycle tops (buy signals), and (2) the average magnitudes of the tops and bottoms over the past year. As you approach the indicated intervals and magnitudes, you are looking intensely for changes in market direction, and you will rarely be disappointed.

An unusual anomaly in the CBOE Volatility Index appeared in the final quarter of 2008. On August 21 of that year the VIX registered a low of 19.82, which would have led us to expect the next cycle high to appear on or about October 9 would be somewhere in the low 30s. The DJIA did make an intraday bottom of around 7770 on October 10, but because of the worldwide mortgage credit crisis and the failure of several large lending institutions coupled with the uncertainties of a presidential election, the Volatility Index actually continued to rise beyond the anticipated magnitude and the anticipated date for a new high. It set an all-time record high of 89.53 on October 24, just prior to the 2008 presidential election.

Not only did the Volatility Index set a higher than expected new high, the low in the stock market and the high in the Volatility Index became asynchronous by about two weeks. It is important therefore to take such news events into consideration when seeking to identify volatility highs and equity market lows. Also, as explained in Chapter 10, use of the VIX as a timing indicator involves the identification of variable peaks and valleys rather than waiting for constant, range-bound tops and bottoms.

SUMMARY

In this chapter we have seen estimated results from the employment of the hybrid trading system of Chapter 6 over the past five years. Results have been compared with results of the S&P 500 Index both for each entire year and for the total of the favorable periods within each year. Trading system results were also compounded with results obtainable through use of leveraged bear funds during the unfavorable periods each year. Further explanation was provided about the process of identifying favorable investment periods, and information was given about advantages of purchasing exchange-traded short funds during the unfavorable periods each year.

CHAPTER 12

A Typical Trading Day

I t may be useful to look over the shoulder of a trader to see what usually happens in any given trading day. Certainly one of the best teaching methods is teaching by example. I, for one, have often wished I had the opportunity to watch a successful trader go through his or her daily routine and ask questions at every step along the way. At the same time it should be recognized that no one trader's approach is the only approach, or even the best approach, for other traders to emulate. Optimal trading styles differ and go through successive refinements. Here again, to repeat a borrowed cliché, trying to understand what an individual trader is doing can be like trying to understand moving water by catching it in a bucket. In a sense, the attempt to copy another trader's approach is also like shooting at a moving target because, hopefully, our daily procedures are continually undergoing refinements. With those caveats, here is what my trading day is like.

BEFORE THE BELL

I typically rise between 6:30 to 7:00 A.M. on market days. Because the market opens at 8:30 A.M. in my time zone, this gives me adequate time to have breakfast, enjoy a time of devotional reading and prayer with my wife, and to rehearse the day's events with her because she is my most important partner.

Review Stage

Around 7:30 A.M., I boot up my computer and review my plan of action set the night before. This includes consulting a list of stocks for potential purchase and a list of stocks for potential sale that I have entered at the bottom of a printed page of current holdings. It is critical to enter each day with a game plan, and my game plan is usually one that was developed the evening before the market opens. Experience has taught me that it is usually always best to have a plan and stick to it as much as possible throughout each trading day.

Pre-Programming Stage

I then program my trading platform to record all stocks above five dollars in price that make new 52-week highs that day so that I can examine each one more critically after the market closes at 3:00 P.M. in my time zone. Next I call up the Excel spreadsheet that shows all my holdings in every portfolio, as well as numbers of shares, current share prices, and both settled and unsettled cash available for transactions. I do this so I can be ready to update holdings quickly with any transactions that may take place that day. I reset this program to show real-time gains or losses in each portfolio throughout the trading day.

Intel Gathering Stage

I am now ready for intel gathering. I first look at my primary brokerage account to get real-time bid and ask prices and sizes for all of my holdings and for each one of the stocks on my candidate buy list. I am particularly concerned to find any stocks that are bid up above the previous day's closing price, or that are asked down below the previous day's closing price. These data alert me to expect further information about those stocks. I then consult the Yahoo! Finance page or my brokerage news facility where I have also recorded portfolio information including stocks held, numbers of shares, purchase prices, dates of purchase, and percentage performances to date. Of primary interest here is any current news reported on any of those stocks. I am also concerned about any general market information that may portend overall market direction, such as current index futures fair value information, commodity trends, international stock exchange performance, and earnings reports. If any special developments are found concerning any of the stocks on my list, I may then also go to the respective Yahoo! message boards to see what traders are saying about those developments.

I always take message board information with a grain of salt because I know there are persons posting who have short positions or long positions in that stock, and are simply trying to move the market for that stock in their preferred direction. Their actions are perfectly understandable, although at times they can be deceptive. Nevertheless, it can be informative to read what they are sharing. I may also turn on CNBC or Bloomberg TV to learn of any other important market developments.

Finally, I take all of the information I have gathered and revisit my plan of action for the day to make refinements. I may delete stocks from my candidate buy list or add stocks to my candidate sell list, or I may simply become more resolved to proceed as planned. I am now ready for the sound of the bell.

THE FIRST HALF HOUR

There is usually a flurry of pent-up trading activity in the first half hour.

Early Selling

It is often a good time to make planned sales because prices of some stocks may bounce at the open in ways that are not warranted by overall market sentiment or appropriate valuation for those stocks. I like to set or adjust limit sell orders at this time to take advantage of this bounce and to supply demand. Some traders wisely wait out the first half hour and make no transactions during that time, in order to avoid being caught up in this opening surge. It goes without saying that no one should place market orders before the open because that behavior tempts market makers to fill those orders from their own stores of shares at prices that are welcome only to them. Also, until market direction is established for the day, it is difficult to make fair valuations of stocks for acquisition or sale.

Direction Finding

During this early time I am eager to discover the opening direction of the general market and of the individual stocks on my buy and sell lists. Human nature being what it is, I am reluctant to buy stocks on my list unless they are showing some positive momentum at the open—or at least unless they have larger bid sizes than ask sizes. At the same time, I try not to chase run up bubbles unless there is a solid basis for the run up. Also during these early minutes, I frequently check my brokerage trading platform to get real-time quotes for all my holdings as well as for my current watch lists of several hundred stocks.

The Hot List

Another productive activity that I begin during these early moments is to construct a "hot list." This is a list of stocks from my stock-selection model that are ranked from "very strong buy" to "hold" and that are gaining in excess of 1 percent on the day. Usually this consists of five to ten stocks, which I list from highest to lowest rank. I am especially keen to follow the progress of stocks on this list that may be gaining in excess of 5 percent on the day. If there is good justification for this move up, in terms of fundamentals such as cash flow or news such as earnings surprises, and if there is also some prospect that the stock will move up in categorical rank according to my analysis systems, I am likely to buy such stocks quickly.

MIDDAY MONITORING

Real-Time Quotes

Throughout each trading day I am continually monitoring real-time quotes of my holdings and of several hundred stocks on my watch lists. I am also closely monitoring my "hot list" as described in the preceding paragraph. This hot list becomes especially important throughout the trading day because it contains a subset of a subset of the most desirable stocks; that is, it shows which of those stocks selected by my computer algorithm are performing best on that particular day. Because of the features of my trading software, I can instantly obtain a ranking of percentage gainers and losers on my lists.

Watch Lists

I have found it useful to maintain several kinds of watch lists. Most of my watch lists are limited to stocks that have at least doubled in price at some point during the past 52 weeks. At the Yahoo! Finance website where quotes are delayed for 15 to 20 minutes, I maintain separate watch lists of stocks organized according to distinguishing features such as superior cash flow, best book value, lowest PE ratio, and most attractive rolling earnings/PE divergence. There I can check performance over time and monitor which selection variables are most predictive of share-price appreciation. I also have watch lists comprised of stocks touted by various stock picking services or held by leading mutual funds. I confess that this latter group of watch lists is something of a comparative performance evaluator or an ego inflator/deflator, because it helps me know how I am doing by comparison with others.

AFTER THE CLOSING

Portfolio Updating

When the final bell sounds at 3:00 P.M. in my time zone, my work really begins. I first enter closing stock prices into the Excel spreadsheet that shows the holdings and cash balances in all of my portfolios. This gives me instant totals to compare with totals at any previous day's closing. I print out this spreadsheet, date stamp it, and place it in a ring binder. Later I will write tomorrow's stock picks, potential sales, and a plan of action on the same paper.

Data Entry

Next, I begin the tedious work of entering closing stock prices and new 52-week highs and lows into another Excel spreadsheet that contains about 200 stocks ranked according to my current mathematical selection model. I am moving towards automated downloads to minimize effort, but this is a bit tricky since the actual list of stocks is modified each day. Because I aim for overall trading gains exceeding 10 percent each month, I next delete stocks from that same list whose price gains over the past three months have now dropped below 30 percent. Then I call up my brokerage watch list for stocks making new 52-week highs that exceed a five-dollar share-price limit and that exceed a daily trading volume of 10,000 shares. From this list I draw out only those stocks that have at least approximately doubled in share price over the past 52 weeks, and I enter them into my Excel selection spreadsheet. For these new stocks I must also enter cash flow, rolling earnings per share/PE divergence, and earnings growth transformations that the algorithm employs to provide final stock rankings. I must also enter revised point-and-figure analysis ratings and other technical ratings because technical ratings may change at the close of each trading day. The entire process of data entry and editing of the stock list can take several hours each day at the height of a bull market, or just half an hour a day at the end of a bear market when few stocks are remaining that satisfy the requirement of a 30 percent gain over the past three months. In the interest of saving time in bull-market periods, I have found it necessary to shorten the list of stocks for analysis by deleting stocks with negative overall ratings or by entering only stocks that have gained in excess of 40 percent over the past three months.

Analysis

Finally, I am ready for the selection algorithm to rank all 200 stocks for investment viability. After all of the data has been updated, the final analysis is accomplished simply by using the Excel "sort" command over the appropriate data column. This ultimately reduces the information to ratings from +7 (very strong buy) to −3 (very strong sell). This final step requires only enough time to press the sort button and eyeball the results. The accuracy of the process in selecting winners has been so dependable that I am almost always driven by curiosity to find the outcomes in preparation for the next day of trading.

This entire process is well worth the effort because it provides me with a list of the most suitable stocks to sell from among my current holdings and a list of the best stocks to acquire from among the stocks that I do not yet own. In addition, the analysis provides me with a current ranking of all of the stocks in my portfolio along with details of their strengths and weaknesses. With all the other normal responsibilities of life, I seldom retire before midnight on weekdays, and often may not finish work until 1 or 2 in the morning.

Posting

Approximately three days each week, depending on available time, when everything is finished for the day, I post a list of all the stocks identified with ratings of +4 (hold) or above in a personal email message to friends and family along with market commentary and devotional reflections. I do this as a public service, as my way of making a contribution to society. I am regularly carrying out the analyses anyway, and it seems only right to share insights that have been every bit as providentially received as the sunshine and the rain. And since this approach to trading is not adversely affected by competition, it is not a problem for me if others are thus encouraged to buy the same stocks that I am pursuing or already holding. This kind of openness also provides a limited measure of accountability, because we traders usually do not have any observers to look over our shoulders and shake their heads at the crazy things we do.

WEEKENDS

Weekends are great for rest and reflection, reading and regrouping. This is when I seek to read and write and conduct research into new projects and ideas. Because trading can be such an intensely competitive and materialistic pursuit, I find it necessary to set aside time for spiritual reflection and restoration so as not to be overly caught up in anxiety and greed. This time has also been necessary to prevent me from frenetically climbing some ladder of success, only to discover much later that the ladder was leaning against the wrong building. Life is so short that it is now of great concern to me that my activities and projects lead to satisfactory and satisfying levels of lasting and meaningful success.

SUMMARY

My daily trading activities are fairly predictable. They consist primarily of early morning pre-market intel gathering, market-hours trading and portfolio monitoring, and after-market data entry and analysis to establish a game plan for the next day of trading. There are always some unique activities that may change from day to day, and there are steps that will be altered by technological developments, but the general process is fairly constant. It should be obvious that my kind of trading is labor intensive, and the profits are proportional to the amount of time invested.

CHAPTER 13

Threats to Success

A s mentioned earlier, in the process of trading stocks there are always variables outside of one's personal control. In the race car analogy, I stated that there may be an oil slick on the track or another race car that is out of control and careening across our path. Although we cannot predict and control such developments, we need to quickly become aware of them and respond accordingly. In this chapter it is my intention to examine some of those most common threats so that the reader will be better aware of some of the dangers inherent in stock trading.

ACTIONS OF THE FEDERAL RESERVE BOARD OPEN MARKETS COMMITTEE

The Federal Reserve's Federal Open Markets Committee (FOMC) has been chartered by the United States government to provide market stability, and thus to contain inflation and deflation through deliberate use of the financial tools put under its control. One of these tools is the target lending rate for use among lending institutions. This target lending rate is sometimes labeled the Fed Funds Target Lending Rate. Here I have chosen to call it the FOMC Target Lending Rate for consistency and ease. It is important to point out that this target rate is not the same as the actual lending rate, but the actual lending rate usually tends to follow the lead of the target rate, so that the FOMC has indirect influence on the actual lending rate through their adjustments in the target lending rate. In Table 13.1, it is possible to view all of the adjustments the FOMC has made to the target lending rate over the 18-year period from 1990 to 2008, and to see the corresponding positions of the S&P 500 Index, the unemployment rate, the inflation rate, and the Misery Index.

You can see from Table 13.1 that there were 77 adjustments made to the Fed Funds Target Rate during the 18-year period between January 1990 and October 2008. Notice also that the table reports a "Misery Index." This is simply the sum of the unemployment rate and the inflation rate at any given time. There are many lessons to be learned from this 18-year historical record of the actions of the FOMC in relationship to the performance of the S&P 500 Index and the other variables reported. Here are a few of those lessons:

1. There is a highly significant negative correlation between the FOMC Target Rate and the performance of the stock market as reflected in the S&P 500 Index. This correlation over the observed period is an amazingly high $-.383$ (N=77, p<.001, two-tailed). Thus, the higher the Fed Funds Target Rate was set to be, the lower the S&P 500 Index tended to be. Of course, we cannot argue causation from correlation and say definitively on this evidence alone that the FOMC Target Rate caused the market to rise when the rate was low and to fall when it was high, but it would make no sense to argue conversely that the FOMC rate itself was caused by the market movement. This latter argument would have us maintain that the FOMC tended to raise rates when they saw that the market was low and to lower rates when they saw that the market was high, which would be wholly unsupportable. Another argument that might be advanced against a negative effect of the FOMC Target Rate on the stock market would be to point out that the same-day correlation between the FOMC Target Rate and the S&P 500 Index does not allow time for the FOMC Target Rate to take effect. However, when an average time lag of approximately 80 days is introduced between the FOMC Target Rate change on the day of change and the subsequent S&P 500 Index measurement, the negative correlation reported above remains virtually unchanged. What do I conclude from this information? There is a lot of truth in the old saying, "Don't fight the Fed." When the Fed is raising rates, it is time to be unusually cautious about market prospects. And when the Fed is lowering rates, it adds a note of optimism about the future. At the same time, it is useful to remember that a correlation of this magnitude suggests that FOMC action in adjusting the target rate accounted for only about 15 percent of the variation in the equity market, or conversely that the equity market variation accounted for only about 15 percent of the variation in the target rate. There are a lot of other variables out there that are worthy investigation as well. Unemployment and Inflation would

	The Relationships between the FOMC Target Lending Rate and the
TABLE 13.1	S&P 500 Index, Unemployment Rate, Inflation Rate, and Misery Index (1990–2008)

Change Date	Rate (%)	Days Held	S&P 500	Unemployment Rate	Inflation Rate	Misery Index
1/1/1990	8.25	193	352.20	5.40	5.20	10.60
7/13/1990	8.00	108	367.37	5.50	4.82	10.32
10/29/1990	7.75	16	304.71	5.90	6.29	12.19
11/14/1990	7.50	23	317.12	6.20	6.27	12.47
12/7/1990	7.25	12	326.82	6.30	6.11	12.41
12/19/1990	7.00	20	331.75	6.30	6.11	12.41
1/8/1991	6.75	24	315.23	6.40	5.65	12.05
2/1/1991	6.25	35	343.05	6.60	5.31	11.91
3/8/1991	6.00	53	373.59	6.80	4.90	11.70
4/30/1991	5.75	98	380.80	6.70	4.89	11.59
8/6/1991	5.50	38	387.12	6.90	3.80	10.70
9/13/1991	5.25	27	387.92	6.90	3.39	10.29
10/10/1991	5.00	27	381.45	7.00	2.92	9.92
11/6/1991	4.75	35	392.89	7.00	2.99	9.99
12/11/1991	4.50	9	384.47	7.30	3.06	10.36
12/20/1991	4.00	111	400.40	7.30	3.06	10.36
4/9/1992	3.75	84	404.29	7.40	3.18	10.58
7/2/1992	3.25	64	411.77	7.70	3.16	10.86
9/4/1992	3.00	518	417.08	7.60	2.99	10.59
2/4/1994	3.25	46	470.18	6.60	2.52	9.12
3/22/1994	3.50	27	460.58	6.50	2.51	9.01
4/18/1994	3.75	29	447.63	6.40	2.36	8.76
5/17/1994	4.25	91	454.92	6.10	2.29	8.39
8/16/1994	4.75	91	463.68	6.00	2.90	8.90
11/15/1994	5.50	78	461.47	5.60	2.67	8.27
2/1/1995	6.00	155	478.65	5.40	2.86	8.26
7/6/1995	5.75	166	556.37	5.70	2.76	8.46
12/19/1995	5.50	43	611.95	5.60	2.54	8.14
1/31/1996	5.25	54	635.84	5.60	2.73	8.33
3/25/1997	5.50	418	773.88	5.20	2.76	7.96
9/29/1998	5.25	16	1002.60	4.60	1.49	6.09
10/15/1998	5.00	33	1056.42	4.50	1.49	5.99
11/17/1998	4.75	226	1163.55	4.40	1.55	5.95
6/30/1999	5.00	55	1391.22	4.30	1.96	6.26
8/24/1999	5.25	84	1348.27	4.20	2.26	6.46
11/16/1999	5.50	78	1422.77	4.10	2.62	6.72
2/2/2000	5.75	48	1424.37	4.10	3.22	7.32
3/21/2000	6.00	56	1516.35	4.00	3.76	7.76
5/16/2000	6.50	232	1406.95	4.00	3.19	7.19

(Continued)

TABLE 13.1 (*Continued*)

Change Date	Rate (%)	Days Held	S&P 500	Unemployment Rate	Inflation Rate	Misery Index
1/3/2001	6.00	28	1298.35	4.20	3.73	7.93
1/31/2001	5.50	48	1349.47	4.20	3.73	7.93
3/20/2001	5.00	29	1139.83	4.30	2.92	7.22
4/18/2001	4.50	27	1242.98	4.40	3.27	7.67
5/15/2001	4.00	43	1291.96	4.30	3.62	7.92
6/27/2001	3.75	55	1224.38	4.50	3.25	7.75
8/21/2001	3.50	27	1184.93	4.90	2.72	7.62
9/17/2001	3.00	15	1040.94	5.00	2.65	7.65
10/2/2001	2.50	35	1071.38	5.40	2.13	7.53
11/6/2001	2.00	35	1120.31	5.60	1.90	7.50
12/11/2001	1.75	330	1123.09	5.70	1.55	7.25
11/6/2002	1.25	231	894.74	5.90	2.20	8.10
6/25/2003	1.00	361	975.32	6.30	2.11	8.41
6/30/2004	1.25	41	1125.38	5.60	3.27	8.87
8/10/2004	1.50	42	1064.80	5.40	2.65	8.05
9/21/2004	1.75	19	1110.11	5.40	2.54	7.94
11/10/2004	2.00	34	1184.17	5.40	3.52	8.92
12/14/2004	2.25	50	1194.20	5.40	3.26	8.66
2/2/2005	2.50	48	1203.03	5.40	3.01	8.41
3/22/2005	2.75	42	1171.42	5.20	3.15	8.35
5/3/2005	3.00	58	1171.35	5.10	2.80	7.90
6/30/2005	3.25	40	1194.94	5.00	2.53	7.53
8/9/2005	3.50	42	1230.39	4.90	3.64	8.54
9/20/2005	3.75	42	1228.81	5.10	4.69	9.79
11/1/2005	4.00	42	1220.14	5.00	3.46	8.46
12/13/2005	4.25	49	1267.32	4.90	3.42	8.32
1/31/2006	4.50	56	1264.03	4.70	3.99	8.69
3/28/2006	4.75	43	1294.87	4.70	3.36	8.06
5/10/2006	5.00	50	1325.76	4.60	4.17	8.77
6/29/2006	5.25	446	1270.20	4.60	4.32	8.92
9/18/2007	4.75	43	1314.78	4.70	2.76	7.46
10/31/2007	4.50	41	1364.30	4.70	3.54	8.24
12/11/2007	4.25	42	1467.95	5.00	4.08	9.08
1/22/2008	3.50	8	1330.61	4.90	4.28	9.18
1/30/2008	3.00	48	1395.42	4.90	4.28	9.18
3/18/2008	2.25	43	1329.51	5.10	3.98	9.08
4/30/2008	2.00	162	1413.90	5.00	3.94	8.94
10/9/2008	1.50	20	899.00	7.30	5.40	12.70

almost certainly be among those variables, and that is why they are also considered here.

2. The average FOMC Target Rate over the 18-year period reported in Table 13.1 was 4.35, unweighted for duration of time held at each level. This suggests that 4.35 could be taken as a kind of pivotal point, above which the rate is a drag on equities, and below which the rate is a stimulus to equities. Admittedly, this conclusion is somewhat speculative, but it helps to permit a better historical perspective on where we are at any given time with respect to the magnitude of the FOMC Target Rate and its potential relationship to equity futures.

3. Another insight that can be gained from Table 13.1 has to do with the duration of time for which the FOMC Target Rate has been held after each adjustment over the 18-year period of interest. During that period the rate was adjusted every 80 days on average. Therefore, when the rate is adjusted more frequently at repeated short intervals, we can conclude that the FOMC is showing some frustration at the perceived lack of effect of their last rate adjustment. Note that this was especially in evidence from October, 1990, through January, 1991, when the FOMC lowered rates six times over a period of slightly more than three months.

4. It is also instructive to notice that the correlation between the FOMC Target Rate and the unemployment rate during this period was a non-significant $-.075$ (N=77, n.s., two-tailed). This non-significant negative correlation suggests that there was no meaningful relationship between unemployment and the FOMC Target Rate during this 18-year period. Perhaps we could even go as far as to say that the FOMC was not particularly influenced by unemployment levels when it set target rates, and unemployment levels seemed relatively uninfluenced by FOMC Target Rates as well.

5. Predictably, the most meaningful and significant correlation here is that between the FOMC Target Rate and inflation. That correlation was a strong positive .475 (N=77, $p<.001$, two-tailed). In this regard, it seems obvious that the FOMC was primarily targeting inflation when it raised rates, irrespective of any negative influence that such action might have had on the equity markets. In this case we may conclude that variation in inflation accounted for 23 percent of the variation in the Fed Funds rate. This was overall inflation, and not simply the core inflation rate. It would appear that there was a distinct tendency for the Fed to raise interest rates whenever inflation reached unusually high levels.

6. The correlation between the Fed Funds Target Rate and the Misery Index was a significant .283 (N=77, $p<.05$, two-tailed). Recall that the

Misery Index is obtained by adding together the unemployment rate and the inflation rate at any given time. Here the positive relationship suggests that the higher the Fed Funds Target Rate was at any given time, the greater the misery by this definition. However, because we cannot argue causation from correlation alone, we cannot conclude whether the FOMC introduced misery or simply responded to misery when it raised interest rates. For sure, however, the rate hikes brought misery to some equity investors. The reason that the correlation between the FOMC Target Rate and the Misery Index was lower than the correlation between the Fed rate and the inflation rate was apparently that the Misery Index incorporates unemployment, which is unrelated to the Fed rate.

These factors help to explain why so many traders have also been called "Fed Watchers." They have historical reasons for believing that FOMC behavior has important consequences for equity markets.

Another Fed tool for regulating markets is the infusion of liquidity capital into the economy. I remember distinctly, as a relevant example, that the Greenspan FOMC was intensely worried about the so-called "millennium bug" in the days leading up to the turn of the millennium mark at the beginning of the year 2000. It was feared that banking and other financial sector computers would cease to function properly because of the limitation of decimals that had been used to record years of transactions. As a consequence, the FOMC pumped massive liquidity into the economy just prior to January 1, 2000. When it was observed by mid January 2000, that there really was no millennium bug effect, the FOMC rapidly withdrew liquidity from the economy. In my opinion, the net effect of this rapid build up of liquidity followed by a rapid withdrawal of liquidity was the final swelling and bursting of the "tech bubble" that began in March 2000. It was a kind of whiplash event brought on in large part by rapid currency stimulus followed by rapid currency depletion. The NASDAQ Composite Index, for its part, ran up to an all-time high of about 5000 by the end of February 2000, but it promptly lost about 70 percent of its value over the next two years beginning in early March of 2000. While Mr. Greenspan labeled the cause of the bursting of the tech bubble to be the "irrational exuberance" of investors, at least some of the blame might equally be laid at the feet of FOMC interventionist policies. One pundit called the subsequent market malaise an "iatrogenic" illness—that is, an illness caused by the physicians. I have subsequently read that it is believed by some authorities that about 20 percent of all illnesses are brought about unintentionally by physicians themselves, and this causes me to wonder whether the same statistics apply equally to the health of the economy and the interventions of regulators. I certainly applaud the presence and activities of both physicians and FOMC regulators, but it seems clear that they also make mistakes with harmful consequences. The point in all of this discussion, however, is that Fed actions are beyond the control of ordinary investors, and it is well for them to stay informed of those actions as much as possible. Whenever the FOMC enters a trend of raising target lending rates and tightening liquidity, it is well for traders to beware and to be especially cautious about entering long positions.

ANALYST DOWNGRADES

Another threat to success is posed by analyst downgrades. Whenever an analyst downgrades a publicly traded company, it tends to have an immediate dampening effect on the share price of that company's stock. However, careful analysis of any company's present condition and future prospects is a tedious and costly process, and because most analyst firms are responsible for the evaluations of multiple companies, it often becomes cost effective and necessary for them to minimize the effort expended on any one analysis. Therefore, too often analysts may never visit the companies they are analyzing, and they may never carry out a detailed examination of operations. Instead, their analysis may be based on previous information gathered, on prior targets set for share-price appreciation, and on the most recent share-price movement. Because of the oftentimes capricious nature of downgrades, it is well for any trader to keep several things in mind:

- It is critical to maintain adequate portfolio diversification. No company's stock is immune from sudden and unpredictable downgrades.
- All analysts are not equal. It is important to examine the track record of any analyst to ascertain whether the upgrades or downgrades are credible. This is especially true if there is a history of the same analyst upgrading and downgrading the same stock.
- Some downgrades are based on insufficient analysis and may result only from a rapid run up in share price beyond prior targets. They may also result from the analyst's perceived need to keep in step with a rapid downturn in share price. In both of these cases the downgrades may be inaccurate and "behind the curve" regarding future price action.
- When there is a sequence of intermittent downgrades followed by upgrades by the same analysts on the same stocks, it may be appropriate to question the integrity of the analysts involved. Analysts are human enough to succumb to the temptation to drive down the price of a stock temporarily for the benefit of clients and customers. This is another

reason why some analyst downgrades may not signify a need to sell the targeted stock, but may in fact permit contrarian inferences.

- Very few stocks ever reach the analyst price targets within the time projected by those analysts. Thus, analyst price objectives tend to be overly optimistic.

Some traders claim that they have developed a knack for predicting when analyst upgrades and downgrades are likely to occur. Some of those traders actually build a trading strategy around their ability to anticipate upgrades. This appears to me to be a highly useful skill to develop, but I personally lay no claim to this ability. The closest thing to this skill that is reported in this book is the ability to identify and capitalize on EPS, PE, and share price divergences that often appear at the time of earnings reports, as is described in Chapter 5—or the ability to time the equity market's movements based on highs and lows in the CBOE Volatility Index and put/call ratio cycles as reported in Chapters 10 and 11.

"PUMP-AND-DUMP" PLOYS

It often happens with micro-cap penny stocks (low capitalization stocks trading under five dollars a share) that certain traders will find such a stock moving up with strong momentum and they will take a large long position in that stock. Then they will seek to promote that stock vigorously on a variety of stock bulletin boards. They frequently target active message boards of other stocks in the same sector or in the same share-price range as their own holding because the participants on those message boards may be most responsive to wild claims about the future potential of the stock being promoted. The objective of these traders is to attract interest in the stock in order to drive the share price rapidly higher so they can sell their position at market as soon as the price movement will permit them to make a profit. Despite their claims about long-term prospects of the stock, they have no intention of holding their position any longer than necessary. This ploy is appropriately labeled a "pump-and-dump" strategy. It is ineffective with larger capitalization stocks with higher share prices because the trader is less likely to be able to take a sufficiently large position in those stocks relative to overall capitalization, and because such stocks usually cannot be driven higher by message board promotions.

Due to several related negative experiences in the past, my own posture is generally to avoid all stocks priced below five dollars a share. Also, I no longer place much credence in bulletin board promotions. Certainly no bulletin board recommendation is worthy of consideration without due diligence and prior analysis.

MESSAGE BOARD PANNING

A trading strategy that is almost the mirror opposite of the "pump-and-dump" approach just described is that of "message board panning." However, this approach is not limited to penny stocks, but is frequently used as well with higher priced stocks that offer options. The idea here is to promote the notion that the company is falling apart, the management is incompetent, the earnings prospects are dismal, the business plan is hopeless, and the share price is about to plummet. Usually traders who post such messages either have a large short position in the stock and they stand to gain from a price collapse, or else they are hoping to drive the price down so they can get in at a lower price. When you think about this for a moment, their motivations can become fairly transparent. Most normal persons who become disenchanted with stocks will sell their positions and move on to greener pastures. They do not hang around to advise shareholders about the wisdom of selling. Sometimes these arguments can be forceful and convincing, and it happens frequently that shorters have also done their homework and have some solid reasons for their negative positions. Nevertheless, it is dangerous to follow their advice without due diligence. It is sometimes frightening to consider that someone could actually profit materially by slandering a company and causing it to lose capitalization. It can be like shouting "fire" in a crowded theater when, in fact, there is no fire. This kind of activity can definitely be a threat to your trading success.

MARKET MAKER MEDDLING

Market makers or specialists perform a valuable service for traders. These specialists maintain markets for thousands of stocks and make it possible for traders to buy and sell those stocks in an orderly and regulated manner. It is also possible for the specialists to make a considerable profit through this activity by means of the unique opportunities they possess. For one thing, they are able to trade their own shares and those of their clients at preferential prices when the right conditions present themselves. In addition, they have great latitude to establish spreads in the marketplace—that is, they can often determine the distance between the bid and ask prices and thereby enhance their profits and regulate the volume of trading activity. Because they are able to see the open orders to buy and sell, market makers are also capable of moving markets in predetermined directions under appropriate conditions.

For example, in a thinly traded stock, if a market maker sees a series of stop-loss sell orders just below the current price of a stock, it is possible for that market maker to trigger one of those orders and launch a cascade of market sell executions. This activity can increase trading volume and, thus, profits, at the same time that it can permit purchase order entry at a lower and more favorable price for the market maker and his clients. This procedure is sometimes called "taking out the stops."

In addition, traders who enter market orders prior to the market open are inviting the market maker to make executions from his own store of shares at prices that are beneficial only to the market maker. It is important to clarify that not every market maker is lacking in integrity. Many go beyond even the limited restraints of the legal system to conduct business in an ethical way. And those who do exhibit questionable behavior are usually well within the dictates of the law. The point here is that traders need to be aware of the threats to trading success that may be posed by the activities of some market makers.

NEGATIVE NEWS EVENTS

Negative news events can have an immediate disastrous effect on share prices, even if the news reported is not accurate. One highly successful trader I know of maintains a team of news watchers, and his primary trading strategy each day is built around capitalizing on ongoing news events, whether the news is positive or negative. In this section, our focus is primarily on negative news events because of the threat they can pose to share prices. It is useful to list some of the more common adverse news events that can affect share prices. The effects of these negative news events can be even more pronounced during a bear market trend because markets tend to be more sensitive during those times.

- Perhaps the most common negative news event is a negative earnings report. If a company fails to reach stated earnings projections, it is likely to bring the share price down, even if the earnings level is still highly respectable. Beyond that, even if a company reports record high earnings, if future earnings guidance is negative, it is likely to affect share price adversely. And, even if no earnings guidance has been provided, if current quarterly earnings fall below prior quarterly earnings, it can have negative implications for share price.
- Word of share price dilution is another negative news event. Share price dilution can occur whenever there is an additional public offering of shares in order for the company to raise capital. This is analogous to what happens whenever the U.S. Treasury Department decides to print more money and place it in circulation. It has as a net effect the

devaluation of the dollar, just as increasing the number of shares in circulation will reduce the value of individual shares. Stock splits will also increase the number of shares in circulation and thereby reduce share price, but this is not necessarily a problem for the trader who holds the stock because the number of shares held will increase to offset the price dilution.

- Reports of analyst downgrades constitute additional negative news events that can affect share prices adversely. Because analyst downgrades have already been discussed above, there is no need for further expansion here.
- Announcements of insider selling are further news events with negative effects on share prices. Although single incidents of small position sales usually have no effect on share price because such minor adjustments may be considered normal, repeated sales of large positions can have a serious negative effect. It has been observed that small position sales by insiders may have less impact on share price than insider purchases of shares. Another way of expressing this is to say that the positive effects of insider buying more than offset the negative effects of insider selling in most cases.
- News reports of instances of company fraud and embezzlement usually have an immediate negative effect on share prices. For this reason also, it is important to scrutinize management for any hint of impropriety. This includes instances of patent violation, false advertising, and failure to satisfy public safety standards for all of the company's products.
- Losses of large contracts or important clients can also have a negative effect on share prices. This is the inverse of the positive effect that word of new contracts or new clients can have on share price. Any development that negatively influences the prospects for future earnings can be considered a threat to trading success.

LARGE POSITION DUMPING

Whenever the holder of a large position sells all of his or her shares at market, it can drive share price sharply downward—especially if the stock is thinly traded. Aside from the fact that such behavior is foolish and wasteful on the part of the seller, it is also an example of bad etiquette because it often has a rude and harmful effect on the fortunes of innocent bystanders. In my opinion such behavior is every bit as immoral as intentionally setting a forest fire because it damages the market environment just as arson can damage the natural environment.

OVERHEAD: TAXES, COMMISSIONS, MARGIN INTEREST, SPREADS

All of the previous threats to trading success presented in this chapter can be labeled "variable threats" because the extent and timing of the damage cannot be predicted in advance. By way of contrast, overhead threats can be labeled "constant threats" because the amount and timing of the losses can be known in advance. There are many different ways to cope with overhead threats.

- Taxes: Taxes can be minimized by moving most of one's trading capital into an IRA. Traditional IRA gains are not taxable until the time of withdrawal, and it is probable that the rate of taxation will diminish at the time of withdrawal—especially if withdrawal happens after retirement. Also, capital gains in a regular, non-IRA stock account are reduced for stocks held two years or more. However, it is also fortunately the case that capital losses can be deducted from capital gains to reduce tax liability.
- Commissions: Commissions can remove a large chunk of your trading capital if you trade frequently with a high-commission broker. Although I maintain several different brokerage accounts, nearly all of my trading is done in accounts with brokerages that have the lowest commissions. There have been times in my own trading experience when I wondered whether I was working for myself in trading, or whether I was laboring on behalf of my stock brokerage. I can remember the huge sense of satisfaction I had when I reduced my trading overhead by 30 percent by moving from one discount brokerage with 10-dollar-per-trade commissions to another discount brokerage with 7-dollar-per-trade commissions. The net difference in overhead was substantial.
- Margin Interest: Margin interest is one of the greatest sources of income for some brokerages. Traders often fail to weigh the cost of margin interest against the gains made possible by margin borrowing. It is important to do this calculation regularly. It may wean you from the temptation to trade excessively on margin.
- Spreads: Spreads may be the single greatest "overhead threat" to trading success. The distance between the bid price and the ask price for any given stock at any given time is one means the market maker or specialist has for deriving income. Whenever you buy or sell at the market price you are helping to support the market maker. This is often inevitable, but it can be burdensome when the spreads for low volume stocks exceed 5 percent of the last traded share price. This can mean that you are effectively forfeiting 10 percent of your trading capital just

in a single round transaction of buying and selling that stock. Cumulatively considered, this can be far more expensive than the combined effects of taxes, commissions, and margin interest put together. The only mitigating steps I know to reduce this threat are to avoid stocks with excessive spreads, use limit orders instead of market orders for such stocks, and to place your limit orders midway between the bid and ask prices.

SUMMARY

In this chapter we have considered some of the threats that can stand in the way of trading success. In particular, we have examined some of the real and potential effects of actions by the Federal Open Markets Committee (FOMC), analyst downgrades, trader "pump-and-dump" ploys, message board panning, market maker meddling, negative news events, and the constraints of the overhead costs of trading.

CHAPTER 14

A Summary of Trading Principles

It is useful and important to establish a set of personal guidelines to regulate trading activity. The following list of trading principles has been hammered out on the anvil of experience over many years and may be suggestive for the construction of your own guidelines. Some of these principles are useful for traders to consult in the same way that a chess master resorts to internalized guidelines when the positions on the chess board become too complex to permit full comprehension of all the alternatives. These points are listed in no particular order of importance. Many of them have been mentioned or implied in earlier chapters.

NEVER FOLLOW A TIP WITHOUT DUE DILIGENCE

Many professionals love to give stock tips. In some cases it is their job to do so. At any given time there are hundreds of websites offering thousands of different opinions on which stocks to buy or sell. If that is not enough, surely we can find some friend who will add his opinion to this list. It is critical that we conduct thorough research on any recommendations regardless of the source or the sincerity of the opinion. You might say that any stock tips should be considered guilty until proven innocent. This is especially true for recommendations from TV stock commentators because, although public mention may move the stocks higher temporarily, we will usually manage to get in only after the initial surge, and such stocks often fall back when it becomes apparent that there was inadequate basis for the recommendation.

DON'T GET GROUNDED ON LOW VOLUME

Buying stocks with low average daily trading volume is inherently dangerous. While we may take comfort in the thought that such stocks have low capitalization and thus often move higher with very few shares purchased, the same is true in reverse, so that one large market sell order can wipe out the gains of several days or weeks. If we wish to avoid driving the share price down as we sell, it may take several days or weeks for us finally to unwind our positions in such stocks. Even posting a limit sell order can drive down the price of the stock before any execution can take place. And the spread for any low volume stock is usually exorbitant. Buying a low volume stock is like mooring a sailboat in a shallow lagoon. You must wait for the tide to rise before you can launch out to sea again. Even then, in the process of becoming ungrounded you may leave your rudder and pieces of your hull buried in the sand at the bottom of the lagoon. Any stock that is regularly trading less than 10,000 shares a day is suspect and should ordinarily be avoided. Fortunately there is no shortage of higher volume stocks with good prospects for the future.

NEVER BUY AT THE HIGH FOR THE DAY

This is a very simple rule that can help you avoid the temptation to chase stock bubbles. Remember that the trader's calling is to supply demand and demand supply. Whenever we offer the high price for the day, we are effectively demanding demand. We are running with the crowd to chase the stock to new highs, and this can be detrimental to overall performance. It is usually better to wait for the stock price to turn down and only then to place your purchase order, or even to place a limit order at a lower price and wait for the stock to come to you. This principle could be stated even more simply as, "Don't chase stocks." Remember, there is always a tendency for stock prices to regress to the mean—especially following a gap up in price movement.

NEVER SELL AT THE LOW FOR THE DAY

This is the flip side of the previous principle. I can remember times when I have sold with the crowd in the panic of the moment, only to watch the stock bounce back a few minutes later in the day or early in the following morning. There may be some valid exceptions to this rule, but it is usually better to pause and take a deep breath and then to sell after the price improves somewhat. This rule will not prevent losses entirely, but it can mitigate them somewhat. Admittedly, it is difficult not to join the panic when it seems like everyone is running for the exit, but I confess that some of my biggest losses have come when I sold at market in a panic. Almost invariably the stock in question rebounded from its lows and was given a better opportunity to sell later at a higher price. This principle holds especially when the decline has no basis in any news report and when the decline has already moved the stock price down 10 percent or more and you have failed to get out earlier.

REMEMBER WHY YOU BOUGHT

Whenever you buy a stock, you should have strong defensible reasons for that purchase. Perhaps you can remember those reasons, but more likely you should record them in writing. When those conditions that justified the purchase do eventually change, this will likely supply the necessary grounds for selling the stock. However, if the original reasons for purchase remain unchanged, then you should be very slow to sell. When you are deciding whether to sell or not, you should always ask the question whether the original grounds for purchase have changed. Often this simple step can spare you the discomfort of watching from the sidelines as a perfectly good stock that you have just sold is subsequently climbing to new heights.

DON'T GET TOO ATTACHED TO ANY STOCK

It is easy to become attached to stocks that have performed well in the past or that you discovered when they were in obscurity and now they are popular. This is especially true for stocks in your portfolio that have delivered comparatively strong gains. Sometimes stocks have special appeal just because of the nature of their underlying business. However, current prospective performance is really the only justification for holding any stock. If your analysis suggests that certain other stocks which you have not yet acquired have a strong likelihood of outperforming stocks which you currently hold, then your course of action is abundantly clear. You should jettison your laggards in a heartbeat. Success in trading is only partially determined by how quickly you acquire good stocks. It is equally dependent on how quickly you unload underperforming stocks.

MAINTAIN DIVERSIFICATION

Don't put all of your eggs in one basket. It is an important feature of capital preservation that you hold a variety of stocks at any given time. Not only should traders diversify over several stocks, but they should also diversify over a variety of sectors and stock capitalization sizes. It is a temptation to hold only stocks from the same leading sector, but this is a mistake because individual sectors often fall into disfavor and quickly take all of their stocks down at the same time. Of course, it is possible to be overly diversified and mirror the performance of a market index fund, and become encumbered with excessive trading expenses and onerous portfolio management responsibility. Limits of diversification are also determined by market conditions and the amount of available trading capital. Ideally, a swing trader should aim to hold a minimum of five to ten stocks at any given time, depending on the amount of trading capital available. Remember, however, that diversification across sectors does not provide absolute protection against a general market downturn. For this kind of protection, the diversification must include other asset classes besides stocks.

DON'T OVERTRADE

As the adage goes, "A penny saved is a penny earned." There are commission and spread costs associated with every trade. Therefore some of your best trading days will be days when you abstain from making any trades. Such days serve to confirm and attest to the wisdom of earlier trading decisions. Also, as we saw in Chapters 9 and 10, there are times of bearish downward trending when it is better to be out of stocks altogether. In those chapters you can see that a trader can actually enhance profits by being out of the market approximately 50 percent of the time. However, just as there are compulsive shoppers, there are also compulsive traders. The word that describes this shopping tendency is "oniomania." It is a compulsive drive to shop. In my earliest days of trading, this was one of my own biggest faults. Currently, I am learning to congratulate myself for doing nothing when nothing is required. One way to measure success is to observe the ratio of total gains to the total number of trades. By this measure, the most successful trader is the one who makes the most profit using the least number of trades. Every tradeless day becomes a cause for celebration.

DON'T HESITATE TO REACQUIRE A WINNER

It is part of the very nature of stock market trading that stocks can quickly fall in and out of favor. When you buy a stock, it should never be your intention to hold it forever. In the same way, when you sell a stock, you should never write it off as a lost cause forever. The best stocks that show the most potential for rapid growth are often the most volatile stocks. Such stocks frequently undulate from making new 52-week highs to dropping more than 10 percent below those recent highs. The challenge is to approach them in such a way that you can make money while they are rising and you can preserve those gains when they are falling. Meeting this challenge often means that you must buy, sell, and reacquire the same stocks repeatedly from time to time.

DON'T GET YOUR GUIDANCE FROM MESSAGE BOARDS

Stock bulletin boards such as those at the Yahoo! Finance website or at several similar sites can provide useful information. There you can often learn why a stock is making precipitous moves in one direction or another. By reading such bulletin board messages you can often find helpful alternative websites with useful stock information. You can sometimes get valuable information about a company's business plan, its governance, its earnings prospects, and about recent analyst upgrades and downgrades. But do not be deceived. Many of the people posting such messages have as their goal a desire to influence you either to buy or to sell the stock. Those who want you to sell usually hold a short position, or they wish to buy the stock after it moves lower in price. Those who want you to buy usually hold a long position, or they are waiting to short the stock after it moves sharply higher. Many times people are employing "pump-and-dump" strategies in an effort to drive the price higher so that they can sell at a profit. The bottom line is that you should visit message boards often and learn all that you can from them, but at the same time you should take everything presented there with a grain of salt.

MAINTAIN YOUR OWN TRADING IDENTITY

As a serious trader, you must maintain your own identity. By this I mean that your success in trading depends more on your ability to choose your own correct path and to follow it consistently than on your ability to emulate others. When a mountain climber stands at the base of a challenging mountain in order to choose a path to the top, he or she must carefully survey the terrain and choose a path that is well suited to his or her stamina and skill and patience. The path must be committed to memory because, once the ascent has begun, it will be dangerous to change course and it may be difficult to recognize the original course as the terrain changes. Above all, the climber must not merely fall in line behind someone else unquestioningly. Other climbers' paths and rates of ascent may not be suited to everyone else's skill and endurance, and may not therefore bring others to the summit. Certainly all paths will not reach the summit within the same time frame and with the same level of risk. This does not mean that trading methods cannot change as skill and stamina improve, but it does mean that such changes should be tested and proven before they are adopted.

READ WIDELY

In stock market trading, as in warfare, there is no substitute for intelligence information. The vast and growing literature in this field can help each trader identify an appropriate philosophy and style. It can suggest techniques that will increase the probability of success under various market conditions. It can point to other evolving sources of information. It can allow the trader to form realistic expectations and to set appropriate goals. Therefore it is essential that traders read extensively. This may be the single most important preparation any new trader can make. I believe it was Thomas Edison who said that he read a great number of books for every creative idea and every new invention he produced. This is equally true in gathering successful trading ideas, and it involves the continual reading of books, articles, and current internet material. Developing extensive reading habits may be the single most important key to success in trading. I once met a Swiss young man who was fluent in seven languages. When I asked him his secret of success at learning languages he replied that he never considered himself to have learned a language until he had read at least 24 books in that language. I have no idea how he came up with that precise number, but I suspect that success at trading may also have some similar threshold reading level.

BACK OFF PERIODICALLY

Trading is a psychologically intense, physically demanding, and emotionally draining activity. This is especially true when you are trading with other people's money, or when you are living off the proceeds of this activity. Thankfully there are weekends and holidays when markets are closed and it is possible to back away and maintain perspective. Beyond this, it is periodically necessary to take time off from this activity and evaluate progress, gain new insights, and plan new approaches. Perhaps the two best times to back off are when you are losing inexplicably and when you are winning exorbitantly. The first situation requires time away from the market in order to regroup and to detect problems and improve procedures. The second situation may signal a market top when it is appropriate to take profits and stand aside.

SELDOM IF EVER BUY WITH UNSETTLED FUNDS

My own journaling suggests that this has been an area of great weakness for me personally. My greatest losses have come at times when I was waiting for funds to settle and I was therefore unable to abandon losing positions. This remains a challenge because it is difficult for me not to reinvest sale proceeds immediately when attractive buys are available. Fortunately it is less of a problem when diversification is fully maintained and when thorough research is conducted on all new acquisitions. Sometimes also the constraint of having to hold a new acquisition for three days for the settling of funds is a positive factor because it provides opportunity for the stock to experience and recover from any initial retrenchment. However, this is still a concern requiring great caution and awareness. Nevertheless, remember that the right to buy stocks before funds settle is akin to the privilege of borrowing money with no interest charged. Therefore, as a rule it is better to trade with settled funds, but there will be some exceptions to that rule.

LOOK TO SELL WITH THE SAME LEVEL OF ZEAL THAT YOU LOOK TO BUY

Selling a stock that has peaked in its performance in order to free up capital to buy a potential winner is an exciting step. It allows you to lock in profits, avoid potential losses, and pursue new opportunities. Cultivating this positive attitude towards selling allows you to avoid a "buy-and-hold" mentality that would be a sure path to disaster. After all, the planting of crops is always done with a goal of harvesting produce. And the buying of stock is not so that we can boast of our holdings, but so that we can sell that stock at a profit. It is not until we sell that our goals can be realized. This is why it has become a daily ritual in my own trading to make a list of all the stocks in my portfolio that are potential sells on any following day. Success is not just a matter of finding and acquiring the best stocks quickly. It is also a reflection of how rapidly we are able to sell stocks that are no longer defensible holdings.

MAINTAIN A TRADING JOURNAL OR DIARY

In addition to taking advantage of the opportunity of learning from others through the reading of books and articles, we should take advantage of the opportunity to learn from our own trading experiences in the market. Keeping a journal is one of the best ways to take advantage of this learning opportunity. Minimally, such a journal should be a diary of winning and losing behaviors in daily trading activity. It can, of course, be a much more elaborate journal and be combined with a record of all trading activity, including dollar amounts of gains and losses. The purpose, however, is mainly to discover areas of success and failure so that trading skill can be enhanced. A good way to begin is simply to enter lessons learned into a log book at the end of each trading day. This should be reviewed periodically to ensure that the lessons are not forgotten.

GATHER INFORMATION ON YOUR HOLDINGS DAILY

Circumstances change constantly concerning any company or stock. Your greatest winner today will often become your greatest loser tomorrow. It is absolutely essential to gather information on each holding daily—possibly even several times each day. For this reason also it is difficult to maintain large portfolios with more than 15 or 20 stocks. I suppose fund managers with extremely large portfolios partially justify their inability to keep abreast of developments in each stock by citing their diversification. They attempt to manage risk by increasing the number of stocks they hold, with the downside that they are thus unable to surpass overall market performance. Others manage risk by continually gathering information on a more limited number of stocks. Knowledge is power. It enables you to limit losses and capitalize on new opportunities.

LEARN FROM YOUR MISTAKES

Most traders are guilty of making a very limited range of mistakes that they repeat over and over again. This is a much easier problem to remedy than if those mistakes were infinite in number and never repeated. The good news here is that if we become aware of our errors, record them in a journal, and resolve never to repeat them, there is every possibility that we can become highly skilled traders. Gaining skill in trading in some ways resembles the learning of a foreign language. To communicate effectively the learner must grasp the vocabulary, the syntax, the morphology, the phonology rules, and the situational appropriateness of the ideas to be communicated. As mistakes are eliminated in all of these areas, the speaker can attain level of fluency approaching that of a native speaker. Similarly, the more we are able to eliminate critical mistakes in trading, the more likely it is that we will become successful traders. Success then becomes a matter of the systematic removal of mistakes. Legendary football coach Joe Paterno used to tell his Pennsylvania State University players that making mistakes was inevitable, but success as players was determined by the ability to overcome those mistakes successively from one game to the next.

DON'T DAMAGE THE ENVIRONMENT FOR OTHERS

We live in a time when people are appropriately aware of the dangers of air pollution, water pollution, and climate degradation. However, there seems to be less awareness of behaviors that may comprise a kind of "market pollution." One such contaminating behavior occurs when a trader dumps a large position in a thinly traded stock at the market price. Not only does this inevitably result in needless losses for the impatient seller, it can also quickly drop the price of the stock to levels from which it may take months to recover, if indeed there is ever a recovery. This is like fishing with dynamite in a small pond. It can kill all of the small players that feed on and sustain that ecosystem. Another way in which we damage the market environment is by shorting individual stocks in failing sectors. For example, when real estate and financial sectors are hurting, it is not helpful to the economy to be shorting individual home builders and banks. Instead, we may be able to satisfy our bearish hedging needs by buying exchange-traded inverse index funds.

DON'T LET YOURSELF BECOME DISCOURAGED

The best traders in the world will inevitably suffer some losses. Sometimes those losses will be large and protracted. There will be times when it will be a great temptation to abandon trading altogether. Therefore a trader must learn to regard losses as valuable learning experiences. If explorers like Columbus could sail only in the direction the wind was blowing, they would never have discovered the New World. They learned through tacking maneuvers to maintain a desired general direction regardless of the way the wind was blowing. A successful trader must also learn how to navigate through the winds of adversity and to succeed in both bearish and bullish market trends. I am reminded of the experience of one trader who lost millions in one trade and fully expected to be fired by his supervisor the next day. Instead, his supervisor informed him that there was no way he could be fired after so much money had been invested in his trading education. It helps to view losses as educational investments in the same way. Of course, this only applies if we learn from our mistakes.

LEARN TO TIME GENERAL MARKET TRENDS

It is critical to success that traders develop some rudimentary skill at timing the market. Equity markets go through regular cycles just like ocean waves rushing towards the beach. A highly successful investment banker recently told me that the real estate market also goes through regular seven-year cycles. Therefore, regardless of the kind of market you trade, it is important that you learn to time the cycles. Whether your timing technique involves watching bell-weather stocks, use of the CBOE Volatility Index, reliance on the Elliott Wave Principle, monitoring advance-decline ratios, watching put-call ratios, or some other approach, it is important for you to understand the direction the markets are trending at any given time. Of course, few if any traders can pick the exact moment of a market turnaround in advance, but it is possible to come within a few days of such events. It is one skill to anticipate the approximate time of a turnaround in advance with a modicum of reliability, and it is another skill to recognize when such a turnaround has occurred. Both of these skills are beneficial and possible to cultivate. I realize that some commentators still maintain that it is impossible to time the markets, and I must sympathize with them because I used to be one of them.

DON'T BEGRUDGE THE PAYING OF DUES

It has been observed that most traders experience losses at the beginning. This phenomenon is so predictable that it is sometimes called "paying dues." Some traders have even expressed regret that they began their trading experience with lucky successes that made them overconfident and caused them eventually to experience greater losses than they would have if they had experienced losses at the beginning. The point here is that it is normal to experience early losses, and this should not be viewed as an indication that trading success is unattainable. This also implies that it is helpful to build up surplus initial trading capital before launching out into a trading career—at least to a point where initial losses will not put you out of the trading business altogether.

SET REALISTIC, MEASURABLE GOALS FOR TRADING GAINS

It is important to set goals for trading gains. However, unless these goals are measurable, it will be impossible to know when trading has been successful and when it has not been successful. And unless these goals are realistic, it is possible that trading may never be successful because the goals may be unattainable. Setting realistic goals can be a challenge, and it should flow out from personal experience rather than from recommendations of others. Goals can be changed with time and experience. This is somewhat like deciding how far you can swim in a specified time. It is probably best to make such decisions as you swim laps in a local pool rather than as you attempt to cross the English Channel for the first time. In the same way it is best to set goals for trading gains after you have been trading for a while and have been able to measure your achievements.

DON'T TAKE ADVICE FROM INVESTMENT PROFESSIONALS

This sounds like a strange principle to find in a book on trading. This principle did not originate with me, but with no less of an investment professional than Peter Lynch, who managed the Fidelity Magellan Fund for many years. Lynch's point was that you would not expect a plastic surgeon to advise you to do your own facelift or a plumber to advise you to install your own hot water tank. In the same way, most investment professionals would prefer to manage your money for you than to train you to do their job. If you are seeking a trading career, you must have a sense that your performance can equal or exceed that of professionals who will still be happy to manage your money on your behalf for a fee. My point in stressing this principle is that it is usually a better practice to trust the predictions of a mathematical trading formula than to rely on the opinions of an investment guru with his finger to the wind.

AVOID BUYING A STOCK IMMEDIATELY AFTER IT HAS MADE A HUGE PRICE RUN UP

Price movement in a stock resembles a pull on an elastic band. When the stock has had an upward run of 20 percent or more in one day, there is often a strong pull in the opposite direction. This tendency towards retrenchment in price is especially pronounced when the run up has not been accompanied by any news, or when the stock price has gapped up. Stocks tend over time to fill these gaps before going higher. A statistician might refer to this tendency for near-term reversal in price as an example of regression to the mean. Elliott Wave theorists have even attempted to set mathematical limits on the likely percentage of retrenchment to be expected after a run up in an individual stock or in the general market averages (Frost and Prechter 1990).

If you still have your heart set on buying the stock in question, it is better to wait until it has fallen in price or to set a limit buy order substantially below the last execution price. If you already hold the stock, it may be a good idea to sell it before the close of trading on the day of the run up. You will likely be able to repurchase it later at a much lower cost if you should desire to do so.

AVOID SELLING A STOCK IMMEDIATELY AFTER IT HAS HAD A HUGE LOSS

This principle is the opposite side of the previous principle. Stocks that have just experienced a one-day decline in share price of 20 percent or more, will often rebound by the end of the day of trading or during the next day or two. This is especially true if the decline was not prompted by any news or if the decline involved a downward gap in share price. If you did not manage to sell the stock earlier, at this point you may be better served by waiting for a price rebound before unloading your shares. Again, in most such situations you may be rewarded for patiently waiting for the regression to the mean to take place. Certainly, this also has implications for selling stocks short as well. You should avoid selling stocks short that have already experienced a sharp decline in price. Such stocks will often experience a near-term rebound in price.

MAINTAIN YOUR DISCIPLINE

Almost invariably my trading losses have come at times when I have yielded to the temptation to violate my own rules. For example, there are few things more difficult for me to do than to sit outside of the market on a day when stocks are moving up. But this is exactly what my guidelines tell me to do when the macro-market indicators have signaled a downtrend. Over time, however, sticking to this discipline has enabled me to avoid many "suckers' rallies" and has thereby paid great dividends. There are many such guidelines that often place a trader in contrarian situations, which lead to temporary anxiety but eventually produce longer-term gains. Another example is when a stock is moving up rapidly in share price, but the stock does not exhibit requisite fundamentals to permit me to make a purchase. If I go ahead and buy the stock anyway in spite of my rules to the contrary, I will usually lose money on the trade.

DON'T HESITATE TO SELL GOOD STOCKS WHEN MACRO MARKET INDICATORS SIGNAL A DOWNTURN

One of the most difficult things to do as a trader is to sell a stock that has great fundamentals and great technicals and is moving up in price. But when macro-market indicators signal that the general market has reversed direction and is about to start a downward trend, that is what my rules tell me to do. Often such stocks may even continue their climb for a short time thereafter, but it usually happens that these great stocks will eventually turn sharply downward with the overall market. It is good to remember that it will still be possible to buy back even more shares of those stocks after the dust has settled and the market downturn has finished.

FOCUS MORE ON AVOIDING GREAT LOSSES THAN ON MAKING GREAT GAINS

In professional football and basketball it is often said that a great defense is better than a great offense. Perhaps this is because if you have a great defense, any average offense will do. In stock trading a few big losses can take you completely out of contention because you will have no more investment capital left. But even small losses are easier to experience than they are to recover from. Another way to illustrate this fact is to point out that if you lose 20 percent of your investment capital, you now must earn a 25 percent return on your remaining capital in order to get back to your starting point. Thus, it is harder to climb out of an investment hole than it is to dig the hole in the first place. This means that it is best to err on the side of caution.

CONTINUALLY BE WATCHING FOR SUCCESS PREDICTORS

It is important to be looking for new variables that predict success in trading. Each new discovery will improve the odds of success. I remember, by way of example, how satisfying it was to observe a positive relationship between cash flow and share-price gain. More recently I have seen that analyst earnings estimates that suggest company earnings will at least double over the coming year can be highly predictive of future success. Doubtless there are many such predictors that need to be gathered like precious gems scattered along our path.

SUMMARY

In this chapter we have been given a set of 30 trading principles. These are offered as tentative guidelines with the proviso that every trader should develop or adopt a set of guidelines consistent with his or her own approach to trading. The trading principles set forth here are presented in no particular order of importance.

CHAPTER 15

Morality in the Marketplace

One critical topic that gets little coverage in most of the trading books I have read is the topic of morality in the marketplace. It is true that many business schools have begun offering courses in business ethics in response to what has been perceived as an erosion of integrity in the workplace. But this does not appear to have stemmed the tide of fraud, deception, greed, theft, tax evasion, bribery, and other misconduct that poses a threat to the survival of our capitalistic system. As of February 2009, the FBI reports that it has 530 ongoing corporate fraud investigations. In this chapter I want to examine what I believe to be the greatest single threat to the stability of our economy and consequently is the greatest threat to any hope of trading success.

As I write this, the ink is barely dry on the headlines regarding the Bernard L. Madoff securities fraud case, in which the former chair of the NASDAQ Stock Exchange was arrested on December 11, 2008 on charges that he defrauded investors of an estimated $50 billion through a decades-long Ponzi scheme. His victims included charities, pension funds, banks, and individual investors. At least one of his victims is known to have committed suicide as a result of being defrauded of a large fortune. Although this was the largest securities fraud case on record, it is by no means the only example of such behavior. Even the continued existence of the Securities and Exchange Commission in its present form has been called into question by its failure to prevent this massive deception. Perhaps Madoff was not apprehended sooner because no one could believe that such devious behavior could ever take place on such a scale over such an extended period of time in a civilized world.

The business arena requires integrity to survive. The severity of the problems of corruption resulting from the decline of integrity and the influences of this trend on our economic well being can hardly be overstated. I believe this is the single greatest threat to our economy. This problem is not limited only to Wall Street. Imagine my dismay some years ago when I was teaching business English at an Asian university where I soon discovered that a majority of the business students routinely cheated on examinations. I promptly lectured the students with a prediction that their national economy would soon be in shambles if they persisted in such behavior because capitalistic economies such as theirs required integrity to function. Subsequent to these events, I have had much time to reflect on the gravity of the effects of declining integrity, conditions that promote the decline of integrity, and possible solutions to this problem. You may wonder what these concerns have to do with success in the trading of stocks, but I believe they have everything to do with successful stock trading and with every other financial activity that involves trust.

INTEGRITY DEFINED

Integrity is usually defined as firm adherence to a code of moral values. High on the list of those moral values is honesty or trustworthiness. Integrity also implies a certain care and concern for the well being of others. So a person with integrity is said to be someone who can be trusted to act in the best interests of those who rely on him or her. It should be evident therefore that there is a strong relationship between integrity and trust. Where there is no integrity, there is no trustworthiness, and where there is no trustworthiness, there can be no trust, and where there is no trust, capital markets cannot exist as we know them. Our economic survival is to a very large extent based upon trust.

For example, if people wish to purchase automobile insurance, they have only to telephone an insurance agent and give him a few details over the telephone. The insurance agent is then authorized to issue coverage, so that their automobile is instantly insured without their having signed any policy or without their payment of the premium having yet arrived in the office of the agent. The entire transaction takes place on the basis of trust. Similarly, when we make purchases of apparel at most clothing stores, we are given a few days or weeks in which we can return the purchased items with no penalty. In this arrangement, the customer is being trusted that he is not acquiring the clothing to wear at one party and then to return it the next day. When there is a breakdown of such trust, it does not necessarily mean that a law has been broken, but it does mean that someone has acted without integrity and the economy suffers damage to some extent.

In the realm of stock trading, when we place an on-line order to buy or sell stock, there is a three-day settlement period for each transaction. We trust the seller to deliver shares within three days. When the seller fails to deliver the purchased stock to our broker within the required three-day time limit, we have a classic failure to deliver (FTD). In practice, we can go about our business without ever really knowing that the stock was not delivered. We can proceed as if the intended transaction had fully taken place. However, the untrustworthy seller stands to gain financially from those undelivered shares during the delinquent period. This kind of behavior can also foster naked shorting, when unscrupulous persons sell stock short that they do not legally possess, and they can benefit financially at the expense of others in this manner. The Securities and Exchange Commission estimates that there are more than six billion dollars worth of FTDs occurring each day on our stock exchanges. This FTD phenomenon has the potential to destroy our capital markets as we know them. Here again we have an example of the critical role of trust and integrity in our economy and how dangerous the situation may become when integrity disappears.

THE GRAVITY OF THE EFFECTS OF DECLINING INTEGRITY

Capitalism, possibly more than other economic systems, depends on the integrity of its participants. Perhaps this is because so much of its functioning as a system is regulated exclusively by laws of supply and demand as they are mediated by the good will of the participants. Admittedly, it would be unrealistic to expect every capitalist to exhibit perfect integrity at all times. In fact, the very costs of non-integrity can be, and ultimately are, built into the system and can be sustained to a point. But there is a tipping point that we may be fast approaching, beyond which these costs can no longer be sustained.

This integrity-decline tipping point is analogous to the growing burden of entitlements such as the non-negotiable costs of social security, Medicare, and service to our national debt that weigh on our national budget and could also reach a tipping point. Imagine, for example, how much of a tax we pay for retail merchandise because of shoplifters. Consider the costs of alarm systems and security guards. Think of how much more expensive medicines and foods become because of security packaging requirements. Even the price of gasoline is higher at the pump because of the cost of required routine pump inspections and accuracy certification. This does not even reflect the cost in taxes required to pay for the justice system and the associated arrest and imprisonment of offenders. What percentage of our national GDP goes to pay for securities fraud and associated costs such as unemployment insurance and welfare payments? I do not profess to know the answer to that question, but I would propose that the percentage is shockingly high and is growing.

Beyond these costs, consider the exorbitant medical costs that are paid due to Medicare fraud or unfair litigation practices, or the added costs of goods and services due to unfair credit card lending practices. Consider also that it is not unusual for people to pay three times the value of their homes when they include mortgage interest payments over the amortization periods. And although many of these costs are legal and accepted charges, it also happens that, because of them, conditions may also arise under which buyers are forced to default on their credit cards and mortgages and send other unwelcome ripples through the economy. A moment's reflection on these difficulties leads one to conclude that some of the immoral behavior that can threaten the roots of the capitalistic system is patently illegal behavior, and some of this questionable behavior is currently perfectly legitimate.

It is important to reflect on the causes of the home mortgage meltdown and resultant credit freeze and economic downturn that began to appear in 2008. Whether you believe these ills were caused by borrower intemperance, by lender abusiveness, by Wall Street greed, by political corruption, or by all of the above, clearly the root of the problem can be traced to a lack of personal integrity. As the problem unfolded and interest requirements ballooned, borrowers realized that their mortgage obligations had exceeded the values of their homes and their capacity to repay the loans. Many borrowers turned their backs on their mortgage commitments and walked away, causing a further glutting of housing inventories and a continuing decline in home values. Government rescue efforts effectively passed the problems on to taxpayers and their children who had not participated in the creation of the problem. International markets suffered from the subsequent inability of the American consumer to acquire foreign goods and services in the same proportions as before. Meanwhile, unethical traders continued to short home builders, realtors, and financial institutions and managed to make huge profits from the misfortunes of others—all the while that they were exacerbating the problem. This catastrophic economic development has been studied by many of the best economic minds in the world.

I noted that Alan Greenspan, in a televised interview in February 2009, stated that at the heart of this largest economic catastrophe in a generation was the problem of human greed. He was therefore not optimistic that any long term solution could ever be found. Current government leaders have proposed a variety of possible solutions, including greater market oversight, government incentives to purchase toxic assets, extensive tax cuts, and massive government spending on public works projects. It amazes me that so few if any of the proposed solutions to this multifaceted economic problem are designed to address the root problem of declining integrity. But realistically speaking, how can anyone address the problem of declining integrity? Minimally, I believe we can study its causes and seek to regulate or eliminate them. This is an approach that involves analysis of the components of the problem in an effort to divide and conquer its sources.

CONDITIONS THAT CAN PROMOTE THE EROSION OF INTEGRITY

If there is to be any prospect of curbing the erosion of integrity in our society, it is imperative that we acknowledge the magnitude of the problem, determine its causes, and understand the ultimate effects of its noncontainment. Declining integrity in society can have many sources, and I can only address a few of the most important ones in a book of this kind.

The Secularization of Society

Most Americans are aware of the doctrine of separation of church and state and of the valid reasons for its acceptance. However, separation of church and state is not the same concept as secularization. In a true secular society, not only is the state separate from religious institutions, but also religion itself is marginalized so as to have no forum in education, in science, business, law, or political decision making. The belief that there is a Supreme Being who observes human behavior and who will one day bring it into account is regarded at best as a superstition and at worst as an affront. Secular humans who have discarded all such beliefs as irrelevant can easily conclude that reprehensible clandestine behaviors are beyond the reach of accountability. They may even applaud those who are able to grow wealthy by cheating the system and getting away with it. For example, I have read that some of the investors in Madoff's Ponzi scheme realized that something illegal had to be happening in order for the hedge fund profits to be so dramatically and consistently positive. However, they believed that Madoff was benefiting from illegal insider trading that was happening beneath the radar of the Securities Exchange Commission, and they wanted to get in on the proceeds. It was their belief that anyone who could so consistently benefit from illegal behavior deserved their acclaim and financial support.

My point is not to claim that only religious persons can show integrity, but it is to point out that American culture is becoming increasingly more secularized, and that this trend toward increasing secularization has had a negative influence on the level of integrity in our culture, which in turn has adversely affected the stability of our economy and our prospects for honest trading gains in the marketplace. I am aware of the fact that the increase of secularization in some Middle Eastern countries has been beneficial to the economies of those countries, but I do not believe that has been the experience of Western civilizations where the movement towards secularization has resulted in a devaluation of human self worth, a diminishing of the so-called Protestant work ethic, and a decline in integrity.

Population Growth and Urbanization

As population grows and becomes increasingly urbanized, it becomes correspondingly more difficult to know one's neighbors and to feel any accountability towards them. Dense populations become increasingly stratified hierarchically to afford living space to both the "haves" and the "have-nots" within the same limited geographical area. Crime rates increase in urban areas along with the growing disparity in societal worth attributed to the wealthy over the poor. As urbanization increases, trust and a sense of personal responsibility towards others tend to diminish. Per capita debt levels also tend to rise. Perhaps these correlates of urbanization are what led Thomas Jefferson to maintain that any city that rises in population beyond 150,000 persons becomes the enemy of the state. Unfortunately, however, with the inevitable rise in population, the tendency towards urbanization seems irreversible. There may even be some societal benefits of urbanization, such as the resulting proliferation of goods and services and the preservation of wilderness areas that might otherwise become over-developed.

Furthermore, not everyone has the luxury of living in a rural or small-town environment because of the location of available employment. Certainly, I do not wish to imply that every city dweller lacks integrity. My point is only that the growth of urbanization has historically been associated with the decline of integrity as it is defined here and should be recognized for this potential threat—especially when someone is looking for a place to raise a family or when appointments are being made to important leadership positions where strong moral character is required.

Recently we have been reminded that it is not only the growth of our cities that poses a threat to the development of personal integrity and to our economic well being, but the growth of our major corporations also presents inherent dangers. A number of large financial corporations have recently been rescued through government bailouts to prevent the xsxs inevitable insolvency that would have resulted from their unethical use of corporate funds. In each case, these corporations were judged to be "too big to fail." That is, the dangers posed to the national economy by their bankruptcy were too great to permit. Therefore, in the case of corporate size also, bigger is not necessarily better. I would speculate that the problems associated with inordinate size also extend to other institutions such as schools and churches and retail franchises. When organizations become too large, there is a decline in interpersonal relationships and associated accountability and trust.

Globalization

There are countries in which corruption is so rampant that it permeates all levels of society. In such countries conducting business can become a challenge to personal integrity. Bribery and corruption often become the price of doing business. Competition to succeed in international commerce with such countries can threaten personal and corporate integrity. In this context, there was a period of several years when I resided in a Middle Eastern country. One day during my time there I received a notice from the post office that a package had arrived for me from America, which turned out to be a shirt my mother had sent for my birthday. The postal official informed me that I must pay him a high customs duty to claim my package. I objected that, being a student, I did not have much money, and besides, the customs fee he was asking exceeded the value of the gift. He then asked me how much I could pay. That question raised certain flags in my mind. I replied that I was not prepared to pay anything for my package and he would therefore have to return it to the sender. He responded that because of my circumstances he would ask his supervisor to lower the customs fee on my behalf. I watched as he walked to the back of the room and hid behind a pillar for a few moments. Soon he returned with the good news that his supervisor had agreed that I would not have to pay this time. I thanked him profusely, took my package, and went on my way wiser for the encounter. I learned later that even many of the doctoral dissertations in the library of the major university of that country were verbatim translations of European dissertations that had been plagiarized to satisfy degree requirements. Also, many of the students at all levels of the public school system were accustomed to the bribing of their teachers in order to get better grades. Even many of the teachers had the practice of offering special exam preparation courses at their homes for a fee that would guarantee that the students would pass the final examinations in their courses.

As noted earlier, in addition to a commitment to honesty, integrity also involves a concern for the well being of others. In the capital city of one country I visited, I once encountered a man lying on the sidewalk in a busy shopping district. The man was unconscious after having suffered an epileptic seizure. Amazingly, shoppers were indifferently stepping over his body as they busily went about their business. I found a police station across the street in full view of the incident. The policemen thought it was strange that I would seek their cooperation in helping the man find medical assistance. I learned then that human life is not afforded the same value in all cultures. This was an example of a breakdown of care for the well-being of others, which is an aspect of integrity that also has bearing on our economic well-being.

My point in giving these examples of the lack of integrity in some countries is not to shame persons that may have known no other way of life, but it is simply to argue that globalization can have devastating influences on the levels of integrity in our own culture if countermeasures are not adopted. Currently our economy benefits extensively from the perception that our markets are managed with greater integrity than many other markets in the world. Wealthy foreigners often trust our economic system more than they trust their own economic cultures, and so they buy U.S. equities and treasury notes. Imagine what could happen to our economy if this perception were to disappear. The preservation of integrity in our capital markets must therefore be one of our foremost objectives.

The Growth of Materialism

There is an ancient Biblical adage that states that a man's life does not consist in the abundance of his possessions. Unfortunately, this was not well understood by those who committed suicide during the stock market crash of 1929, or by Edwin LeFevre, author of the classic stock trading book *Reminiscences of a Stock Operator*, who subsequently took his own life following several large trading losses. More recently the investor in Madoff's Ponzi scheme was not convinced of this either when he took his own life on learning that he had been defrauded by Madoff of a large fortune. None of these individuals had in place a firewall between their possessions and their self worth. For them self worth and net worth were identical concepts. This is a tragic mistake that is a very real potential threat for all stock traders. Contrary to popular belief, not only are net worth and self worth different constructs, but also wealth and wisdom are different. Part of my motivation in including this chapter is that I feel great compassion for those traders who experience financial stress resulting from the confusion of these concepts, and I would spare them as much pain as possible. I certainly wish to prevent suicidal behavior on the part of those who suffer losses in the market.

In modern society we experience a great deal of pressure to keep up with the Joneses. We are bombarded daily by mass media with messages to the effect that, unless we buy some advertised product, we will continue to be less than beautiful, we will remain behind the times, our intelligence may be called in question, we will lack optimum health, we will be unpopular, and we will miss out on the normal pleasures of life. It is easy to see how we may arrive at a philosophy of life that was aptly summarized on a bumper sticker I saw on the back of a pricey sports car. It said, "He who dies with the most toys wins." The thought was that life is a game with its object being the gathering of material goods. The reality is that material goods not only fail to bring happiness, but they actually bring anxiety regarding how we may be able to maintain them securely. The more expensive and extensive the goods, the greater the anxiety will be. Often, rather than winning friends for us, the acquisition of goods only serves to separate us from those who have less.

There is another ancient Biblical adage that states that the love of money is the root of all evil. We need to recognize that money itself is a neutral commodity that is harmless in itself. It is like education, in that its value depends on how it is used. Rather, the love of money is the real problem posing a threat to integrity and well being. Think of the ultimate fates of many of the winners of windfall fortunes in public lotteries. For many of them, their good fortune has not only moved them into a higher tax bracket, but it has also brought alienation from family, unhappiness, and even divorce, and it has made them the targets of unscrupulous merchants and thieves. Financial gain is not wrong, but the amassing of wealth takes advance preparation to manage the societal responsibilities and opportunities that are associated with wealth. Windfall profits can be destructive of integrity if protective measures are not taken, whether those profits come from public lotteries or from the trading of equities.

The point in this section is that the rise of materialism in our society has a devastating impact on the presence of integrity. To the extent that the highest goal in life becomes the acquisition of wealth and possessions, honesty and concern for the well being of others will be pushed aside as impediments, and integrity will disappear in society.

Failure to Cultivate the Inner Dialogue

In our haste to acquire more wealth, we often fail to allocate sufficient time for lasting inward concerns. To illustrate, let me suggest that individuals and institutions in some ways resemble trees. Just as trees have branches and leaves above ground and roots beneath the ground, we all have public and private personas. The part above ground is in full public view and constitutes our image seen by others. The part that is hidden beneath the ground is that which upholds and nourishes the superstructure. The underground part of us often needs to be as large and well formed as that part above ground. In harsh and dry environments, the part underground may need to be even larger than the superstructure in order to support life and maintain growth. However, the root system is seldom seen and is even less often admired for what it accomplishes. In addition, unless the root system is firmly established, any strong wind will blow the tree over. We might say that any fierce market correction could have us jumping out of windows if our root system is inadequate. Believe me that I have seen persons who were absolutely terrified about the status of their bank assets or their stock portfolios during inclement weather in the economy. That terror is a sure sign that they have not cultivated the inner dialogue.

Maintaining our private root systems is what I here label "cultivating the inner dialogue." It sounds mystical, but all I mean by this is that we need to take the time to strengthen and expand our hidden spiritual roots in order to prosper in our visible lives. Otherwise, with inadequate root structure, any strong wind of adversity can blow over the entire tree, and that would be the end of the whole trading program. Furthermore, unless we cultivate the inner dialogue, the voice of conscience will become inaudible. There is more to be said about this important matter later. For now, I simply wish to point out that failure to cultivate this inner dialogue, to develop strong spiritual roots, or to build our lives on a strong foundation, can have dire consequences when adversity comes. Integrity is a responding to the voice of conscience, and unless we have cultivated the capacity to hear and respond appropriately to the voice of conscience, integrity will elude us.

Individual, Corporate, and National Indebtedness

Debt can easily become a form of bondage, whether for individuals, corporations or for nations. Some persons might well argue that the very assumption of debt is evidence of a lack of integrity. Stock traders are not immune here because the need for trading capital may predispose them to borrow, to trade on margin, or to leverage excessively. We all seem to be carrying out a kind of juggling act in which our liabilities are balanced against our incomes and assets. Too often, however, it is only when our indebtedness exceeds our ability to repay that we become embarrassed about acquiring debt. Interestingly, Thomas J. Stanley in his bestselling book, *The Millionaire Mind*, concludes from many interviews with American millionaires that the single greatest uniform quality of those he interviewed was an absolute and passionate commitment to integrity. They especially avoided excessive consumption and the perils of debt. The conclusion reached was that, "You cannot enjoy life if you are addicted to consumption and the use of credit."

Heavy debt obligations, in addition to becoming a kind of slavery, predispose people to a "victim" mentality. By this I mean that debtors can develop a mindset that argues that "the system" has taken advantage of them and therefore they are justified in getting revenge on the system. This mentality has many expressions—all the way from shoplifting to credit card fraud to tax evasion. In the marketplace we see it when traders feel justified in shorting companies out of existence or in running Ponzi schemes or in carrying out "pump-and-dump" strategies. Their feeling is that, since they have not been the recipients of good will, they are not about to show it to others. Indebtedness then, if not a cause of the decline of integrity, becomes at least one of its most acute symptoms.

POSSIBLE SOLUTIONS TO THE PROBLEMS THAT PROMOTE THE EROSION OF INTEGRITY

It is often easier to identify problems than it is to find their solutions. It is also said to be easier to fix the blame for a problem than it is to fix the problem itself. If we can become aware of the seriousness of the problem of integrity decline, and can begin to understand some of its root causes, then perhaps we will find the courage to take the medicine that could effect a cure. In the preceding paragraphs, I have listed six potential causes of the decline of integrity in society. For each of those causes we need to examine possible cures.

Adopting Historical Judeo-Christian Values

If, as I believe, secularization constitutes a genuine threat to integrity and the resulting well being of our economy, then we do well to examine some alternatives. Minimally we need to respect and emulate persons who have adopted historic Judeo-Christian values. Otherwise, we risk the possibility that predatory practices will continue to weigh on our economy. I often think of the example of an African brush fire, where lions and gazelles can be seen running shoulder to shoulder to flee the common threat. It has been said that a greater fear drives out all lesser fears. My view is that a modicum of the fear of God is the best cure for predatory practices and social incivility that seem so common in our culture today. It can mark the beginning of true wisdom. The founding fathers of this country were not far off when they claimed that Western democracy required a heavy dose of religious values in order to survive. The need is for people to be guided by principles that will be exercised in their secret moments when they are not in public view, and this is the essence of integrity. Certainly such values would spell the end of Ponzi schemes and all other forms of corruption in the marketplace.

In this connection, I was amazed to learn that, during the religious revivals that took place in Britain at the beginning of the last century, it was not uncommon for the citizenry to hold "white glove" ceremonies (Riss 1988). A white glove ceremony was one in which local police constables were called in and each was presented with a pair of white gloves. Then they were gratefully dismissed from service. The reality of the situation was that, because of the religious revival, the jails were all empty and no one any longer had a predisposition to commit crime. Can you imagine the boost to our own economy that could result from such a development if it became pervasive? It would also constitute a renaissance of integrity. And our economy would no longer suffer from the consequences of the corrupt behavior that currently poses such a serious threat to the survival of capitalism. Of course, this kind of sociological renewal is not something that can be staged, but its historical occurrence serves to verify the value of religious influences for the restoration of integrity in society.

Developing Community Relationships

If urbanization is indeed a threat to the cultivation of integrity as I believe it to be, we may have any one of several approaches to counteract this threat. The most obvious solution consisting of moving to a small town or a rural setting may not be an option for most city dwellers. However, there is a lot of data to suggest that such a move could improve their health, happiness, and longevity. But if this is not possible for you, one alternative approach is to cultivate a local network of close friends. The object here is to promote accountability, cultivate trust, and demonstrate trustworthiness. The idea is that such a network of interpersonal relationships presents a climate for the cultivation of integrity. This worthwhile endeavor requires more than casual acquaintanceships. We cannot justify trust in persons whom we do not know. I am advocating that we make the effort to get to know our neighbors, our bankers, our brokers, our grocers, our physicians, our coworkers, and even our auto mechanics at a personal level. We are really not experiencing community relationships unless we encounter friends whenever we go about our daily business. It is useful to this end to visit with those persons with whom we have regular business and to record their names and phone numbers or e-mail addresses in order to establish and maintain meaningful relationships with them. In this endeavor, we need to remember that the goal is not to cultivate popularity and an inordinate number of relationships and thus actually fall prey to the delusion that bigger is better. I believe it was Emerson who wrote that anyone who by the end of his lifetime has cultivated five deep and meaningful friendships is a wealthy person indeed.

In an effort to follow my own advice, I had an interesting encounter with a bank manager in a small town near my home. On learning that he had always lived in this small town—apart from a short stay at a nearby university—I mentioned that he must like his town or he might easily have moved elsewhere. He replied that he liked his town well enough, but there was one thing he did not appreciate. While he was away at university, he had developed a strong appetite for alcoholic beverages. Because this small Southern town was in the Bible belt and because everyone there knew everyone else, there was no way that he could go to the local grocery store and purchase a case of beer without news of his purchase getting back to friends and family. Therefore, he was forced to drive to a nearby city to make his purchases. I reminded him that he must be aware of the advantages of his situation. For example, many of the people in his town did not even find it necessary to lock the doors of their homes. And a mugging in the streets was virtually unheard of. I cite this whimsical example to highlight some of the differences between urban and rural life, and the bearing these differences can have on the presence of integrity. As an aside, it is interesting to note that this young man's stay at university did not appear to make any positive contribution to the existence of integrity in his community.

There is a small island approximately three miles off the coast of Mainland China known as Quemoy or Kinmen. Because this island is a province of Taiwan, during the Cold War it was constantly under threat of invasion from China and was often attacked and bombed. The island became well fortified and many of its beaches were mined. But its greatest defense stemmed from the fact that all of its citizens were acquainted with one another. No one could infiltrate the island without being recognized as an intruder. There is a certain safety that grows out of meaningful interrelatedness.

If urbanization and growth in the sizes of corporations can be perceived as being problematic for the cultivation of integrity, there is another step that can be taken that may help to promote accountability and trust. Wherever possible, it can be advantageous to choose smaller institutions over larger institutions. This holds true for schools, universities, churches, synagogues, banks, retail stores, and many other institutions. To the extent that bigger is not necessarily better in societal institutions, the implications for behavior should be obvious. We should often make a conscious choice to go small.

Promoting Integrity Abroad

If globalization can be perceived to be a threat to integrity, then why not use globalization to export integrity rather than to import corrupt business practices? To some extent this is already happening. Whenever a foreign company wishes to be listed on any U.S. stock exchange as an ADR (American Depository Receipt), the company must provide disclosures and satisfy American accounting standards. The company becomes regulated by the same rules and standards applicable to any U.S. company. As you can imagine, there are immense economic advantages to be gained from complying with those rules and standards and becoming listed on any U.S. stock exchange. In this way integrity can be exported to some countries where it may not commonly exist in the public marketplace.

Beyond that example, it is often possible to require the signing of a mutual code of ethical practices before entering into international business relationships. Such a code could specify enforceable penalties for bribery, fraud and other related corrupt business practices—including such penalties as the firing of those who engage in such practices. The premise here is that trust must be maintained in order for business partnerships to prosper. As it becomes apparent that integrity is a recognized ingredient in such prosperity, other companies will adopt similar standards.

To the extent that integrity reflects care and concern for the well being of others, U.S. companies engaged in international business partnerships should continually be on the lookout for charitable opportunities to promote societal improvements in the countries where they are partnering. The provision of jobs to international employees is one obvious benefit, but beyond that there may be opportunities to provide scholarships, medical benefits, infrastructure, and social services.

Valuing and Cultivating Simplicity of Lifestyle

Materialism is a terrible threat to happiness as well as to integrity. Our very possessions can bring with them a kind of bondage. The most obvious way to gain victory over possessions we do not need is to give them away to people who actually do need them. If that is a daunting prospect, then you may be in material danger. Let me give a simple illustration to explain.

Near my home there are many artificial ponds that have been created by landowners for a variety of valid utilitarian reasons. Some are for irrigation and some are for recreation, and some may be just for aesthetic charm. In most cases the ponds were created by damming up streams or small rivers. However, if the ponds do not have a spillway to pass on the flowing water, they soon tend to become stagnant and they breed mosquitoes, algae, and disease. They lose their charm and may even develop a stench. My point is that stock traders also must create artificial ponds of capital for utilitarian purposes. They gather investment capital from those streams that may happen to come their way. But the goal of trading should not be to make a large lake that swallows up all the land in sight. We also require

TABLE 15.1 Levels of Personal Consumption

Levels	Descriptions	Ratings
1	Consumption Exceeds Needs and Income Level	Total Failure
2	Consumption Exceeds Needs but Remains Within Income Level	Poor
3	Consumption Is Limited to Needs and Remains Within Income Level	Average
4	Consumption Is Limited to Needs and Remains Within Income Level With Some Excess Income Distributed to the Needs of Others	Good
5	Consumption Is Limited to Needs and Remains Within Income Level With All Excess Income Distributed to the Needs of Others	Excellent

a capital spillway that passes on the flow to those beyond who also have needs for water. In this case the spillway should be some kind of managed charitable giving or the sharing of resources with others. Otherwise our assets can become like the Dead Sea that can no longer support life. Ideally, once the pond has served its intended purpose and satisfied our needs, the spillway should match the volume of the inflow.

In this connection, I once had a conversation with a very wealthy person about the need to live within one's means. He proudly announced to me that the money he spent on his personal consumption was a smaller portion of his income than was the case for many of his friends. I commended him for living within his means, but reminded him that his income was much larger than that of his friends, and therefore he should compare his consumption level to his needs rather than to his income level. In retrospect, Table 15.1 might have been helpful to explain what I meant by ideal levels of personal consumption.

Of course, in all such discussions the identification of "needs" is beyond my wisdom to specify or define for other persons. Distinguishing between needs and wants is a lifetime pursuit. It may be useful for us to travel to third-world countries to see what constitutes needs in other environments. I have found many cultures in which maintaining a good credit rating or owning a car or a credit card did not constitute a need. One way to evaluate needs is to consider whether the object of the need is required for the fulfillment of one's life goals or objectives. For example, to fulfill my calling in life I may need to show up for work. This requires that I have a car, decent clothing, nutrition and sleep. At the same time, it is not necessary that my car, clothing, food, and housing be of the most expensive variety. In fact, over-expenditures on such items may actually be counterproductive to my life goals.

Ordering Our Private Worlds

Earlier I suggested that the failure to cultivate an inner dialogue was another source of the decline of integrity, and it was a recipe for disaster. We need to take time to cultivate our hidden spiritual roots lest some unanticipated economic storm with all of its fury should blow over the trees of our lives. Gordon MacDonald, in his bestselling book, *Ordering Your Private World* (2003), shares vital truths for living that came to him as the result of his experiencing the tragedy of a nervous breakdown. He tells how he became too busy maintaining his public image to care for more important concerns. The terrible chaotic pressures of urgent matters crowded out the essential quiet moments he needed to order his private world. He compared his life to a sinkhole that was caused by hollowness underneath that one day brought his whole life crashing down. I suppose that stock traders and fund managers are especially susceptible to this same syndrome. With our avid attention to net worth, we often neglect more lasting matters of self worth. This neglect is a proven formula for allowing the voice of conscience and the standards of integrity to fade from our lives.

My own prescription for this problem is to establish and maintain priorities that favor lasting concerns over passing matters, eternal things over temporal things. For example, family relationships are usually more lasting that other personal relationships, so they need to be given priority. We often can only fully understand who we are and what our gifts can be when we are in close relationship and in regular communication with our families. Such relationships are also empowering.

Truth and beauty also seem to go together hand in hand as lasting preoccupations that can be empowering as well. But it takes time to cultivate the capacity to see and hear the truth and beauty all around us. The intricate and elegant patterns in nature speak of a creative design that encourages people to see ordered beauty in market motions and stimulates them to explore and learn more about practical market empowerment. For example, whenever I gaze at Mendeleev's periodic chart of the elements I am moved with awe at the creative beauty and mathematical design that predisposes all of the elements to function in predictable patterns. There is truth and beauty there that has an infinite number of practical applications. It is at the same time a masterpiece of art and a library of truth. To find similar patterns in the arena of stock trading and other activities of life also has great practical and aesthetic value.

An elegant formula like Einstein's familiar $E = mc^2$ is a similar expression of truth and beauty. It defines dependable relationships in a concise and empowering way. A simple regression equation that shows an ordered relationship between cash flow and share-price movement also shows truth and beauty with demonstrable practical power. Perhaps this is why I personally love mathematical trading systems that employ formulas to convey truth and represent artistic patterns of predictable outcomes. However, I confess that for me the greatest and most beautiful mathematical formula of all is found in the words of the ancient epistle, "Draw nigh to God, and He will draw nigh to you." There is awesome symmetry, truth, and beauty in that expression that has great power to produce practical outcomes and to cause integrity to flourish in our society. It is also a proven way to bring order out of chaos in our personal lives and to value the eternal over the temporal.

Getting Out of Debt's Enslavement

Getting out from under the bondage of debt can be one of the most liberating experiences in life. I have read that some skiers have avoided perishing in an avalanche of snow merely by maintaining a kind of backstroke arm motion that kept them near the surface of the descending snow. In the same way, a few reasoned actions may help to promote our own survival in an economic downturn or in the descending crush of unanticipated expenses.

My first suggestion is that we turn off the faucets of unnecessary expenditures. We can save hundreds of dollars monthly by simple steps such as replacing incandescent lighting with fluorescent lighting, by conserving water usage with proper shower heads and toilet mechanisms, by shopping for cheaper telecommunications packages, by regularly replacing heating filters so that our heating and air conditioning becomes less costly, and by limiting shopping purchases to items on prepared lists of actual needs. Some telecommunications charges are especially destructive of our well being. For example, by insisting on large screen and high definition television sets, we not only pay more for our viewing time, but we are also drawn into wasting more of our precious time commodity on unnecessary viewing. Another destructive habit comes in the form of our insistence on buying new. For example, we can save thousands of dollars by limiting automobile purchases to cars that have already suffered the heavy depreciation costs of the first three years of usage. And it may not be good business to fly business or first class when coach seats are available.

We should shop for sales and never make purchases on credit, and we should avoid credit card debt like the plague. It is a good idea to destroy all of your credit cards and use a single debit card for purchases. When we buy on credit we are effectively paying a much higher price for all of our purchases. Not only do we pay interest on outstanding debt, but the credit card lenders invariably charge exorbitant penalties if we are ever late in paying. By waiting a few more months to make necessary furniture or appliance purchases until after we have cash in hand and we are able to find a discount sale, we can save hundreds of dollars and maintain great peace of mind. It is also a good idea to take our children with us when we shop for groceries. When presented with an array of possible choices, we can point out which items are cheapest and then ask them to choose which items they believe we should buy. Of course, children should be allowed to experience how the money they save can be made to work for them in productive investments.

The issue of delay of gratification is an immensely important concern. Educational experiments have been conducted with children to find a correlation between the ability to postpone gratification, such as that of eating candy, and their actual learning achievement in the classroom. Children who could forego the consumption of a small piece of candy on their desks before them in anticipation of a much greater amount of candy as a later reward were able to achieve more in study. It turns out that the ability to delay gratification is one of the best predictors of learning success. In the realm of stock trading I am certain that there is also a strong positive correlation between the ability to postpone transactions until more beneficial prices appear, and eventual trading success. There may also be a positive relationship between trading success and the ability to avoid trading on margin. Certainly there is also a positive correlation between trading success and the ability to postpone buying stocks until favorable market trends occur.

At a broader level, I was captivated to learn that there was a law in ancient Israel stipulating that every 50 years there should be a year of jubilee. What this meant effectively was that all debts had to be cancelled once every 50 years. Thus nearly every person in society had the opportunity of experiencing freedom from debt at least once in a generation. Beyond that, predatory lenders had to release their grip on the poor people in society periodically. Undoubtedly those lenders were still able to arrange schedules of payment in such a way that they made a profit. However, one cannot help but consider how beneficial such a custom would be for our own national economy if there could ever be a way to implement similar practices.

SUMMARY

In this chapter it was maintained that the systematic erosion of integrity is the greatest single threat to our economic well being and to capitalism in general. The underlying premise of this chapter has been that, unless we realize the seriousness of this threat, we are unlikely to take the steps required to defend against it. We have examined six different potential sources of the decline in integrity and have proposed several ways in which these influences may be overcome. The sources of the erosion of integrity were identified as secularization, urbanization, globalization, materialism, inadequate spiritual development, and growing indebtedness. The fact that this chapter is a comparatively large one is a reflection of the fact that the author considers the practice of maintaining moral integrity in the market-place to be of paramount importance.

CHAPTER 16

Random Walk or Rational Wager

Y ou probably did not get far in the reading of this book before you
detected my own personal bias concerning the ordered predictability
of capital markets. Surprisingly, not everyone shares this view—not
even every economist, as you have probably already discovered. The bril-
liant economist John Maynard Keynes (1921, 1936), for example, wrestled
long and hard over the concept of predictability and ultimately came out of
this contest with the belief that ordered patterns in past market phenomena
did not permit mathematical probability statements about future market
phenomena. Keynes exhibited a certain disdain for mathematical formulations of economic phenomena. He called the arithmetic mean a very inadequate axiom (Bernstein 1996), and the Newtonian notion of "regression to
the mean" was loathsome to him. Keynes also condemned the assumption
of classical economists that human nature is reasonable as "flimsily based
[and] disastrously mistaken."

Another famous economist who opposed attempts to quantify and predict economic outcomes using mathematical methods adopted from the
physical sciences was Frank Knight of the University of Chicago (1964). He
bitterly attacked what he considered, "the near pre-emption of [economics]
by people who take a point of view which seems to me untenable, and in
fact shallow, namely the transfer into the human sciences of the concepts
and products of the sciences of nature." Interestingly, although Keynes and
Knight shared disdain for quantitative approaches to economic forecasting,
they remained professional adversaries throughout most of their careers.
The point that I am attempting to make by citing them is that not every

economist is sanguine about the possibilities of constructing successful mathematical models for the trading of stocks.

Similarly, random walk theorists maintain that stock prices move in unpredictable ways. Much of the impetus for this view was drawn from a study conducted by Professor Harry Roberts of the University of Chicago in the 1950s (Stigler 1986). Roberts found that real price movements of stocks and a series of random numbers he generated by computer were indistinguishable. He concluded from this limited data set that stock market behavior was random and unpredictable. Perhaps his conclusions suffered from the failure to recognize that there can be a grand normal distribution that is composed of identifiable subsets of data that depart from the normalcy of the total. Ironically, Random Walk Theorists, who also disavow the efficacy of attempts to predict market behavior by scientific means, require the efficient market hypothesis (EMH) to justify their theory (Peters 1991). The EMH maintains that there is a kind of equilibrium in the equities markets such that prices similarly regress to a median point established by offsetting pressures of supply and demand at any given time. In this way random walk theorists also rely on a similar scientific concept derived from Newtonian physics—that any natural system left alone will seek equilibrium. Perhaps this concept even has roots dating back to Aristotle, when he said that nature abhors a vacuum.

For a long time it has seemed to me that academicians generally belong to one of two main groups. There are those who propound theories like young children making miniature boats to sail in a pond. And there are those who debunk theories like young children throwing rocks at the boats that are sailing in the pond. Occasionally there are those who do both, building their own boats and then throwing rocks at the other boats. A cursory inspection of the doctoral dissertations of any major university will support this view. Among these academic boat builders are both deductive and inductive thinkers. The deductive thinkers tend to concoct a theory and then go looking for data to confirm their theory. Perhaps they are like children who build a boat and then go looking for a place to sail it. The inductive thinkers tend to gather data and then attempt to propose a theory to explain the patterns in the data or a model to capture the practical implications of the data patterns. Possibly these inductive thinkers are the ones who first find a beautiful pond and then try to imagine and construct boats that will sail there. Ultimately, the most important concern should be that durable boats and beautiful ponds eventually do come together. For my own part, I have found a beautiful market pond and have subsequently been constructing reliable trading systems that I trust will not quickly capsize whether as the result of flying rocks or vicissitudes of the pond itself.

In any case, I am not at all troubled by these mathematical and scientific controversies because, as you will see later in this chapter, I regularly rely on concepts such as regression to the mean on almost a daily basis to extract profits from the stock market. However, because the notion of predictability is so central to the thesis of this book, I need to discuss it more thoroughly and explore with you its meanings, its promises, and its limitations.

PREDICTABILITY AND PROBABILITY

Webster (1979 edition) defines *predictable* as "capable of being foretold on the basis of observation, experience, or scientific reason," and the infinitive form *to predict* is defined as "to declare in advance." The definition of *probable* has arrived at its present-day meaning a bit more circuitously. It has come to us from the Latin *probabilis*, meaning to test, approve, or prove. Originally it did not have its current definition, "supported by evidence strong enough to support presumption but not proof." Nor did *probability* mean as it does today "the (mathematical) likelihood that a given event will occur." When Galileo wrote that the theory of Copernicus that the earth revolves around the sun was "improbable," he did not mean that he disagreed with that theory or that its veracity was unlikely, but he meant instead that the theory did not meet with the approval of society in general (Hacking 1975). It was not until after the foundational work by Pascal and Fermat on gambling odds in the 1650s that current views about probability became widely established. Bernstein (1996) in his superb book on the origin of risk management expressed amazement that probability theory was never developed by the Greeks or the Arabs with their advanced mathematical skills. He attributes the eventual derivation of probability theory to the spread of Christianity and its belief in the orderliness and predictability of a future controlled by a non-capricious Deity. The very use of numbers for purposes of calculation as we know it today was unknown in the West until the appearance of Fibonacci's book entitled *Liber Abaci* in Italy in 1202. In tribute to Fibonacci, the Fibonacci ratio, *0.618*, appears at the bottom of the front cover of this book. As was mentioned earlier in this book, this ratio is of great significance today to certain technical traders and adherents to Elliott Wave Theory (Frost and Prechter 1990).

What does it mean to say that some market phenomena are predictable or probable? When pollsters predict the election of any candidate to public office, they do it within a certain margin of error. They cannot say for sure what is going to happen in the future, but they are able to quantify the likelihood of certain voting outcomes within specifiable limits of accuracy. Pollsters' predictions of election outcomes are based on sentiments expressed by potential voters in the period immediately prior to the election. If enough potential voters are canvassed to constitute a representative sample of the general voting population, and if those potential voters are found to favor one candidate by a sufficient margin, and if the gathering of the poll is close enough in time to the actual election, and if the individual responses are trustworthy, then the pollsters can claim with reasonable certainty that this most favored candidate will win the election. A similar process is followed when mathematical systems are designed to pick stocks that are considered likely to succeed and rise in price in the near future.

Consider the elements of this process. Observations are made of past market phenomena. If those observations are timely, repetitive, sufficient in number, accurately gathered, and representative of future phenomena to be predicted, then it may be possible to predict the same future phenomena within certain limits of confidence or levels of likelihood that we call probabilities. Von Mises (1957) in his classic work on the nature of probability states that there must be a *collective* of repetitive observations of the same phenomenon in order to make probability statements of the likelihood of its reoccurrence. He notes that no one can estimate the probability of a single individual's death because it is a non-repetitive phenomenon. However, by gathering data over many persons in the same age cohort, gender group, occupation, and health category, insurance companies can successfully set life insurance premiums at a level that will indemnify against the risk of dying on the part of any one person in the same group. When we predict with a certain level of confidence that the stock of a particular company or that a general market index average is going to rise or fall, it has both similarities to and differences from the example of the work of the insurance actuary. The process is similar in that it is based on the observation of repetitions in past phenomena, whether in the individual company stock price movement, in the price movement of stocks having important characteristics shared with the stock of focus, or in patterns of movement of the general market index of reference. However, the process is different in that, in the case of individual stocks, we are not predicting that the company will die, which would be a non-repetitive phenomenon, but we are predicting that its share price will rise or fall, which has happened many times in the past and has certainly happened across the cohort of stocks of reference.

THE LIMITS OF PREDICTABILITY

Some events in life are indisputably predictable. For example, given the right input data and measurement equipment, someone can predict the time of the rising of the sun within a nanosecond at any temperate zone location and can verify the accuracy of the prediction, regardless of wind velocity, temperature, or seasonality. However, this prediction is still subject to a small probability of error because the sun might implode or a comet might strike the earth and alter its rotational cycle or the shape of the horizon. But for all practical purposes, the prediction would be highly reliable. Why is it that we are so confident in this prediction? It is because we have so much past data demonstrating the dependability of this outcome. All such mathematical estimates of the probability of future events are based on patterns of occurrence in the data observed in the past. Admittedly, not all events in life are as predictable as the rising and setting of the sun.

What about human behavior? Is it also predictable? This is a relevant question because market movement is driven by human buying and selling behavior that reflects human sentiment at any given time. A strict psychological behaviorist might claim that, given enough information, all human behavior is predictable. My own belief is that some human behavior is predictable and some is not. For example, it is highly likely that every reader of this book is going to ingest food, breathe air, and sleep sometime in the next week. That is predictable human behavior. Furthermore, if we had enough information about the numbers of dog owners at every location on earth, it would be possible within quantifiable limits of error to predict how many persons would be out walking dogs at any given time. However, I would defy anyone to predict whether I will walk my own dog sometime within the next 30 minutes. You could say that some aspects of dog-walking behavior are predictable and some are not—especially when time limits are imposed. An even more basic question is whether anyone really cares enough to pay money to know how many people are walking their dogs at any given time. Aside from some company that manufactures dog leashes, there probably are not many persons interested in that piece of information. Whereas, information about an approaching hurricane or an impending stock market rally could be of vital interest to many affected persons. These considerations raise questions about the kinds of behavior that may be predicted, the value of predicting such behaviors, the cost and accuracy with which the predictions can be made, and the effects of time constraints on the predictions. These are all critical concerns for the stock market trader.

Von Mises (1957) has asserted that the theory of probability, or what in practice we may call the use of inferential statistics, is an exact science. However, we know that it has some limitations of a mathematical nature. For example, those inferential statistics that are parametric in nature assume that the data in the population of phenomena to be predicted or estimated are both normally and independently distributed. This means in practice that we would hope that fluctuations in the stock market would have a distribution approximating that of a normal bell curve and that price movements of individual stocks would be independent of the movements of other stocks in the same population. Unfortunately, we know that neither of these assumptions is perfectly satisfied by stock market data. For example, variation in market averages often exceeds the predicted bounds. And we know that individual stocks, with a few notable exceptions that are especially evident among microcap stocks, often rise and fall in tandem and in positive correlation with major market averages. We often hear it said about the movements of prices of individual stocks along with major averages of the stock market, that "a rising tide lifts all boats." These irregularities impose constraints on the predictability of stock market phenomena. In my own work, I recognize these constraints and attempt to get around them in various ways. First, with respect to irregularities in variability, I attempt to recalibrate the ranges of variation as they shift. For example, because I rely on the CBOE Volatility Index as a timing indicator, in seasons when volatility makes dramatic departures from normal expected ranges, I shift the expected ranges accordingly. With regard to the lack of independence in the price movements of individual stocks, I attempt to overcome and actually harness this irregularity by being fully invested in the market only in favorable seasons when my timing indicators suggest that the overall market averages are moving upward. In other words, I go with the flow.

I suspect that Keynes, when he observed the irregularities in variation of market phenomena, decided that such phenomena were therefore too unpredictable for the application of mathematical and scientific methods of prediction. In effect, he saw the data of market variation like ocean waves beating upon the shore. He understood that some economists were approximating these waves in their probability function models. But then he saw that the occasional tsunami defied predictability in all of those models. Perhaps he wished to spare us from the devastation of the unpredictable economic tsunami. For my own part, I refuse to abandon all attempts to enjoy the seashore just because it is likely that an occasional unanticipated tsunami will strike. Furthermore, I suspect that even tsunamis have some predictability, if only for a few minutes or hours in advance rather than for longer periods of days or weeks as may be the case with hurricanes or cycles in the CBOE Volatility Index. To the extent that the time focus of prediction is narrowly defined, the dangers of unanticipated economic tsunamis may be minimized. Such a narrow time focus may also be sufficient for stock trading purposes.

FOLLOWING THE NUMBERS OR FOLLOWING THE GURUS

A lot of our trading behavior will depend on whether we have greater trust in the numbers or in the market gurus. Relying on mathematical trading systems is a radically different approach from relying on the opinions of investment professionals. Recently I have read that a non-specialist has been able to develop a regression equation for predicting the quality of wines before the grapes are even harvested (Ayres 2007). The formula takes into consideration the annual rainfall and the average summer temperature in the Bordeaux region of France. It turns out that there is a high positive correlation between low rainfall amounts and high summer temperatures and the quality of wines produced each year. As you can imagine, the wine tasters association is not pleased with the resulting growing reliance on formulaic predictions of wine quality. They insist that they are the final judges of the quality of wines, and no mathematical formula can replace their expertise. Unfortunately for them, the wine must age at least six months in wooden casks and ideally even several years beyond that before the experts' judgments can be applied. And even beyond this timeliness advantage for the regression equation over the wine tasters, it has been found that the regression equation is often more accurate than the palates of the wine tasters. This is one of many possible examples of the triumph of numbers over the judgments of gurus.

In yet another field of endeavor, professional baseball, a mathematician has developed a successful formula to predict professional batting averages while the players are still amateurs. His formula takes into consideration more than just the number of hits in relation to the number of at-bat opportunities. He was able also to incorporate the number of walks, in consideration of the fact that pitchers will often walk dangerous batters. As it happened, the formula has been a great aid in the recruitment of talented professional baseball players, and the formula has even outperformed professional scouts who often travel great distances and stay in cheap motels in order to observe the amateur players in actual games. Again, you can imagine that the scouts might understandably take exception to this innovation since they have many years of training and experience. Here is another example where mathematical formulas have routinely outperformed the judgments of professional experts.

In the realm of stock trading there are also a great many expert investment advisers and professional stock pickers. It could easily be perceived as threatening to them if a mathematical formula could be developed to rank order stocks for acquisition or sale in a reliable manner. If such a mathematical trading system could be found to outperform the gurus consistently, there might be fewer persons standing in line for trading seminars, or consulting investment planners, or faithfully viewing TV experts' stock-picking programs. Of course, the development and correct use of such a trading system would be a tall order; but, if sufficient dependable data on past stock performance can be applied to estimate future stock price movement in a reasonably accurate manner, then this would certainly be within the realm of possibility. At least that is the position that is advocated in this book. And that is what has been attempted here.

In my own personal experience as a social scientist, I frequently encountered disagreements over whether to trust the scores of university entrance examinations over the impressions of professional interviewers. No one has argued that the test scores always perfectly reflect the achievement and aptitude of the students, and regrettably some admission mistakes certainly do occur when such tests become the only basis for admission. But most educators agree that the use of test scores has made the process of university admission fairer than it was in the days before such tests were given. In bygone eras it was not uncommon to admit students for university study solely on the basis of whether or not they came from upstanding families. I have subsequently become so convinced of the value of admissions testing that I could wish that all elected officials were required to pass a battery of tests before they could be allowed to enter government service. Admittedly such tests would require careful design to contain relevant questions and to discourage a disproportionate tendency towards cheating. It should be acknowledged in this example, however, that tests lose predictive validity with time. Tests that manage to predict first year grade-point averages of incoming students tend to lose some of their predictive accuracy with each successive year of university study. For this reason most universities also require that test scores be current within six months before they can be deemed valid for university entrance decisions. This relationship between timeliness and accuracy raises important issues that will be revisited later in this chapter.

There is also a subliminal tension between academic researchers who advocate quantitative research methods and those who advocate using "qualitative" research methods exclusively. Perhaps some of the antipathy of qualitative researchers towards quantitative research has to do with a general distrust of mathematics. In fact however, quantitative and qualitative research methods do have a lot in common. Both approaches attempt to learn from observations of data. Both have established systems for the collection and analysis of the data. Both have techniques for establishing the reliability of the conclusions of analysis. However, there are several important differences. For one, quantitative researchers use statistical methods to generalize their findings from a subset of the observable data to the larger population from which their sample of observations has been drawn. Quantitative researchers speak in terms of mathematical probabilities that their generalizations and conclusions will hold true beyond the limited sphere of observations made. In this way they are making a kind of prediction that similar outcomes will take place in future observations and they are quantifying their level of certainty or uncertainty about their generalizations. You can imagine how this can relate to mathematical predictions about the stock market and about the price movements of individual stocks. Observations have been made in the past that are being used to estimate within quantifiable bounds of probability what is likely to happen in the future.

In this connection, I remember once being invited as a keynote speaker to an academic conference that was focused on research methods in the field of linguistics. To my chagrin, I soon discovered that I was the only quantitative researcher who had been invited. I considered the possibility that there was an agenda by the qualitative research organizers to discredit quantitative research methods, and that would have been easier to accomplish when there were fewer voices in opposition. However, I was pleased to discover early on that everyone was gracious and tolerant and no one in the audience threw anything. During the discussion period at the end of the program it occurred to me to ask a question that had been bothering me for a long time. I asked the qualitative researchers how they knew when their students had mastered their methods since they did not believe in objective tests and quantitative measures. I explained that when my own students had completed the requisite semesters of formal study, I could give them an examination and could know immediately whether they had gained sufficient knowledge and skill in the methods of quantitative research to be certified as competent. And if they failed the examination, I could even estimate the amount of additional study that might be required for them to master the subject matter.

There was a long silent pause after my question, and it appeared for a time that no answer would be forthcoming. Finally one of the most knowledgeable participants replied that his students were required to serve an internship under his direction. At the end of their internship they were certified in much the same way that an airplane pilot is certified after he has had the prescribed number of hours of flying time. I found that answer honest and insightful. His approach to evaluation ensured his status as a guru and a gatekeeper to his profession, but it did not appear to me to guarantee the learning mastery of his students. My own approach to evaluation did not ensure my guru and gatekeeper status, but by focusing on the numbers it did assure the learning mastery of my students. In fairness, whenever I board an airplane, I am thankful the pilot has been certified as having completed the requisite flying time under authoritative supervision, but I always find myself hoping that this internship was also accompanied by an abundance of aptitude and objectively measured learning achievement. In the case of stock trading, I always find myself hoping that traders will be able to do the math and not merely to follow the advice of experts.

The point of these examples is that stock trading is also a realm of professional activity in which there may well be room for mathematical models to at least challenge the authority of stock-picking gurus. The result of reliance on mathematical trading systems is likely also to be more consistently accurate than strict reliance on the experts, at the same time that it is unlikely to promote the guru status of any trader. To the extent that mathematical models can be accurate and feasible to apply, they can be extremely useful, liberating, and profitable.

THE ACCURACY AND USE OF MATHEMATICAL MODELS

In the late 1990s there was a hedge fund that was often in the news, and the news often reflected a measure of awe at the sheer magnitude of the fund and its profitability. The name of the Fund was Long-Term Capital Management, which was founded in 1994 by John Merriwether, and among the members of its board of directors were Myron Scholes and Robert C. Merton, two Nobel-Prize-winning economists who gained that distinction for their development of the Black-Scholes Model for the pricing of derivatives. Because of the success of their mathematical models, these traders were able to leverage their vast holdings in derivatives markets and bond markets and thereby make billions of dollars. However, there came several days in 1998 when the volatility of the markets exceeded the predictions of their formulas. In a word, their mathematical models failed. In a very short time their losses ran into the billions of dollars and they began desperately to seek backing from wealthy individual investors like George Soros. By this time, however, their losses exceeded the ability and willingness of individual investors to come to their rescue. In the end a consortium of banks was able to close out their liability in order to keep the derivatives markets afloat. Did their experience indicate that mathematical models are never appropriate for use in equities trading? I think not. At issue were the accuracy and the use of their particular mathematical models—not to mention the integrity of their business practices. In the end the participating banking institutions were able to close out all of the positions of LTCM at a profit by the year 2000.

In hindsight, there were two steps that could have averted the entire crisis. First of all, it turns out that the LTCM mathematical models had been promulgated through the backtesting of market data going only five years into the past. Had their backtesting extended several decades into the past, it is likely that their models could have had appropriate timeliness to capture at least some of the volatility they had underestimated. In the second place, had they been much more moderate in their use of leverage, it is also likely that the fund's losses would not have exceeded the reach of its assets. It is interesting in light of the previous chapter on morality in the marketplace that these two mistakes could be said to be reduced to the ethical problems of laziness (failure to do sufficient backtesting) and greed (excessive leveraging). In fairness to the fund managers, they may have believed that the preceding five years of market data were more representative of future market trends than were the data before that time, so that their failure to do sufficient backtesting may not have been simply the result of laziness. And they may have considered that their use of leverage was within acceptable bounds given the supposed accuracy of their models, so that the appearance of excessive leveraging may not have been the result of greed. However, it is hard for me to imagine that their leveraging in excess of a 25-to-1 ratio was not an expression of greed.

The matter of timeliness of market data is a concern that I promised earlier to revisit. Just as the accuracy of achievement testing for university admission has time constraints, the accuracy of any stock-selection model also has time constraints. These time constraints have both a forward and a backward reach. In the case of achievement testing, the test data cannot be too old and outdated or it will lose validity for estimating university success. This is the backward reach of time constraints. At the same time, even current achievement test data cannot be used to predict success much beyond the first year of university study because too many factors may encroach upon prediction accuracy. This is the forward reach of time constraints. In the case of designing stock-selection models, the backward reach of time constraints dictates that the data upon which the models are based must be sufficiently current and sufficiently representative of possible trends. This is why in my own models technical data are updated each day and fundamental data are updated every month or so. The forward reach of time constraints explains why the stock recommendations themselves are updated each day and why no buy-and-hold strategies can ever be supported by this approach. The models simply do not work in most cases to tell us much about what is going to happen with individual stocks beyond a few weeks into the future. Fortunately, a lot of predictive accuracy is gained by adding macro-market timing indicators. This is because most stocks have positive betas, or in other words, because they tend to move in the same direction as the overall market.

PREDICTABLE MARKET PHENOMENA

As you might suspect, traders have expended a lot of time and effort in search of predictable market phenomena. For example, Rudd and Clasing (1982) documented several kinds of phenomena where disequilibria existed in the stock market. They labeled these phenomena the January effect, the PE effect, and the low-capitalization effect. It turns out that there is a measurable and dependable tendency for market averages to move higher in the month of January. There is also a consistent tendency for stocks with low price-earnings ratios to outperform stocks with higher price-earnings ratios. And they found that small cap and micro cap stocks on average outperformed large cap stocks. If markets maintain constant equilibrium such that no measurable market phenomena can provide any advantage to investors, then these reliable phenomena should not occur. To the extent that they do occur, they pose challenges to the random walk theory and the associated efficient market hypothesis.

In my own trading experience, there are many additional market inefficiencies that result in predictable trading advantages or disequilibria that permit consistent trading gains. I am constantly seeking even more market inefficiencies to enhance profitability of mathematical trading systems. It is because of the existence of such inefficiencies that many stock traders and equity fund managers can achieve returns that regularly surpass the overall market averages. My own list of predictable market inefficiencies that are useful in stock trading and in the construction of mathematical trading systems includes the following examples.

Cash Flow

I have found that stocks of companies with outstanding cash flow and free cash flow regularly outperform stocks of companies with low or negative cash flow, when other considerations are held equal. Because exchange-listed companies are required to report cash flow information, it is possible to capitalize on this information in a consistent manner. I found this particular example of market inefficiency through the use of multiple regression analysis.

Momentum

Stocks that are moving up in price with unusual volume, celerity, and regularity are predictably likely to continue their upward motion. This may indicate some sort of self-fulfilling prophecy phenomenon as investors see the regular upward price movement of these stocks and gather confidence that they will continue to perform in the future as they have in the past. Alternatively, it may have to do with earnings predictability within the economic sector of the particular stock, or even with management methodology. The point is that this too is a phenomenon that is sufficiently reliable and predictable so that it can be employed to make trading gains.

EPS/PE Divergence

As described in Chapter 5, when companies show a growth in rolling earnings per share that has outpaced price-earnings ratio movement, there is usually value present that has not yet been priced into the market. This divergence may result from the buying back of shares by the company, as well as from growing revenues or from a cutting of operation costs. It is considered an example of inefficiency because it has not yet been recognized by the market.

Share-Price Regression

When stocks show a sudden large price movement upwards or downwards on a given day, there is a distinct tendency towards panic buying or selling respectively. This panic trading quickly results in overbought or oversold conditions from which the stocks predictably regress shortly thereafter to more reasonable share prices. This is particularly evident when the share price gaps up or gaps down. There is a consistent tendency for individual stocks and major market averages to fill those gaps in subsequent trading. Related to this tendency, there is also an evident tendency for the market to rebound after a series of down days, or to fall back after a series of up days. For example, after three or four consecutive down days, there is a reliable expectation that the market will experience a positive day. These may be considered examples of market inefficiency because there is a strong likelihood that the market will move in the predicted direction in each case.

Volatility and Put/Call Ratios

As demonstrated in Chapter 10, there is a distinct and regular tendency for fluctuations in the CBOE Volatility Index (VIX) and the put/call ratio to reflect levels of investor fear or complacency. These fluctuations can also signal fluctuations in overall equity market trends in a reliable manner. I have shown how those signals can be used to time entry into and exit from the market and thereby to enhance investment profits. In general, when there is excessive volatility it usually constitutes inefficiency because it portends a coming rise in market averages as the volatility subsides.

Analyst Earnings Estimates

I have observed recently that the stock of companies for which analysts have made strong positive estimates of future earnings performance will predictably see share-price gains. It can be shown empirically that companies with strong positive future earnings estimates will on average outperform companies with weak or negative earnings estimates. For this reason, I have given preference to companies with strong future earnings estimates.

These observations are being shared as empirical evidence that market phenomena are not entirely random and that sufficient market inefficiencies exist to permit consistent trading success. In other words, stock selection and market participation can be governed by principles that are much more orderly and predictable than rooms full of monkeys throwing darts at lists of stock symbols. I have noticed that even Malkiel (1996) in his classic scholarly defense of Random Walk Theory concedes that "there is some evidence that stocks with low price-earnings multiples outperform those with high multiples." He also agrees that technical analysis appears to succeed insofar as it can identify stocks with momentum. Thus, he effectively concedes that momentum constitutes yet another kind of inefficiency in the market. He goes on to offer possible reasons why this happens.

Trends might tend to perpetuate themselves for either of two reasons. First, it has been argued that the crowd instinct of mass psychology makes it so. When investors see the price of a speculative favorite going higher and higher, they want to jump on the bandwagon and join the rise. Indeed, the price rise itself helps fuel the enthusiasm in a self-fulfilling prophecy. Each rise in price just whets the appetite and makes investors expect a further rise.

Second, there may be unequal access to fundamental information about a company. When some favorable piece of news occurs, such as the discovery of a rich mineral deposit, it is alleged that the insiders are the first to know and they act, buying the stock and causing its price to rise. The insiders then tell their friends, who act next. Then the professionals find out the news and the big institutions put blocks of the shares in the portfolios. Finally, the poor slobs like you and me get the information and buy, pushing the price still higher.

I am gratified when random walk theorists do concede the possibility of inefficiencies in capital markets—even if I can cite only a few examples of this concession. It is encouraging to note however that it takes very few of these inefficiencies to exist in order for well positioned traders to make a lot of money. For my own part, being a pragmatist, it is enough for me to observe that any market inefficiencies do exist. It is not necessary for me to produce a comprehensive theory explaining why they exist. Like Edison, I am looking for an element that will produce light in an incandescent bulb, not for a theory that explains why the light is produced. Once I have found market inefficiencies, I try to harness them to the best of my ability in order to produce trading gains. I will leave it to others to explain why they work as intended.

Finally, there is a very old joke about a finance professor and two of his students who were out walking together one day. On the sidewalk in front of them they spied a ten dollar bill. The finance professor, who was a strong proponent of random walk theory and the efficient market hypothesis, told his students, "Don't bother to pick it up because, if it were a real ten dollar bill, someone would have picked it up by now." Fortunately, the students were skeptical of random walk theory and they picked it up anyway. My sincere hope is that faulty theories will not prevent trading gains.

SUMMARY

In this chapter we have considered arguments in favor of the view that market behavior is not entirely random, and that there exist sufficient market inefficiencies to permit the design of successful mathematical trading systems and to reap consistent trading gains. It was argued that just as all scientific predictions of natural phenomena entail probability statements about future occurrences of such phenomena based on past patterns of their occurrence, so certain stock market phenomena may also be predicted under certain similar circumstances. Six examples of market inefficiencies were provided and these included stocks with cash flow advantages, momentum, EPS/PE divergence, share-price regression opportunities, positive analyst earnings estimates, and the tendency of market averages to move in response to sentiment indicators such as the CBOE Volatility Index and the put/call ratio.

CHAPTER 17

On the Nature of Risk

The systematic measurement and management of risk is a comparatively new development in the history of civilization. Most scholars trace the beginnings of this endeavor to the work of Blaise Pascal and Pierre de Fermat in France in the 1650s, as they solved the problem of how casino winnings should be distributed among players when the game is left unfinished. Obviously, recognition of the existence of risk itself goes back much further in history. And certainly earlier civilizations have sought to understand and minimize risk even if they were unable to measure and manage it in any scientific sense. The English word *risk* is said to be derived from the French word *risqué*, denoting the same possibility of loss or injury inherent in our term. The English word *hazard* is said to be derived from the older Arabic word for dice, *al zahr*.

The foundation of scientific risk management lies in the concept of the Gaussian normal distribution of natural events that was introduced around 1848. This simple yet profound concept is the basis for all advances in risk management and permits insurance actuaries to promulgate suitable insurance rates to cover liabilities for all kinds of property, medical, casualty, and life insurance. Without the concept of the normal distribution we could not measure the risks and rewards attached to medical treatments, bridge construction, election campaign strategies, dietary supplements, fertilizer applications, airplane travel, or stock trading. The properties of the normal distribution also permitted Karl Pearson (1901) to develop the correlation coefficient to further his study of genetics. The correlation coefficient in turn became the building block of social science and economics.

The properties of the normal distribution are illustrated in Figure 17.1.

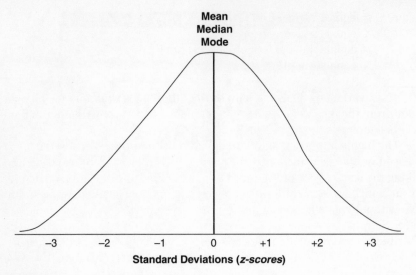

FIGURE 17.1 The Normal Distribution

If you think of the normal distribution as a pile of homogeneous data observations, the mid point of the data is where the pile is highest and most of the observations occur. If a data distribution is truly normal, it will have several important properties that are useful to us (Henning 1987). First, the mid-point or mean of the distribution denotes a perfect center and should have the same location whether it is determined as the mean (the arithmetic average), the median (the middle score), or the mode (the highest point). Second, the distribution will have perfect symmetry, so that the right side is the mirror image of the left side. This is one of those many examples in life where truth and beauty come together in harmony. The third property of this distribution is that it is *asymptotic*, that is, the ends or tails of the distribution never intersect the horizontal axis. Thus, in theory, there is always the possibility that some data point will appear that is infinitely above or below the mean.

This exact normal distribution rarely if ever occurs in nature, and we seldom have opportunity to gather enough observations to verify whether a given distribution is truly normal or not. But even when the natural distribution can be said to approximate a normal distribution, it has important implications for the management of risk. First of all, notice that the variation of data points around the mean of any representative sample drawn from a normal distribution can be expressed as follows:

$$s^2 = \sum (X - M)^2 / (N - 1)$$

where   s^2 equals variance
        X equals a given observation
        M equals the mean of all observations
        N equals sample size

Thus, variance equals the sum of the differences squared of each data point from the mean of all data points, divided by the total number of data points minus one.

The highly important standard deviation of a normal distribution is expressed as the square root of the variance. The process of squaring and taking the square root of the result is done so that the deviations from the mean, which are sometimes negative and sometimes positive, will be additive without canceling one another out. If I seem to be belaboring minutia here, there is good reason. It turns out that any data point found in the distribution can be located in terms of the numbers of standard deviations (*z*-scores) that it lies above or below the mean of the distribution. Because the proportion of data under the curve at any point of the distribution is constant, we can determine the probability or likelihood that any observation will occur at any particular *z*-score distance from the mean of the distribution. In other words, given a normal distribution in the population of interest, we can determine the likelihood of the occurrence of any individual events within the distribution. This generally holds true for us whether the events of interest are IQ test scores, human height measurements, automobile accidents, crop yields, or monthly movements of major stock market indices. The power of this simple arrangement for the management of risk can hardly be overstated.

We often go astray and get into trouble in situations where we attempt to apply these natural relationships to events that are not normally distributed. However, a lot of computational work has been done to show that the underlying principles are sufficiently robust so that they can safely be applied to distributions that approximate normal distributions, but may not be perfectly normal. Obviously, actuarial science is sufficiently accurate that insurance companies have been able to balance risks in ways that allow them to make a profit at the same time that they manage to indemnify their policy holders against those risks. Gambling casinos can make a predictable profit at the same time that they allow for the possibility that some gamblers will occasionally win. Medical science has succeeded in producing medicines that can be expected to cure far more people than they kill. And it is reasonable to expect that certain stock trading procedures can be consistently more successful than other trading procedures. In other words, by taking advantage of what is known about probability distributions, we can trade stocks in ways that greatly skew the odds of success in our favor. For example, with regard to efforts to time the market, when we see that market indices or volatility indices have moved a certain number of standard deviations above or below their means, we can reasonably expect that there will eventually be a regression back towards the mean.

THE RISKS OF RISK MANAGEMENT APPLIED TO MARKET PHENOMENA

Bernstein (1996) in his exceptional book on the history of risk management noted three important challenges associated with using the principles of the normal distribution and the regression-to-the-mean phenomenon for decisions on investing. First, he points out that this regression process may proceed at such a slow pace that it could be disrupted by an unanticipated shock. Second, the regression may be so forceful that it does not come to rest at the mean, but may proceed to the other side of the mean. Third, he notes that the mean itself may be unstable so that yesterday's normality may be supplanted by a new normality that we know nothing about. Another related challenge that one might add to his list occurs when the regression proceeds towards the mean, but does not actually reach the mean. Additionally, it seems to me that the greatest challenge occurs when the regression does not proceed in the time or direction expected. In my experience none of these challenges precludes the possibility of successful stock trading except perhaps the final challenge. Fortunately, that challenge appears to be less common than the others. Fortunately also as we have seen in the previous chapter, the inefficiencies in the market on which we can capitalize to make profits in stock trading are not limited to regression-to-the-mean phenomena.

By way of example of the greatest challenge, such as when regression does not occur in the time and direction expected, Bernstein recounts that investors in 1930, who jumped in after the market had lost 50 percent of its value and could have been considered ripe for regression to the mean, would have been dismayed as they watched the market fall another 80 percent. Similarly, investors who sold out in 1955 after the Dow Jones Industrial Average (DJIA) had regained its 1929 highs would have been frustrated on the sidelines as the DJIA doubled again over the next nine years.

It has also been observed as an example of the instability of means that the stock market has over many years experienced an upward drift in its mean by about 7 percent per year on average, or about 12 percent if calculated on the basis of total return of individual stocks. Happily, this drift is in a favorable direction, so that it could be argued that, if an individual investor is not realizing gains of at least 7 percent per year on average, he or she is definitely doing something wrong. It is an interesting parenthetical observation that, if you based market gain expectations on the Fibonacci ratio, 0.618, annual gains of about 11.8 percent would be expected, which is the difference in that proportion above a 50/50 equilibrium. Perhaps again this is another example where truth and beauty go together. In fact, from 1970 to 1993, the average annual return of the S&P 500 stocks including both capital appreciation and income was 11.7 percent.

RISK AND VARIANCE

In the evolution of portfolio management, *risk* has come to be identified with *variance*. This development may be attributed to the work of Harry Markowitz (1952), a Nobel Laureate. Markowitz reasoned that most investors and fund managers are concerned about variance in returns and like to limit that variance so that returns would not be subject to wild swings from quarter to quarter and year to year. Because life is short, many investors prefer comparatively smaller gains that are predictable from year to year over larger average gains that, due to market volatility, might actually be large losses in some periods. Of course, Markowitz himself did not define risk as variation, but that has been a subsequent interpretation by others. Identifying risk with variance or volatility is intuitively satisfying because stocks with greatest average returns are often stocks with greatest price volatility or risk by this definition. Perhaps related to the greater returns from volatile stocks is the finding that increased volatility causes stock prices to go down and stocks to become undervalued (Sorenson, 1995). In this way it can be shown that the ability to assume more risk over time is associated with the capacity to reap greater rewards. Markowitz determined that portfolio diversification plays a key role in variance or risk reduction.

As a result, diversification has become the holy grail of present-day portfolio management. Remember, however, that there is a dynamic tension between risk reduction and maximizing returns. As a portfolio becomes increasingly diversified, it will increasingly approximate the same returns as the major market indexes. To the extent that you are determined to beat the returns of the major indexes, you must also be prepared to limit diversification. Also, as attractive and empowering as the identification of risk with variance may be, there is more to risk than variance in return. It may well be, for example, that true risk cannot be understood without recognition of the capital liabilities of each individual investor.

RISK AND COMPASSION

Most people desire to minimize risks in their lives. Risk denotes the possibility of loss or injury, and is generally believed to be something to be avoided. Of course, some persons are more risk averse than others, and there will always be sky divers and roller coaster riders and mountain climbers and day traders and dice rollers who derive pleasure from potential hazards. But, whether we seek them or not, many risks in life are unavoidable. Most of these risks are not ones that we can insure against because they are not sufficiently repetitive or measurable to permit loss-probability estimates, or because the cost of insuring against them would exceed our ability to pay. Reducing uncertainty and risk can be very expensive.

Kenneth Arrow (1971), an economist at Harvard University and later at Stanford University, won a Nobel Prize for his speculations about an imaginary insurance company that would insure against any loss of any kind and any magnitude. He reasoned that the world would be a better place if we could insure against every possibility in what he described as a "complete market." He believed that people would take more risks in that kind of a world and this in turn would result in more economic progress. Such a utopian world would then become more altruistic and democratic. Accordingly, Arrow welcomed the spread of insurance coverage and other risk-sharing arrangements such as commodity futures contracts and derivatives that enabled farmers, mine owners, airline companies, and factory managers to limit pricing risks and stabilize their enterprise revenues. His work recognized the monumental role that risk management has played in modern economic progress. Imagine a world in which affordable insurance could be obtained against every possible negative outcome in life. Perhaps we could then insure not only against accident, fire, theft, sickness, and death, but also against traffic tickets, failed marriages, depression, and unhappiness. We could also insure against financial insolvency and against all losses in stock trading, and this would preserve our trading capital so that we could eventually make more trades and find more winning strategies. Such insurance could reduce our fear of loss or of experiencing any negative consequences in life, and we could then proceed confidently in any entrepreneurial endeavors.

Unfortunately, such a utopian world would not be without its own problems. There would still be cheaters who attempt to take advantage of the system. Imagine people who would sue to collect liability insurance because someone made them unhappy. Or picture those who would perpetrate automobile accidents or bouts of heartburn from overindulgence in order to collect insurance settlements. Likely there would be those who would sue because the work of the hairdresser or tailor or lawn care specialist did not bring them sufficient satisfaction. Ultimately, these negative possibilities return us to Chapter 15 and the paramount need for integrity in the marketplace. There it was maintained that integrity consists of trustworthiness and concern for the well being of others, and that capitalist markets cannot exist without some degree of integrity.

Nevertheless, the requirement to reduce or eliminate risk and uncertainty is a universal need of humanity. It explains in part why we buy insurance, install alarm systems, take prescribed medications, contribute to retirement accounts, employ statistical trading systems, build networks of friends, seek solace in religion, and read books about maximizing odds of success in stock trading. Because risk is the common lot of us all, regardless of our age, education, or income level, we cannot but feel compassion for others who are seeking protection from risks that they may face. Certainly we can identify with those who may at some point have lost money trading stocks or are even now confronted with the possibility of such loss. Or we can sympathize with those who have lost a loved one, become terminally ill, or who have been involved in a traffic accident. In some ways the management of risk is the most pervasive concern of us all. It is a very natural and humane preoccupation to seek to manage risk. This is especially a concern of active stock traders.

RISK AND TRUST

As we contemplate the management of risk, at some point a degree of trust must enter the risk-taking equation. For example, after we have taken out an automobile insurance policy, we can drive our vehicle in city traffic more confidently because we have trust that the insurance company will come to our rescue if we are involved in any accident. We can also trade stocks more confidently if we trust our stock-picking guru or our mathematical trading system to be accurate. We can confidently purchase inventory for our retail sales business and assume greater advertising costs if we trust that increasing demand will reward us with greater sales revenues. Even a gambler has trust that the casino will honor its promise to reward winners, and a sky diver has trust that his parachute will open. There can be no risk-taking without trust. Embracing risks without trust is not risk-taking behavior, but it is suicidal behavior. This is why trustworthiness is so essential to economic progress. Perhaps this is also why faith or trust is said to be such a key ingredient in the practice of religion, or as expressed elsewhere, "Without faith [trust] it is impossible to please God" (Hebrews 11:6). Trust can be said to moderate the relationship between risk and reward. This relationship is illustrated in the contingency table (see Table 17.1).

Table 17.1 illustrates a set of relationships that I call the risk/reward/ trust contingency. Notice that this contingency presupposes that there is usually a reward associated with risk-taking behavior. Therefore, in the first quadrant we can see that high risk is associated with high reward. But notice that this outcome is to be expected only under a condition of

TABLE 17.1	The Risk/Reward/Trust Contingency	
	High Reward	**Little or No Reward**
High Risk	1. Trust	2. Over-Trust (Mistrust)
Little or No Risk	3. Super-Trust (Faith)	4. Under-Trust (Distrust)

trust. This is what happens when a stock trader finds inefficiencies in the market, trusts in the potential rewards from those inefficiencies, and takes warranted and creative trading positions that effectively capitalize upon those inefficiencies.

The second quadrant portrays a situation in which high risk-taking behavior is not rewarded commensurately. This is what happens when a stock trader blindly follows the advice of a stock-picking guru or employs an untested stock-selection algorithm or follows gut instinct. The trader trusts his information source enough to take great risk, but his trust is misguided and unfounded and usually goes unrewarded. This is the outcome that can be expected to take place on average when trust is misplaced.

The third quadrant illustrates a situation where very little risk can be expected to yield great reward. This is a highly uncommon and perhaps supernatural situation. One example of this happened in Biblical times when Jacob was being cheated out of his salary as a herdsman by his father-in-law Laban. Jacob prayed and received a dream or a vision from God. In his dream he saw that Laban's bulls of one color or marking were breeding with Laban's cows of another color or marking. Jacob concluded that the next generation of cattle offspring would be of mixed color or mixed marking. He therefore proposed to Laban that he be given as his salary only cattle of mixed color or mixed marking. Laban, being miserly and unfair and knowing that there were currently few if any such cattle in his herd, readily agreed to Jacob's request. Laban later regretted this agreement because the next generation of cattle was entirely of mixed color and mixed marking. So Jacob effectively took possession of the herd by capitalizing on a supernatural revelation by faith. I can offer little advice to stock traders about entering into this kind of arrangement. I would only say somewhat facetiously that, if you get this kind of inspiration, I would strongly recommend that you highly leverage your positions.

The fourth quadrant is one in which little or no risk yields little or no reward. This is what may be expected to happen when a stock trader has no trust in his own stock-picking skill or in anyone else's. He is therefore unable to pull the trigger and take a position involving risk. In the end he is an example of the adage, "Nothing ventured, nothing gained." He refuses to assume risk, he is unable to exercise trust, and he never realizes any gains.

Of the situations depicted in the four quadrants of Table 17.1, the first situation involving high risk and high reward is perhaps the most creative situation. It requires an abundance of research to find market inefficiencies and to enter positions that effectively capitalize on those inefficiencies. It involves trust that entering those positions will produce a great reward. This is the only quadrant that this particular trading book seeks to address. By identifying market inefficiencies and incorporating what is known about those inefficiencies into trading systems, we creatively stimulate trust and a willingness to assume risk. This in turn hopefully leads to above average returns in trading.

RISK AND WEALTH

There is a tendency for persons with more acquired wealth to be unwilling to assume as much risk proportionately as those with less acquired wealth. Or expressed in terms popularized by Bernoulli (1738), the utility of additional wealth is inversely related to the amount already possessed. Perhaps this explains why many wealthier individuals may be more inclined to choose fixed income investments over day-trading and options-trading ventures. Their unwillingness to assume greater risk is related to their perception that they have much to lose in the realm of personal possessions and not much to gain in the realm of personal needs.

This assumed inverse relationship between risk-taking behavior and wealth provides another argument in favor of sharing wealth. It brings us back to the analogy introduced in Chapter 15 of trading capital being like an artificial pond. If we are unwilling to introduce a spillway to our capital pond in the form of charitable giving, the pond will become a source of algae, mosquitoes, bacteria, and disease. One of the symptoms of this malady consists of our becoming unwilling to assume a level of risk that is required for future productivity. When we have allowed our pond to become too large and self-contained, we lose the capacity for creative risk taking. Productivity often requires us to be lean. To further illustrate this point, I have two dogs. One is lean and the other is fat. When we go for a walk together, the lean dog always pulls me forward and the fat dog always pulls me backward. Also, it often happens that small companies that are idea rich and cash poor become the drivers of innovation in our economy.

SUMMARY

In this chapter we have explored some aspects of the nature of risk. In particular we have examined early origins of attempts at scientific risk management. We have examined some of the properties of the normal distribution, and we have considered some of its implications for risk management. We have seen how departures from the mean of expected events can be interpreted in terms of probabilities of the occurrence of those events. We have considered some appropriate and inappropriate applications of risk management to the trading of stocks. We have looked at some of the relationships between risk and variance, risk and compassion, risk and trust, and risk and wealth. We have examined a risk/reward/trust contingency table as it may have bearing upon the trading of stocks.

CHAPTER 18

Trading in the Information Age

A ges come and go. By all accounts, we no longer live in the Bronze Age or the Iron Age or the Industrial Age or the Atomic Age or the Space Age, but in the Information Age. We have access to more information today than was the case at any point in the history of civilization, and the amount of information is growing logarithmically each day. Most of us have more computing power in our homes than was available to the scientists of the Manhattan Project when they developed the atomic bomb. We have access to more print material than resides in the Library of Congress. We certainly have access to more current stock trading information than any brokerage firm could have imagined ten years ago. This information access brings amazing opportunities for the stock trader, along with some dangers. We might say that the Information Age has its own risks and rewards.

THE ECONOMY OF ABUNDANCE

When Stuart Chase (2007) wrote *The Economy of Abundance*, he had in mind the transition to an abundance of choices due to the growing advantages and rapid expansion of access to the Internet. In *The Long Tail: Why the Future of Business Is Selling Less of More*, Chris Anderson (2007) writes of the niche products that are readily available electronically to the present-day consumer. The comparison is frequently made between Blockbuster, with its limited shelf space for CD and DVD movie rentals, and

Netflix, with its nearly unlimited inventory of internet-accessed movies. Blockbuster is compelled by shelf-space limitations to discard old movies of limited appeal in order to make room for more popular new movies. Netflix does not face this same constraint because its wares may be accessed digitally. Therefore, Netflix can display an inventory that is seemingly infinite in size. Similar comparisons have been made between the storage inventory of Tower Records and that of iTunes with more than 3 million songs available over the Internet. The older marketing model represents the economy of scarcity, wherein the choices are far more limited. The transition to the economy of abundance from the economy of scarcity provides not only a marketing edge to those companies that can make the transition, but it also gives more choice to the consumer at lower prices.

Interestingly, Anderson writes that the 80/20 rule of inventory sales no longer applies to internet sales. That is, it is no longer the case that 20 percent of inventory accounts for 80 percent of sales. In the economy of abundance, digital entertainment participants now speak of the 98 percent rule because 98 percent of inventory normally sells at least once a month. This seems to be the ultimate expression of a consumer-driven economy. Anderson also speaks of the "tyranny of locality" that has been the curse of traditional retail operations. Location is critical when it comes to setting up a traditional store. The internet effectively overcomes this limitation because everyone occupies the same space, unless one considers possible advantages in listing order associated with Google searches.

The appeal of the economy of abundance is linked to the view that goods and services will continue their explosion of availability at the same time that prices will continue to come down. The notion of abundance is attributed to this development because there is the promise of infinite selection at prices approaching zero. It is not hard to imagine this new scenario as we see a multiplicity of books available for discounted prices at Amazon, unlimited discounted movies available at Netflix, discount travel options available at Travelocity, viewing and viewer-producing options available for free at YouTube, buying and selling opportunities available at auction prices at eBay, and news information available free at Drudge Report or any one of a thousand other sites.

It is even rumored that the day is fast approaching when there will be zero commissions for the on-line trading of stocks and options. Perhaps the most empowering aspect of this new development is the abundance of information that is now available to us at no cost. If information is power, then we must be the most powerful generation of all time. However, it is important to understand both the benefits and drawbacks of this development because these innovations will also affect the success of our participation in the trading of stocks.

A PERSPECTIVE ON ABUNDANCE

There is little doubt that the emergence of the economy of abundance and the related Information Age has brought permanent change to our lives. And yet, this is not the first time something like this has happened. Think of the time when the early colonists settled America. That too was a time of abundance. Only that was not a time of abundant information or of digital access to abundant goods and services. Rather, it was a time when land was abundant. Any settler who could work the land could have access to a parcel of land for a homestead. Comparisons can be made to the Gold-Rush eras in California and Alaska. There, any miner who found gold could stake out a claim and become wealthy. From each of those earlier examples lessons can be drawn that may have bearing on our current circumstances. Although land was abundant for the early settlers, claiming and clearing and planting and building was backbreaking work. There were both uncertainties and risks at every turn. There were dangers of wild beasts and fires and floods and marauding bands of Native Americans. In case of illness or attack, it was not possible to dial 911 on a cell phone. No one had health insurance, and given the state of medical science at the time, they were probably better off for not having access to a physician to bleed their illnesses away. And for the early gold miners, there was the ever-present danger of claim jumpers and thieves—to say nothing of the often-prevailing risk that they would never even discover gold. Many miners in Alaska died of exposure during the fierce winters. The majority of gold seekers were not even successful in their search. In fact it is said that the merchants who sold goods to the miners ultimately managed to gather more wealth than the miners themselves. In the same way it seems today that the paratrading industries such as brokerages, stock newsletter venders, and cable TV market news channels often stand to make more money than the actual traders they serve.

There are similar uncertainties and risks associated with the threshold of abundance we have entered in this digital age. For example, Stephen Baker (2008) has written that the gathering of information via the internet is a two-way street. He points out that companies like Yahoo! and Google are harvesting an average of 2,500 details about each of us every month. When we surf the web, our interests and preferences are classified and catalogued. Advertising agencies install spyware tracking "cookies" into our computers that will give them information about our individual interests and values. Advertisers are thereby enabled to pitch products to us that we might be more inclined to purchase, and politicians are also enabled to steer their campaign advertisements and speeches in directions that may make it more likely that they will gain our votes. When we go to most websites to order a book, we are told that people who have purchased that particular book have also purchased several other similar books that are listed for us. In this way the booksellers manage to increase the odds that we will make additional purchases. At the same time, the booksellers elicit reviews from us that will help future buyers decide if that is indeed the kind of book they are seeking.

Think of some of the dangers associated with this harvesting of consumer information. Imagine, for example, if records were kept of persons who made large purchases over the internet or through cable shopping networks, who would therefore be considered to have large amounts of discretionary capital at their disposal. If advertising agencies knew who these people were and what their preferences were, presumably those consumers could become easy prey for additional targeted sales attempts or promotion schemes. Of course this happens.

Imagine what might happen if the trades of successful investors were recorded so that others could tell which positions they were holding and what kinds of trades were most profitable. This information could greatly influence the purchases of other traders seeking to emulate the performance of those successful traders. This also has happened. Imagine if the e-mail correspondence of company CFOs could be "hacked into" so that others knew in advance what future earnings releases would contain. Certainly this kind of insider information would put the hackers at great advantage in trading. Many kinds of electronic surveillance might be attempted to provide a trading edge. You can be sure that all of this has been attempted.

What if some of the information you managed to gather on the internet was false information, and you used it to make important stock trading decisions? For example, what if disreputable individuals wishing to drive down the price of a stock in which they held a short position could log on to a stock bulletin board and anonymously post false messages about the future prospects of that company. You and other stockholders who were uncertain about their investment in that stock might certainly be influenced to sell and drive the price of the stock down and deplete the capitalization of the company. This kind of behavior happens daily on stock bulletin boards. Consider the possibility that someone might use Internet purchasing information to gain access to your credit card account or your social security number and be enabled in this way to steal your money or your identity. This too has happened with frightening frequency.

My point here is not to detract from the economy of abundance, and certainly not to dissuade individuals from taking advantage of internet innovations. It is merely to indicate that with every advent of an economy of abundance there are dangers and uncertainties like sharks lurking in the waters. At the same time, if we fail to take advantage of these innovations early, we may fail to reap the full benefits. So it is that today many of the land-acquisition opportunities available to the early settlers are no longer available to us. And many of the gold-rush opportunities available to the early prospectors are no longer ours. Therefore, it is important to us as stock traders to keep abreast of new innovations, at the same time that we keep them in perspective and become aware of potential hazards.

TAKING ADVANTAGE OF INFORMATION-ACCESS OPPORTUNITIES

As suggested earlier, the information available to us via the Internet is virtually unlimited. This also poses certain challenges related to time and focus. None of us has time to consume all of the information available, so we need to be focused in our inquiries. Table 2.1, a list of frequently visited websites that will be useful to any stock trader. Indeed, without regular access to some of those websites it will not be possible to employ any of the trading systems advocated in this book. It was recommended there that every trader diligently compile a list of current websites for frequent reference. Obviously websites come and go, so it will be necessary to update your list regularly.

Another practical way to take advantage of the abundance of free information is by looking over the shoulders of fund managers and other trading establishments. For example, as I write this it is the end of February 2009 and we are in the middle of one of the worst bear markets in trading history. If I access the Yahoo finance website at http://finance.yahoo.com and click on "Investing," followed by "Mutual Funds," followed by "Top Performers," followed by "Large Growth" under U.S. Stock Funds, I can see that the Monteagle Informed Investor Growth Fund (MIIFX) is leading all funds in its category with three-month gains of 34.37 percent. It occurs to me that this is a pretty amazing accomplishment under current market conditions, and gains exceeding 10 percent per month are consistent with my own trading objectives. Therefore I click on the fund symbol and click on the "Holdings" for this fund. It is not surprising to me that fully 35 percent of the fund is in short positions, and that probably accounts for much of the fund's success during this period. However, I notice also that the fund holds two long positions that have been profitable during this period: Myriad Genetics, Inc. (MYGN) and Life Technologies Corporation (LIFE). As it happens, MYGN is already in my watch list and among my prospective holdings, but LIFE is totally new to me. I run my analysis and find it to be a viable holding according to my own stringent criteria. Presumably, it has escaped my notice because it is currently more than 10 percent below its 52-week high. Nevertheless, I determine that I can add it to my watch list and possibly acquire it as the biotech sector continues its leadership position. My point in this example is that the information explosion over the internet has enabled me in this way to find yet another stock to add to my list.

Another example of this "looking-over-the-shoulder" phenomenon is provided as I go to the http://barchart.com website and click on "Signals." There I find a list of 100 stocks arranged by desirability for acquisition according to the technical criteria employed at that website. I notice that the stock at the top of the list, Sturm Ruger and Company (RGR), is a relative newcomer to this list. After running my own analysis, I see that this company has just come out with very favorable earnings results and the stock qualifies for inclusion in my list, not only on the basis of technical information, but also because of its fundamentals. This is another case where I can supplement my own findings by looking over the shoulders of other traders at no cost to me. The possible examples of information access for stock selection are limited only by our time and creativity. Notice, however, that in every case it is necessary to run one's own personal analysis to be sure that the stocks so identified actually do measure up to the criteria one has established.

Yet another example of this kind of "over-the-shoulder" snooping that can lead to outstanding stock selections can be provided at http://clearstation.etrade.com. There you will find a list of stocks labeled the "A-List." These are stocks selected by reference to about 34 different criteria to suggest that the prices should climb. Similarly, there you will also find a list of stocks labeled the "Z-List." This list is comprised of stocks that are considered to be suitable shorting candidates. Of course, here again it is necessary to conduct your own personal analysis before adopting any recommendations from others. Nevertheless, you are likely to find some good trading ideas from these lists.

SUMMARY

In this chapter we have examined some of the implications of the Information Age and the Economy of Abundance as they may relate to the trading of stocks. The necessity of keeping abreast of current technological changes was emphasized and some of the risks and uncertainties associated with these new innovations were identified.

Examples were provided concerning how traders can take advantage of specialized stock information available over the Internet at no cost and thereby effectively look over the shoulders of other traders or trading institutions.

CHAPTER 19

Using a Trading System with an Excel Spreadsheet

Y ou have no doubt noticed that this book is accompanied by a CD with an Excel spreadsheet that provides sample data and formulas for the implementation of the trading systems described in the earlier chapters. Specifically, the CD will allow you to implement the hybrid technical-fundamental system described earlier in Chapter 6 of this book. In this chapter I provide instructions on how to use the CD to begin systematic stock analysis, ranking, and selection as described earlier in this book. Of necessity, the initial database provided on the CD will become dated and outmoded quickly because many of the stocks in the database will fall out of favor or become no longer listed on any stock exchange. That will not be a problem because you will learn in this chapter how to quickly update the spreadsheet with current stock data.

STEP 1: LOADING THE EXCEL SPREADSHEET CD INTO YOUR COMPUTER

For this step you will need to have a current version of Microsoft Excel or compatible software. It is a good idea to make a backup copy of this CD in case you accidentally erase information in any of the cells. After you load the CD onto your computer, what you see next should correspond to the information presented in Tables 19.1, 19.2, and 19.3. You will notice that these three tables comprise one single spreadsheet when placed side by

TABLE 19.1 Sample Excel Spreadsheet with Initial Momentum Segment of Analysis for 50 Stocks as of October, 10, 2008 (Part 1)

	A	B	C	D	E	F	G	H	I
1	Symbol	Price	High	Low	Multiple	%Lag	Inv V	3MG	Fin R
2	REV	11.90	14.85	0.67	17.76	0.20	134.11	1617	−1
3	EDV	106.10	124.37	15.53	6.83	0.14	69.85	583.32	2
4	BBX	5.50	11.82	0.81	6.79	0.53	19.05	579.01	0
5	SMN	90.48	90.50	25.82	3.50	0.00	23785	194.05	4
6	ZYXI	5.00	6.14	1.11	4.50	0.19	36.39	151.26	2
7	GEHL	27.16	29.77	11.17	2.43	0.09	41.60	143.15	0
8	EEV	178.00	178.86	58.82	3.05	0.00	950.53	129.65	4
9	SSG	133.00	136.18	46.46	2.86	0.02	183.89	125.23	6
10	SJH	141.38	143.09	63.03	2.24	0.01	281.54	124.31	3
11	SKK	138.29	140.22	57.06	2.42	0.01	264.12	121.51	4
12	TWM	128.98	129.00	58.47	2.21	0.00	21342	120.59	3
13	DUG	64.70	65.81	25.41	2.55	0.02	226.44	119.84	6
14	SJL	168.82	170.00	69.20	2.44	0.01	527.20	117.55	4
15	SDD	120.00	121.28	54.98	2.18	0.01	310.20	115.63	3
16	SIJ	122.87	124.25	48.43	2.54	0.01	342.64	115.56	6
17	QID	82.05	84.00	33.80	2.43	0.02	156.85	114.40	4
18	SDP	112.81	113.40	46.80	2.41	0.01	694.95	113.37	4
19	EFU	190.00	192.61	65.23	2.91	0.01	322.43	112.12	4
20	CDLX	45.25	50.50	21.00	2.15	0.10	31.09	115.48	2
21	UB	73.39	74.58	34.81	2.11	0.02	198.20	110.83	5
22	REW	116.45	127.16	0.23	506.30	0.08	9017.00	104.30	3
23	MZZ	109.90	111.04	40.50	2.71	0.01	396.47	103.59	4
24	RRZ	141.98	145.80	0.21	676.10	0.03	38707	102.83	3
25	AGA	42.75	45.48	18.73	2.28	0.06	57.04	101.56	3
26	EWV	155.05	157.60	66.16	2.34	0.02	217.27	95.25	3
27	SCC	155.00	157.09	48.80	3.18	0.01	358.10	92.55	2
28	SCRX	31.01	31.21	16.89	1.84	0.01	429.76	83.60	6
29	SDS	110.00	110.77	47.50	2.32	0.01	499.71	80.33	3
30	SIG	15.45	26.50	8.60	1.80	0.42	6.46	79.65	2
31	LBAS	8.10	10.61	1.30	6.23	0.24	39.51	77.24	3
32	LDG	68.93	77.00	36.65	1.88	0.10	26.92	74.51	3
33	DXD	93.20	95.09	44.63	2.09	0.02	157.60	69.42	2
34	EUM	126.31	126.33	0.20	631.55	0.00	59838	63.23	2
35	UFI	3.82	5.09	1.79	2.13	0.25	12.83	60.50	1
36	QCOR	6.32	7.81	0.75	8.43	0.19	66.25	59.19	2
37	IKN	16.40	17.50	6.73	2.43	0.06	58.15	52.13	3
38	BESN	6.55	12.10	2.60	2.52	0.46	8.24	54.12	−1
39	EFZ	120.39	121.12	0.25	481.56	0.01	11984	48.61	4
40	MYY	87.39	87.86	41.52	2.10	0.01	590.19	46.19	2
41	ALO	31.00	38.34	17.55	1.77	0.19	14.15	45.75	0

(Continued)

TABLE 19.1 (Continued)

	A	B	C	D	E	F	G	H	I
42	MITI	4.00	7.74	1.22	3.28	0.48	10.18	42.35	−2
43	TWP	12.56	21.73	5.34	2.35	0.42	8.36	42.24	−1
44	BXS	21.00	31.90	15.15	1.39	0.34	6.09	38.61	2
45	WIBC	10.93	16.50	6.01	1.82	0.34	8.08	38.88	1
46	CRD/B	10.89	22.50	3.07	3.55	0.52	10.31	33.46	1
47	ENSG	13.80	18.39	7.50	1.84	0.25	11.06	31.93	2
48	THOR	21.74	27.72	12.92	1.68	0.27	9.40	31.68	1
49	BWLD	32.29	44.98	18.25	1.77	0.28	9.41	31.31	1
50	BECN	12.43	18.73	6.70	1.86	0.34	8.27	30.43	2
51	EBS	12.39	15.17	4.40	2.82	0.18	23.05	29.06	2

side in ascending numerical order. To save space, some of the numerical data in the book tables have been rounded.

You can see in Table 19.1 that information is provided for 50 stocks of interest based on information available on October, 10, 2008. Incidentally, the Dow Jones Industrial Average hit a low of 7774 intraday on October 10, 2008, which I had projected as a near-term low based on the CBOE Volatility Index high reached that day, and that is why the sample list was chosen for that day. This list of stocks is expected to grow to as many as 200 stocks during bull-market trends, and may contract to 40 or less during bear-market trends such as the one experienced in 2008. You can tell that this list of stocks was compiled during a bear market because comparatively few stocks are included in the list and because many of those stocks that are included on the basis of analysis are exchange-traded bear funds that rise in price when the market is falling. Table 19.1 corresponds to the first page on the Excel spreadsheet included on the CD. As you scroll to the right, you will see the same information that is displayed in Tables 19.2 and 19.3. Numerical data concerning each of the stocks are displayed in the spreadsheet cells, but many of the cells also have underlying formulas embedded that are visible only on the formula bar. You will want to be careful not to erase or alter information in the cells accidentally because that may remove underlying formulas and introduce unintended errors into the analysis. For this reason also, I recommend that you make a backup copy of the CD.

STEP 2: RECOGNIZING INFORMATION ON THE SPREADSHEET

In this step you will learn to recognize and identify the information already present on your spreadsheet. Beginning in Column A, you can see the

TABLE 19.2 Sample Excel Spreadsheet with Technical Segment of Analysis for 50 Stocks as of October, 10, 2008 (Part 2)

	J	K	L	M	N	O	P	Q	R
1	IvRnk	3-ML	Symbol	%LS	IVS	3MGS	IRS	PFS	TRS
2	0.06	0.67	REV	0	1	1	1	−1	−1
3	0.17	15.53	EDV	0	0	1	1	−1	1
4	0.18	0.81	BBX	0	0	1	1	−1	1
5	0.53	30.77	SMN	1	1	1	1	−1	1
6	0.71	1.99	ZYXI	0	0	1	1	0	0
7	0.71	11.17	GEHL	0	0	1	1	−1	0
8	0.79	77.51	EEV	1	1	1	1	−1	1
9	0.81	59.05	SSG	1	1	1	1	1	1
10	0.82	63.03	SJH	1	1	1	1	−1	0
11	0.84	62.43	SKK	1	1	1	1	−1	1
12	0.85	58.47	TWM	1	1	1	1	−1	0
13	0.85	29.43	DUG	1	1	1	1	1	1
14	0.87	77.60	SJL	1	1	1	1	−1	1
15	0.88	55.65	SDD	1	1	1	1	−1	0
16	0.88	57.00	SIJ	1	1	1	1	1	1
17	0.89	38.27	QID	1	1	1	1	−1	1
18	0.90	52.87	SDP	1	1	1	1	−1	1
19	0.91	89.57	EFU	1	1	1	1	−1	1
20	0.94	21.00	CDLX	0	0	1	1	0	0
21	0.96	34.81	UB	1	1	1	1	0	0
22	0.98	57.00	REW	0	1	1	1	−1	1
23	0.98	53.98	MZZ	1	1	1	1	−1	1
24	0.99	70.00	RRZ	1	1	1	1	−1	0
25	1.00	21.21	AGA	0	0	1	1	0	0
26	1.07	79.41	EWV	1	1	0	1	−1	1
27	1.10	80.50	SCC	1	1	0	1	−1	0
28	1.24	16.89	SCRX	1	1	0	1	1	0
29	1.27	61.00	SDS	1	1	0	1	−1	1
30	1.28	8.60	SIG	0	0	0	1	−1	−1
31	1.32	4.57	LBAS	0	0	0	1	1	−1
32	1.40	39.50	LDG	0	0	0	1	0	−1
33	1.47	55.01	DXD	1	1	0	0	−1	1
34	1.61	77.38	EUM	1	1	0	0	−1	1
35	1.72	2.38	UFI	0	0	0	0	0	−1
36	1.72	3.97	QCOR	0	0	0	0	0	0
37	1.96	10.78	IKN	0	0	0	0	0	−1
38	2.03	4.25	BESN	0	0	0	0	1	1
39	2.10	81.01	EFZ	1	1	0	0	1	1
40	2.21	59.78	MYY	1	1	0	0	−1	1
41	2.23	21.27	ALO	0	0	0	0	0	0

(Continued)

TABLE 19.2 *(Continued)*

	J	K	L	M	N	O	P	Q	R
42	2.41	2.81	MITI	0	0	0	0	1	1
43	2.51	8.83	TWP	0	0	0	0	0	0
44	2.64	15.15	BXS	0	0	0	0	−1	0
45	2.73	7.87	WIBC	0	0	0	0	0	−1
46	3.11	8.16	CRD/B	0	0	0	0	−1	0
47	3.19	10.46	ENSG	0	0	0	0	−1	−1
48	3.28	16.51	THOR	0	0	0	0	1	0
49	3.26	24.59	BWLD	0	0	0	0	0	1
50	3.42	9.53	BECN	0	0	0	0	−1	0
51	3.51	9.60	EBS	0	0	0	0	0	−C

symbols given for all of the stocks of interest. These stock symbols are repeated in Column L and Column X for convenience so that you can always see the stock symbol regardless of where you are scrolling on the spreadsheet. In Column B are given the current share prices of all of the listed stocks, as of October 10, 2008. Column C reports the highs in price for all 50 stocks in the preceding 52 weeks. Similarly, Column D reports the lows in price for all stocks over the same preceding period. Column E reports the multiple for each stock—that is the number of times the share price has multiplied from the low to the high. Notice that almost all of the stocks have at least doubled in price over the last 52 weeks. That was part of the basis for initial selection of these particular stocks, although you can see that some of them have subsequently fallen back in price somewhat since they first entered the list. Column F is the percentage lag column. There we can see the proportion of 1.00 that each current stock price has dropped below its 52-week high. Multiplying this value by 100 would give us the percentage the stock has dropped below its 52-week high. Column G is the Investment Value column. This column gives us an initial rating of each stock based on momentum, according to the formula explained in Chapter 6. Column H is the three-month gain column. Here we can see the percentage by which the share price has grown over the past three months. As explained in Chapter 6, this information is used for curve fitting to ensure that the stocks in the list are showing the desired rate of ascent in share price. It is also used to screen the stocks so that, when the values in Column H drop below 30, the stock is normally deleted from the list. Column I is an initial selection rank value of each stock on a scale of about −10 to +10. This Column is identical to Column AA, but it is repeated here to permit you to see changes

TABLE 19.3 Sample Excel Spreadsheet with Fundamental and Final Segments of Analysis for 50 Stocks as of October 10, 2008 (Part 3)

	S	T	U	V	W	X	Y	Z	AA
1	DVS	GRS	BVS	PES	Rnk 1	Symbol	CF	CFS	Final
2	0	0	−1	−1	−1	REV	5\−3	−1	−4
3	0	0	0	0	2	EDV	**	0	0
4	−1	−1	1	−1	0	BBX	12\8	1	−1
5	0	0	0	0	4	SMN	**	0	2
6	1	0	−1	0	2	ZYXI	**	0	0
7	−1	1	−1	0	0	GEHL	20\9	0	−2
8	0	0	0	0	4	EEV	**	0	2
9	0	0	0	0	6	SSG	**	0	4
10	0	0	0	0	3	SJH	**	0	1
11	0	0	0	0	4	SKK	**	0	2
12	0	0	0	0	3	TWM	**	0	1
13	0	0	0	0	6	DUG	**	0	4
14	0	0	0	0	4	SJL	**	0	2
15	0	0	0	0	3	SDD	**	0	1
16	0	0	0	0	6	SIJ	**	0	4
17	0	0	0	0	4	QID	**	0	2
18	0	0	0	0	4	SDP	**	0	2
19	0	0	0	0	4	EFU	**	0	2
20	1	0	0	−1	2	CDLX	24\4	0	0
21	−1	1	1	0	5	UB	16\12	0	3
22	0	0	0	0	3	REW	**	0	1
23	0	0	0	0	4	MZZ	**	0	2
24	0	0	0	0	3	RZZ	**	0	1
25	0	0	0	0	3	AGA	**	0	1
26	0	0	0	0	3	EWV	**	0	1
27	0	0	0	0	2	SCC	**	0	0
28	0	1	1	0	6	SCRX	13\7	1	5
29	0	0	0	0	3	SDS	**	0	1
30	1	1	1	0	2	SIG	**	0	0
31	1	1	−1	1	3	LBAS	**	0	1
32	1	1	1	0	3	LDG	13\9	1	2
33	0	0	0	0	2	DXD	**	0	0
34	0	0	0	0	2	EUM	**	0	0
35	0	1	1	0	1	UFI	13\−4	−1	−2
36	1	1	−1	1	2	QCOR	9\87	−1	−1
37	1	1	1	1	3	IKN	9\5	1	2
38	−1	0	−1	−1	−1	BESN	**	0	−3
39	0	0	0	0	4	EFZ	**	0	2
40	0	0	0	0	2	MYY	**	0	0
41	−1	−1	1	1	0	ALO	38\−5	−1	−3

(Continued)

TABLE 19.3 (*Continued*)

	S	T	U	V	W	X	Y	Z	AA
42	−1	−1	−1	−1	−2	MITI	*\-56	−1	−5
43	−1	1	−1	0	−1	TWP	8\-30	−1	−4
44	1	1	1	0	2	BXS	13\9	1	1
45	−1	1	1	1	1	WIBC	14\26	0	−1
46	1	1	0	0	1	CRD/B	15\3	1	0
47	1	1	1	1	2	ENSG	11\12	1	1
48	0	1	0	−1	1	THOR	43\1	0	−1
49	1	1	−1	−1	1	BWLD	17\13	0	−1
50	1	1	1	0	2	BECN	12\4	1	1
51	1	1	0	1	2	EBS	10\12	1	1

in rank values immediately as you update prices at the close of trading each day.

Table 19.2 provides us with a continuation of information from Table 19.1 available on the same Excel spreadsheet as you move across from left to right. Column J is the pivotal column for the entire analysis. This column employs a formula given in Chapter 6 in order to provide a momentum ranking of all stocks on the list. Column K is where the lowest daily price of each stock over the past three months is entered. This information is subsequently used to generate three-month percentage gain in Column H, and is used as one variable in the momentum ranking formula to produce the ranking data in Column J. As was explained earlier, Column L is a repetition of the symbol list in Column A. It is repeated here for convenience so that it is not necessary to scroll back to the beginning in order to determine which stocks are described at this point on the spreadsheet. Columns M through R are used to provide summary scores on a variety of technical variables on a scale of plus one to minus one as described in Chapter 6. Specifically, Column M scores percentage lag, Column N scores investment value, Column O scores three-month gain, Column P scores investment rank, Column Q scores point-and-figure analysis from http://stockcharts.com, and Column R scores technical opinion over 13 technical variables at http://barchart.com, as explained in Chapter 6. Occasionally this website is unable to provide technical information for stocks that have not been publicly traded for a sufficient period of time. In those cases, it is necessary to copy the data entry from Column Q into Column R on the assumption that, since both of these columns record technical suitability, their results should be highly correlated.

Table 19.3 is a continuation on the Excel spreadsheet from Table 19.2 above. In it we can see scores for the fundamental data on each of the 50 stocks in accordance with the scoring procedure explained in Chapter 6, and we can see a final ranking of the stocks based on the combined technical and fundamental information incorporated into the selection model. Note that in Column S we have the score for divergence, in Column T we are given the score for growth, in Column U we see the score for book value, in Column V we have the score for Price/Earnings ratio, and in Column W we have a preliminary ranking of the stocks as a sum of all of the scored variables tabulated so far. As explained earlier, Column X is a restatement of the stock symbols provided for ease of reference so that it is not necessary to refer back to Column A to identify the stocks in each row. Column Y records data on cash flow. Recall that it is useful at this point to consider both cash flow and free cash flow in ranking stocks for acquisition. Accordingly, two numbers are recorded in this column, separated by a backwards slash (\) so that Excel does not interpret this separation mark as requiring some mathematical operation. The first number is the ratio of cash flow to share price, and the second number is the ratio of free cash flow to share price as provided at http://clearstation.com.

Column Z is the score for cash flow as explained in Chapter 6. Column AA is the final ranking of all stocks, which is the sum of all technical and fundamental scores minus a constant of 2.0 for purposes of alignment. For ease of interpretation, you can always use the sort command in Excel to arrange these stocks from highest to lowest in terms of their desirability. You will see on your spreadsheet that there is one additional column that does not appear in Table 19.3. Column AB reports a tentative short statistic for the stocks in the list. Since most of these stocks have had rapid run ups, it is logical to expect that some may be overdue for a correction. Accordingly, stocks with the highest values in Column AB are considered most likely candidates for shorting from among these stocks. Please bear in mind, however, that I am not advocating the shorting of individual stocks, and these data in Column AB have not been tested or validated in any way.

STEP 3: UPDATING YOUR SPREADSHEET

Now that you recognize the kinds of data in the columns of your spreadsheet, in this next step you will see how to add new stocks to your spreadsheet as they qualify for inclusion, and you will see how to delete stocks from the list that are no longer relevant. This is a process that can take place almost daily as you use the CD and run the analysis. To add new stocks you will first want to visit any number of internet sites that provide stock screening tools to find stocks that are making new highs, that are priced above 5 dollars, and that have at least doubled in price from their lows over the past 52 weeks. An excellent example for gathering this information free of charge is found at http://stockcharts.com/charts/scans. Plan to spend an hour or two updating your spreadsheet the first time. After that it can be done in a few minutes at the close of trading each day.

- First, you will want to return to Column A of your spreadsheet and begin to input current share prices and 52-week highs and lows in Columns B, C, and D for each stock. You can get this information from Yahoo! Finance or Google Finance.
- As you input the current share price and 52-week high and find that they are identical values, you must reduce the current share price by two cents in order that the computational formulas can work because otherwise the algorithm will attempt to divide with zero, which is not possible.
- If you encounter any stocks that are no longer listed on any exchange (and there may be several such stocks on the list that have been acquired by other companies), you can place the cursor on those stock symbols, press the edit command, and then press delete, and delete the entire row for each stock that is no longer listed. If deleting any row causes an error message to appear in Columns I and P, you can copy the value above the error message in Column P and paste it over error value in that Column so that the underlying formulas will continue to function. I usually wait to do this until all of the deletions are finished, and then I use the edit, copy, and paste commands one time in Column P to replace all error messages with values from cells above them.
- Next you need to add any new qualifying stock symbols and their share-price information in Columns A through D. These are the stocks that are making new highs, that are priced over five dollars, that are trading in excess of 10,000 shares per day, and that have at least doubled in price over the past 52 weeks. Yahoo! Finance, http://stockcharts.com, and dozens of other sites have stock screening pages that are useful for this process. If you are updating your spreadsheet for the first time and if equities are entering a bull-market phase, there could be scores of new stocks to add to the spreadsheet. Otherwise, daily additions will seldom number more than three or four new stocks, if any.
- Next you should update the three-month low prices in Column K for all the remaining stocks, and add this information for any new stocks you have added to the spreadsheet. You can find this information at Yahoo! Finance and at several other sites by requesting a quote for each stock and clicking on the three-month interactive chart. As

you move the cursor to the low point on the three-month chart, you can see the share price at that point displayed above. This lowest price over the past three months is what you should enter for each stock in Column K. You will need to update Column K about once a week for stocks already existing in the list, and you will need to enter Column K information for each new stock you are adding to the list.

- After updating Column K as indicated, you should revisit Column H to delete any stocks whose three-month percentage gain has dropped below 30 percent. This is because the goal of the system is to realize trading gains in excess of 10 percent per month. Stocks that do not suggest by their rate of ascent that they will contribute to reaching this goal should ordinarily be deleted from the spreadsheet. During bull-market periods when the numbers of stocks in your list becomes unmanageable, you may decide to eliminate all stocks with three-month percentage gain below 40 percent.

- After updating Column K and deleting unsuitable stocks on the basis of Column H data as mentioned above, it is time to run the analysis for the updated list of qualified stocks.

STEP 4: RUNNING THE ANALYSIS

The analysis phase consists of updating technical data in Columns Q and R, and then simply sorting stocks on Final Rank in Column AA. Also it will be necessary to add data in Columns Q through Z for any new stocks that have been added to the list prior to sorting. This may sound like a lot of work to do daily; however, because there are some useful shortcuts to follow, it is really not that much work. And the payoff in terms of obtaining a valid ranking of investment-grade stocks is tremendous.

- To update technical data in Column Q, follow directions for point-and-figure analysis in Chapter 6. This may involve going to http://stockcharts.com/charts/pointfigure and awarding in Column Q a value of 1 for all green signals, a value of −1 for all red signals, and a zero for colorless, unchanged signals. As a timesaving shortcut, you need not update any stocks with rank values less than 3 in Column W because they are already so low in cumulative rating that changes in the technical analysis of Columns Q and R will not affect their desirability as acquisition targets. Similarly, to update technical data in Column R, follow directions for technical ratings in Chapter 6. This may involve visiting http://barchart.com and asking for a quote and an opinion on each stock with a value of 3 or higher in Column W. If the cumulative technical rating at Barchart is 96 or above, you should award a rating of 1 in Column R. If the rating is from 25 to 95, you should award a zero in Column R. If the rating is below 25, you should award a minus 1 in Column R. If you are updating existing data, you should make changes as they occur in each reported value.

- For all new stocks that you have added to the spreadsheet, you should enter the indicated technical values for Columns Q and R. Then you will need to enter either a 1, a zero, or a minus 1 in Columns S through V for Divergence, Growth, Book Value, and PE, respectively, following the directions in Chapter 6. When all of these entries are completed, an initial rating for all stocks should appear in Column W. If any stock rating remains blank in Column W, you should go to a cell near the top of Column W, hit "edit" and copy the cell information including the underlying formula to all of the blank cells. Then, after you hit the "enter" key, all of the desired information should appear in Column W.

- Only one piece of information is still missing for the new stocks, and then the analysis will be complete. You must now enter information on cash flow in Column Y and score cash flow in Column Z. As indicated in Chapter 6, the best way to do this is to go to http://clearstation.com and enter the stock symbol at the top and request "ratio" information. When the ratio page appears for each stock, find and enter the cash flow and free cash flow ratios sequentially in Column Y. The two values should be rounded and separated by a backwards slash (\) to prevent any unintended mathematical operations. Note that when cash flow data is not given for a stock or an exchange-traded fund, an asterisk (*) is used to indicate missing data. To score cash flow and free cash flow recorded in Column Y, you should award a 1 in Column Z if the sum of the cash flow and free cash flow ratios is less than 12.5. You should award a zero in Column Z if the sum of the cash flow and free cash flow ratios is between 12.5 and 25 or if the information is not given. You should award a minus 1 in Column Z if the sum of the cash flow and free cash flow ratios exceeds 25, or if either ratio is negative. Following the entries in Column Z, the final analysis ranking should appear in Column AA.

- To sort stocks on Investment Rank, simply click on AA above Column AA and use the Excel sort command, sorting from *Z to A*, from the highest values to the lowest values. The highest values are the most desirable, so they appear at the top of the column. Use the automatic "expand the selection" option because you are sorting all columns based on information in Column AA.

STEP 5: INTERPRETING THE RESULTS

The final results of the technical/fundamental analysis appear as a rank value for each stock in Column AA. These values will range from approximately plus 10 to minus 10 for any given stock. The values are interpreted as follows:

- Any stock rated 7 or above in Column AA is considered a "very strong buy." These are the highest-rated stocks, and although they are the most desirable acquisitions, they rarely appear, and almost never appear in a bear-market period.
- Any stock rated 6 in Column AA is considered a "strong buy" and is a highly desirable acquisition.
- Any stock rated 5 in Column AA is considered a "buy" and is usually a worthwhile acquisition.
- Any stock rated 4 in Column AA is considered a "hold" and should not normally be purchased for the first time, but if it is already in your portfolio, it may be worthwhile to keep it as a holding.
- Any stock rated 3 in Column AA is considered "speculative" and may be acquired or held only if you are willing to assume unusual risk.
- Any stock rated below 3 in Column AA is considered a "sell" and should normally be sold at the best available opportunity.

Note that, when there are several stocks listed within any rated category, the stocks at the top of the list within the category are considered preferable to those at the bottom of the category list. These top-listed stocks have greater relative strength than stocks in the same category that appear lower on the list.

STEP 6: MAINTAINING THE SPREADSHEET

You may wish to save the results file for each day to maintain a daily record. To do this you simply click on "File" and then on "Save As . . ." You should specify a title of the record to be saved, preferably with the date of that record.

In addition to the daily updating of technical information in Columns Q and R, you will need to update the three-month-low Column K approximately once a week. And you should consider updating the fundamental information in Columns S, T, U, V, Y, and Z approximately once a month. Of course, you may skip an updating cycle and resume it at a later date, but the accuracy of the system recommendations may be reduced during the period that input data is not timely.

CAUTIONARY REMINDERS

As you run the analysis and calculate the results, remember that this program will produce recommendations at any given time; however, as indicated earlier in this book, there are times when it may be best to be out of the market or to be short the market. Often during bear markets, the stocks that will surface by this system as the best investments will actually be exchange-traded bear funds. Also, it has happened during bear market periods that not a single stock can be found as a recommendation in Categories 4 through 7, and at such times it is necessary to be completely out of the market. I recommend that market timing based on the CBOE Volatility Index or the put/call ratio, or another method as explained in Chapter 10, should become an over-riding concern. In order to maximize returns, it may be best to be completely out of the market as much as 50 percent of the time.

One final set of disclaimers that have been mentioned at several points in this book: Although the stocks in the final ranking column represent the best mathematical ranking of stocks for acquisition or sale at any given time according to the most reliable criteria I have found, there are always variables outside of human predictability and control. For example, if an analyst downgrade or a negative earnings report is announced between the time an analysis is run and a trade is executed, there can be no expectation that the system analysis results will hold. Furthermore, as also mentioned earlier, success at trading depends on many more factors than just identifying the best stocks to acquire. Getting favorable trade executions and properly maintaining one's portfolio are at least equally important concerns. And finally, the trading system included here is the result of many years of systematic refinement and improvement. I fully intend to continue to improve upon the procedures reported here. The reader is also encouraged to make experimental adaptations and enhancements that will cause the system to conform more to his or her trading objectives, temperamental idiosyncrasies, and stylistic preferences. One such enhancement I am currently considering is to add a column to award points for analyst estimates of future earnings. The possibilities for adaptations and enhancement are unlimited.

SUMMARY

This chapter was designed to serve as an instruction manual for the implementation of the trading CD software program accompanying this book.

It was noted that the CD will require Microsoft Excel or compatible software to be resident on your computer. It was also noted that, due to the fact that individual stock data are in constant flux, there will be a necessary updating task at the beginning of the installation phase. This chapter provides complete instructions on how to update stocks, input new data, run the analysis, and interpret the results of the analysis on a daily basis.

CHAPTER 20

Afterthoughts

I n the midst of an economic recession that is deeper than any recession experienced in more than three-quarters of a century, no doubt many stock traders have lost money, or they have given up on trading altogether. It is a fair question to ask how traders would have fared in the present economic environment if they had relied on the mathematical trading systems advanced in this book. We now have the advantage of hindsight to obtain the answer to this question.

TIMING

Recall that one of the primary teachings of this book is that traders should normally hold long positions about 50 percent of the time, and be out of the market or in index short funds the rest of the time. Thus, "buy-and-hold" strategies are not advocated here. You can see in Table 11.1 of Chapter 11 that our five-year performance record ended at the beginning of a "favorable" investment period on October 24, 2008. By using the VIX timing method described in Chapter 10, you can see that the particular favorable period that began on October 24, 2008, ended on December 12, 2008. During that challenging period, the S&P 500 Index climbed from 876.77 to 879.73, a gain of 0.3 percent. The next favorable investment period began on January 20, 2009, and extended to February 12, 2009. During that period, the S&P 500 Index increased from 805.22 to 835.19, a gain of 3.6 percent. The next favorable investment period began on March 2, 2009 and is continuing at the time of this writing. So far during this period the S&P 500

217

has gone from 700.82 to 768.54, a gain of 9.7 percent, and this favorable investment period still has a lot of room to run. Altogether, if you had invested in an S&P 500 Index fund during the favorable periods described, you would have gained more than 13.6 percent in four months. That may not sound like much, but remember that this would have happened during one of the worst economic downturns in the history of U.S. equity markets. If you had bought and held your index-fund investment throughout that same period, you would have lost 12.3 percent, as the S&P 500 Index went from 876.77 to 768.54.

If you had decided to use a mathematical trading system such as the one in the CD program included with this book, and if you had made appropriate individual stock entry and exit decisions, instead of realizing an index-fund gain of 11.4 percent over the four-month period described above, your trading gains would have been more than 26 percent. Furthermore, if you had made the aggressive decision to invest in an index bear fund such as RYTPX during the two "unfavorable periods" (from December 12, 2008, to January 20, 2009, and from February 12, 2009, to March 2, 2009) you would have realized additional gains of 52.3 percent during that four-month period, bringing your total gains to more than 78.3 percent in four months. By comparison, if you had invested in a safe stock like Warren Buffett's Berkshire-Hathaway Class A shares, you would have lost 27 percent of your investment during the same period. Or you could have chosen a blue-chip stock like GE or Citigroup and lost 57 or 93 percent of your investment, respectively.

OPPORTUNITIES

Even though we are experiencing the worst economic downturn in more than three-quarters of a century, there are still many amazing stock opportunities. As I examine my own personal watch list, I see that there are currently more than 70 stocks that have gained over 30 percent in the past three months. Recall that this is one of the qualifying criteria adopted here for investment in individual stocks. Even more amazingly, there are more than 12 stocks that have gained over 100 percent in the past three months. In addition, one of those stocks, an exchange-traded gold fund, has gained over 700 percent in the past three months. Why didn't I put all of my money in that fund and go merrily on my way? Three reasons: First, the fund failed to satisfy my investment criteria; second, because such a move would not have permitted sufficient diversification; and finally, because on principle I seldom invest in gold. My aversion to gold stocks is based on my experience that they seldom have positive earnings and they usually seem to give back gains when economic anxiety subsides. Also, investing in gold removes capital from more productive sectors of the economy. But those sentiments are nothing more than personal idiosyncrasies, and are not intended to discourage more astute traders from making 700 percent gains in three months.

MARKET TRENDS

The economic downturn we are currently experiencing is without precedent in my lifetime. Although our government has approved financial bailout packages that could cost the American taxpayer more than 3 trillion dollars when foreign loan interest is included, I am told that U.S. equity market capitalization actually has already lost 11 trillion dollars in 2008 and an additional 5 trillion so far in 2009. I read recently that the total number of billionaires worldwide has also diminished by 40 percent in this downtrend so far. The total loss of personal wealth worldwide is staggering to consider. I can only hope that those in charge of our own government spending machine will seriously consider these stock market trends as one key indication of the health of our economy. Perhaps when government leaders finally see the high positive correlation between tax revenues and stock market gains they will be less inclined to turn a blind eye to the vicissitudes of the stock market.

To the extent that those in authority learn the importance of market indices as a reflection of the health of our economy, I am optimistic that measures will eventually be taken to enable the stock market to continue its upward growth at a sustainable rate. Hopefully we will learn a lesson from Japan that saw its market capitalization fall more than 80 percent in value in the two decades from 1989 to the present. Economic decision makers in Japan were unwilling to allow unprofitable banks and other corporations fail, so they provided artificial financial support that not only failed to stimulate growth in those institutions, but also brought the entire market lower by removing the competitive advantage from more productive institutions. This is a classic example of iatrogenic malaise—that is, a situation in which the economic physicians themselves caused the illness. Hopefully our leaders will take a broad historical look at other economies in order to avert such failure in our own economy.

One encouraging fact for stock traders to remember is the historical record that the stock market has actually registered gains in the majority of recessionary periods in our nation's history. Thus, just because we are experiencing an economic downturn is no reason to stand aside from stock market trading. Also, we have at this time entered another favorable investment period that may mark a bottom of the present decline.

LESSONS FROM HISTORY

There are some very clear lessons from history that could provide guide-posts to our leaders as they attempt to negotiate their way through the murky waters of economic decline. Here are some suggestions that might prove helpful towards economic health:

Promote Personal Integrity by All Means Available

We have considered earlier the assertion that the greatest threat to capitalism and societal economic health is the erosion and decline of integrity in society. Integrity has been defined as trustworthiness and care for the well-being of others. Because of this threat we must find ways to promote integrity in our society at all costs. I would welcome such measures as the proliferation and requirement of business ethics courses, and the providing of tax incentives and other awards for ethical leadership. Additionally, it might even help to promote prison or courtroom tours as a requirement for chief financial officers, certified financial planners, certified public accountants, lobbyists, and congressional banking committee members so that they could see the ends of those persons who practice securities fraud. Minimally, qualified fraud felons might also be given released time to visit high schools and universities and to give lectures on the consequences of wrongdoing and how best to maintain integrity and to prevent fraudulent activity. It is probably also past time to take a hard look into finding legal ways to promote religious schools and charities, or at least to promote basic religious instruction. Marginalizing the influence of religion in society is not consistent with our need to promote of personal integrity. Community service volunteering could also be rewarded by a reduction in the cost of college tuition or by other appropriate means.

Don't Foment Class Warfare

We are all together in the same boat, so it makes no sense at all to drill a hole spitefully in the bottom of that end of the boat that belongs to labor or to management, to wealthy persons, or to indigent persons. Class warfare serves no purpose other than promoting anarchy, installing extremist regimes in government, and raising the ratings of vituperative media outlets. Signs now appear in our society that some persons are learning this lesson. A leading labor union leader was heard to say recently that demonstrating for ever-increasing wages and ever-diminishing working hours is a "dead-end street." It cuts productivity and drives businesses and jobs overseas. At the same time it is apparent from U.S. Congressional hearings that management leaders are also learning that the era of obscene incentive bonuses and exorbitant executive salaries is ending. Stockholders from all socioeconomic strata are looking for pragmatic corporate leadership that promotes growth and provides value for all. Furthermore, contrary to the ranting of those who promote class warfare, it is not the case that all wealthy persons obtained their wealth by the oppression of the poor. Most of them got where they are by hard work and creative enterprise.

More importantly, obtaining wealth is not a zero-sum game. It is not necessary to rob Peter to pay Paul. Wealth can be generated in society in such a way that all individuals have greater access to that wealth through their own industry. We need to take a hard look at the economies of such nations as Haiti, Cuba, Venezuela, and the former Soviet Union that fomented class warfare as a means of installing leftist regimes. We should consider the negative economic results of such trends and learn the important lesson that class warfare never benefits the majority of the citizens of any country.

Eliminate Capital-Gains Taxation

Capital-gains taxation reduces the profitability of investments, and dampens all economic growth. It discourages would-be savers from investing their money in the stock market and stimulating entrepreneurship. Another problem is that it represents a kind of immoral double-dipping by the government. In fact, government has often already taxed investment capital as income when it was first acquired, and now it is endeavoring to tax it a second time as it is being invested. The zeal to tax capital gains only serves to restrain investment, drive it abroad, and reduce government tax revenues from corporations that would otherwise have been more profitable. How can we encourage personal savings if we systematically eliminate the value of personal investing? There may be some exceptional instances where taxing corporate capital gains may be justifiable, but it seems especially deleterious and unjustifiable to tax capital gains from individual retirement savings.

Regulate the Derivatives Industry

Protecting life and property is one of the most important roles of government. When government fails to regulate a derivatives industry that might otherwise destroy wealth, that government fails in its fiduciary responsibility. Consider that following the Great Depression of the 1930s regulations were introduced limiting the ability of private citizens to leverage their stock investments. As a result we cannot now buy stocks in a margin account in excess of two-to-one leveraging of our underlying capital. Moreover, if the falling value of our investments causes our capital asset base to drop below 35 percent of our investments, we are required by law to add capital or sell investment equity to restore that balance. Those are useful and important regulations, and they have served to prevent a repetition of the 1929 stock market crash. As we know, prior to the 1929 stock market crash individuals were allowed to leverage investments by purchasing stock with as little as 5 percent of the requisite underlying capital, and this was one of the primary causes of that economic calamity. My obvious question then becomes, "How is it that some of our public financial institutions have been allowed to leverage their investments at a ratio exceeding forty-to-one of investment exposure against underlying capital?" The recent economic decline has been attributed to this kind of promiscuous leveraging that still goes on largely unregulated by designated government agencies. Unregulated over-leveraging is a manifestation of unbridled greed that has the power to destroy our capitalistic economic system. Historically, whether it has taken the form of tulip options in Holland, stock options in 1929, or real estate credit default swaps in our current economic crisis, failure to regulate derivatives has had devastating effect. We need a regulatory system that can prevent all such manifestations of greed in the future.

Regulate the Size of Public Sector Employment

It should be obvious that both public and private-sector employment are important and necessary in society. Without public-sector jobs we would be limited in our capacity to defend, educate, and protect our citizens and their property. At the same time, without private-sector employment, we would be unable to provide salaries for the public sector jobs. The problem then becomes one of determining how many public-sector jobs can be and should be supported by our current level of private-sector employment.

In many societies citizens prefer public-sector employment over private-sector employment because of the presumed higher job security of public-sector employment. Also public-sector jobs entail a regulatory control function over the private sector, and thus such jobs may include a level of power and prestige. However, because public-sector jobs do not generate wealth but only serve to regulate, defend, and consume it, it is counterproductive for any society to have too many public-sector jobs in relation to private-sector jobs. I do not pretend to know what the exact ratio of private-to-public sector employment should be, because there is a sliding scale that implies that the fewer public-sector jobs possible within a margin of regulatory safety, the greater the potential gross domestic product could be. Serious research needs to be dedicated to ascertaining appropriate limits of public-sector employment.

One historical model with which I am familiar was that of ancient Israel, where one tribe in twelve was supported by the public in order to conduct priestly, educational, and judicial functions, and later a king was established who levied a tax of about 10 percent to support national defense and diplomacy. I believe it was Sir Francis Bacon who lamented in print that any state that levies taxes in excess of 10 percent reduces its citizenry to bondservants. In socialist countries, everyone effectively becomes an employee of the state, and this has been shown historically to be an unsustainable model for many reasons—absence of entrepreneurial incentive being only one of those reasons. This problem of determining the size of government reminds me of the hypothetical situation that could occur if the number of persons in society living on social security benefits or welfare benefits exceeded the number of wage earners. Also the problem is analogous to what might occur with a rising prison population when the number of persons incarcerated exceeds the number of free persons. These examples also represent unsustainable models.

Regulate the Capitalization Size of Corporations

Historically, this process has at times taken the form of "anti-trust legislation." This was originally enacted to prevent corporate monopolies from obtaining unfair pricing power. In our current economic environment a similar situation has occurred in those cases where financial institutions and automobile manufacturers have been considered "too big to fail." This size problem has made it necessary for government to "bail out" institutions whose failure has been interpreted as entailing "systemic risk" to our economy. One way in which this problem might have been averted is if regulators had placed a capitalization limit on the size of any corporation. This would have forced such large corporations to spin off subsidiary divisions as a preventative measure. As it is, the government is being forced to subdivide corporations such as AIG after the fact, as a corrective measure.

There are currently many reasons why a limit on capitalization size could be beneficial. One of those reasons is that it would be a way of preventing corporations from becoming "too big to fail" as a matter of systemic risk. Another reason would be to prevent inordinately large corporations from exerting unfair lobbying influences on government officials. Excessive political campaign contributions by entities such as AIG, Fannie Mae, and Freddie Mac can be shown to have limited regulatory oversight of the policies of those institutions.

CONCLUSION

It is hoped that you have found in this book tools helpful to you in experiencing trading success in any stock market conditions. We have looked at quantifiable variables that can help us to construct mathematical trading systems and to capitalize systematically on market inefficiencies. We have examined reliable timing methods that can help us know when to be fully invested and when to be out of the market altogether or to be in index short positions. We have considered moral and ethical concerns related to successful trading. We have looked into specific details related to buying and selling stocks and maintaining stock portfolios. We have studied some of the historical origins and implications of probability, risk, and trust as they relate to the trading of stocks. For me the journey has been meaningful and enjoyable, and I trust it will result in greater success for you, both in trading and in life.

Bibliography

Anderson, C. *The Long Tail*. New York: Random House Publishing, 2007.

Arrow, K.J. *Essays in the Theory of Risk-Bearing*. Chicago: Markham Publishing Company, 1971.

Ayres, I. *Super Crunchers*. New York: Bantam Books, 2007.

Baker, S. *The Numerati*. Boston: Houghton Mifflin Company, 2008.

Bernoulli, J. *Exposition of a New Theory on the Measurement of Risk*. Translated from the Latin by Louise Sommer in *Econometrica*, Vol. 22, 1954 (pp. 23–36), 1738.

Bernstein, P.L. *Against the Gods: The Remarkable Story of Risk*. New York, NY: John Wiley & Sons, 1996.

Binnewies, R. *The Options Course: A Winning Program for Investors and Traders*. New York: Irwin Professional Publishing, 1995.

Chase, S. *The Economy of Abundance*. Whitefish, MT: Kessinger Publishing, LLC, 2007.

David, F.N. *Games, Gods, and Gambling*. New York: Hafner Publishing Company, 1962.

Frost, A.J. and R.R. Prechter. *Elliott Wave Principle*. Gainsville, GA: New Classics Library, 1990.

Fullman, S.H. *Options: A Personal Seminar*. New York: New York Institute of Finance/Simon & Schuster, 1992.

Graham, B. *The Intelligent Investor: A Book of Practical Counsel*. New York: Harper Collins, 2003.

Hacking, I. *The Emergence of Probability: A Philosophical Study of Early Ideas about Probability, Induction, and Statistical Inference*. London: Cambridge University Press, 1975.

Harnett, D.L., and J.F. Horrell. *Data, Statistics, and Decision Models with Excel*. New York: John Wiley & Sons, 1998.

Henning, G. *A Guide to Language Testing: Development, Evaluation, Research*. Boston: Heinle & Heinle, 1987.

Jurik, M. (Ed.) *Computerized Trading: Maximizing Day Trading and Overnight Profits*. New York: New York Institute of Finance, 1999.

Keynes, J.M. *A Treatise on Probability*. London: Macmillan, 1921.

Keynes, J.M. *The General Theory of Employment, Interest and Money.* New York: Harcourt, Brace, 1936.

Knight, F.H. *Risk, Uncertainty and Profit.* New York: Century Press, 1964. Originally published in 1921.

Lapin, D. *Thou Shall Prosper: Ten Commandments for Making Money.* Hoboken, NJ: John Wiley & Sons, 2002.

LeFevre, E. *Reminiscences of a Stock Operator.* New York: John Wiley & Sons, 1994.

Lynch, P. *One Up on Wall Street: How to Use What You Already Know to Make Money in the Market.* New York: Penguin Books, 1989.

MacDonald, G. *Ordering Your Private World.* Nashville, TN: Thomas Nelson, 2003.

Malkiel, B.G. *A Random Walk Down Wall Street.* New York: W.W. Norton & Company, 1996.

Markman, J.D. *Swing Trading: Power strategies to cut risk and boost profits.* Hoboken, NJ: John Wiley & Sons, 2003.

Markowitz, H.M. "Portfolio Selection." *Journal of Finance* VII, No. 1 (March, 1952): 77–91.

Markowitz, H.M. "The Utility of Wealth." *Journal of Political Economy* LIX, No. 3 (April, 1952): 151–157.

Maturi, R.J. *Divining the Dow: 100 of the World's Most Widely Followed Stock Market Prediction Systems.* Chicago: Probus Publishing Company, 1993.

Maturi, R.J. *Stock Picking: The 11 Best Tactics for Beating the Market.* New York: McGraw-Hill, 1993.

Muir, J. *Of Men and Numbers: The Story of the Great Mathematicians.* New York: Dodd, Mead, 1961.

Nassar, D.S. *Rules of the Trade: Indispensable Insights for Online Profits.* New York, NY: McGraw-Hill, 2001.

O'Neil, W.J. *How to Make Money in Stocks: A Winning System in Good Times or Bad.* New York: McGraw-Hill, 1995.

Pearson, K. Editorial. *Biometrika*, Vol. 1, 1901.

Peters, E.E. *Chaos and Order in the Capital Markets: A New View of Cycles, Prices, and Market Volatility.* New York: John Wiley & Sons, 1991.

Riss, R.M. *A Survey of 20th-Century Revival Movements.* Peabody, MA: Hendrickson Publishers, 1988.

Rudd, A., and H.K. Clasing. *Modern Portfolio Theory.* Homewood, IL: Dow Jones-Irwin, 1982.

Schwager, J.D. *Market Wizards: Interviews with Top Traders.* New York: Harper & Row, 1990.

Schwager, J.D. *The New Market Wizards: Conversations with America's Top Traders.* New York: Harper Collins, 1992.

Schwager, J.D. *Getting Started in Technical Analysis*. New York: John Wiley & Sons, 1999.

Schwager, J.D. *Stock Market Wizards: Revised and Updated*. New York: Harper Collins, 2003.

Smith, G. *How I Trade for a Living*. New York: John Wiley & Sons, 2000.

Sorenson, E. *The Derivative Portfolio Matrix—Combining Market Direction with Market Volatility*. Institute for Quantitative Research in Finance, Spring 1995 Seminar.

Sperandeo, V. *Trader Vic: Methods of a Wall Street Master*. New York: John Wiley & Sons, 1993.

Sperandeo, V. *Trader Vic II: Principles of Professional Speculation*. New York: John Wiley & Sons, 1994.

Stanley, T.J. *The Millionaire Mind*. New York: Simon & Schuster, 2000.

Stigler, S.M. *The History of Statistics: The Measurement of Uncertainty Before 1900*. Cambridge, MA: The Belknap Press of Harvard University Press, 1986.

Tanous, P.J. *Investment Gurus: A Road Map to Wealth from the World's Best Money Managers*. New York: New York Institute of Finance, 1997.

Train, J. *The Money Masters: Nine Great Investors: Their Winning Strategies and How You Can Apply Them*. New York: Harper & Row, 1980.

Von Mises, R. *Probability, Statistics, and Truth*. New York: Dover Publications, Inc., 1957.

Zweig, M. *Winning on Wall Street: How to Spot Market Trends Early, Which Stocks to Pick, When to Buy and Sell for Peak Profits and Minimum Risk*. New York: Warner Books, 1990.

About the Author

G rant Henning is a retired professor of measurement, statistics, and applied linguistics. He has served as Senior Research Scientist at Educational Testing Service in Princeton, New Jersey, as Professor and Chair of the Applied Linguistics graduate program at American University in Cairo, Egypt, and as Visiting Professor of Applied Foreign Languages at Kinmen Institute of Technology in Taiwan. In addition, he has taught for many years at the Pennsylvania State University and the University of California at Los Angeles. He holds a doctorate in Educational Psychology and a master's degree in Applied Linguistics from UCLA. He has been an avid stock trader for more than 20 years.

About the CD-ROM

INTRODUCTION

This appendix provides you with information on the contents of the CD that accompanies this book. For the latest information, please refer to the ReadMe file located at the root of the CD.

SYSTEM REQUIREMENTS

- A computer with a processor running at 120 MHz or faster
- At least 32 MB of total RAM installed on your computer; for best performance, we recommend at least 64 MB
- A CD-ROM drive

NOTE: Many popular spreadsheets programs are capable of reading Microsoft Excel files. However, users should be aware that a slight amount of formatting might be lost when using a program other than Microsoft Excel.

USING THE CD

To install the items from the CD to your hard drive, follow these steps.

1. **Insert the CD into your computer's CD-ROM drive.**
   The licence agreement appears.
   Note to Windows users: The interface won't launch if you have autorun disabled. In that case, choose Start>Run. (For Windows Vista, choose Start>All Programs>Accessories>Run.) In the dialogue box that appears, type **D:\Start.exe**. (Replace *D* with the proper letter if

your CD drive uses a different letter. If you don't know the letter, see how your CD drive is listed under My Computer.) Click on OK.

Note for Mac Users: When the CD icon appears on your desktop, double-click the icon to open the CD and double-click the Start icon.

2. **Read through the license agreement and then click on the Accept button if you want to use the CD.**

The CD interface appears. The interface allows you to browse the contents and install the programs with just a click of a button (or two).

WHAT'S ON THE CD

The following sections provide a summary of the software and other materials you'll find on the CD.

Content

The CD holds an Excel spreadsheet named "Stocks_Worksheet.xls" that provides sample data and formulas for the implementation of the trading systems described in the book. Specifically, the CD will allow you to implement the hybrid technical-fundamental system described earlier in Chapter 6. See Chapter 19 for detailed instructions on how to use the CD to begin systematic stock analysis, ranking, and selection.

Applications

The **Excel Viewer** application is on the CD. Excel Viewer is a freeware viewer that allows you to view, but not edit, most Microsoft Excel spreadsheets. Certain features of Microsoft Excel documents may not work as expected from within Excel Viewer.

Shareware programs are fully functional, trial versions of copyrighted programs. If you like particular programs, register with their authors for a nominal fee and receive licenses, enhanced versions, and technical support.

Freeware programs are copyrighted games, applications, and utilities that are free for personal use. Unlike shareware, these programs do not require a fee or provide technical support.

GNU software is governed by its own license, which is included inside the folder of the GNU product. See the GNU license for more details.

Trial, demo, or evaluation versions are usually limited either by time or functionality (such as being unable to save projects). Some trial versions are very sensitive to system date changes. If you alter your computer's date, the programs will "time out" and no longer be functional.

CUSTOMER CARE

If you have trouble with the CD—ROM, please call the Wiley Product Technical Support phone number at (800) 762—2974. Outside the United States, call 1(317) 572—3994. You can also contact Wiley Product Technical Support at http://support.wiley.com. John Wiley & Sons will provide technical support only for installation and other general quality control items. For technical support on the applications themselves, consult the program's vendor or author.

To place additional orders or to request information about other Wiley products, please call (877) 762-2974.

Index